Legitimate Sexpectations

Legitimate Sexpectations

the power of sex-ed

Katrina Marson

SCRIBE
Melbourne • London

Scribe Publications
18–20 Edward St, Brunswick, Victoria 3056, Australia
2 John St, Clerkenwell, London, WC1N 2ES, United Kingdom

Published by Scribe 2022

Names have been changed, identifying details and backgrounds have been altered, and stories combined out of respect for the privacy of individuals and couples.

Typeset in Adobe Caslon Pro by the publishers

Printed and bound in Australia by Griffin Press

Scribe is committed to the sustainable use of natural resources and the use of paper products made responsibly from those resources.

Scribe acknowledges Australia's First Nations peoples as the traditional owners and custodians of this country, and we pay our respects to their elders, past and present.

978 1 922585 51 6 (Australian edition)
978 1 922586 74 2 (ebook)

A catalogue record for this book is available from the National Library of Australia.

scribepublications.com.au
scribepublications.co.uk

For our younger selves

Contents

Legitimate Expectation

When should a promise be kept?

This is what the legal doctrine of 'legitimate expectation' is concerned with in the common law world. In Australia it is a little more fraught than elsewhere, but in essence it asks:

> When are individuals entitled to rely on promises made by public bodies? Promises from those with the power to make decisions that impact individual lives? When is it reasonable to expect those promises will be kept?

I failed Administrative Law at university, so indulge me as I co-opt its concept for my own purposes.

To me, it speaks to the idea that we make promises to each other at a collective level, through the institutions we continue to uphold as instruments meant to represent and serve us as a community. The idea that we create expectations, both high and low, for ourselves and each other.

This book asks:

What expectations do we have of the way we will behave in a sexual encounter?

What do we expect of how sexual violence unfolds and why it happens?

How do we expect our institutions to respond?

What expectations do young people have of their futures?

Can we promise our kids that they will live a life free from sexual violence, that their sexual wellbeing will be protected at all costs?

Can future generations hold a legitimate expectation that we will make good on that promise, to do everything in our power to give them the very best chance?

When should a promise be kept?

It Takes a Village

I walk on stage to polite applause. If trepidation is audible, I think I can hear it in the clapping.

I am nervous. Not because 400 people are watching, waiting for me to speak. But because I recognise the significance of this moment. For the next half-hour, I will have the attention of some very important people.

Usually when I am speaking from a lectern, I am at a bar table in the sombre environment of the courtroom — a place where adrenaline starts to hum the moment you walk through the doors. What I say there may be the difference between guilty and not guilty, and the questions I ask have a particular power: they must be answered. It is a responsibility I feel keenly.

But on this day, as I approach the middle of the stage, my powers of advocacy will be put to the test. The questions I ask here demand no answer, and I can only hope the words I say will make a difference.

The judge and jury I face today are Year 12 students from three Sydney schools. Two girls' schools, one all-boys. They have come together on neutral turf for 'Respect Day', where they will hear from speakers and have discussions about respectful relationships and sexual consent.

It is May 2021, and this event is happening during a storm of intense public concern about the stubbornly high rates of sexual violence and harassment in our community.

Nearly a quarter of all Australian women and 5 per cent of Australian men have experienced sexual violence in their lifetime.[1] More than half of transgender and gender-diverse people have experienced sexual violence or coercion, at a rate nearly four times that of the general Australian public.[2] Overwhelmingly, perpetrators of sexual violence are male.[3]

There is a dearth of data about the prevalence of sexual violence in particular population groups, but the research we do have shows that Aboriginal and Torres Strait Islander women are between three and three and a half times more likely than non-Indigenous women to be victim survivors of sexual violence.[4] Research suggests that certain populations are more likely to experience sexual assault, including people who: are homeless; have disability; identify as lesbian, gay, bisexual, trans, or gender diverse, or have intersex variations; have previously been victims of sexual assault at any point throughout life.[5] Breaking it down by age, almost one in five Australian women have experienced sexual violence and more than half have experienced sexual harassment since they were 15 years old. At least one in 20 men have experienced sexual violence and one in four have experienced sexual harassment since age 15. That's a lot of Australians who have been subjected to sexual violence and harassment since at least the time they were in Year 8 or 9, before they could even get a learner driver's permit. And before that age, at least one in six women and one in nine men have been physically or sexually abused.[6] The Royal Commission into Institutional Responses to Child Sexual Abuse revealed just how vast the scale of sexual offending against children is, and has been for decades, in this country.

These numbers only reflect those who have been able to report their experiences, something which can be incredibly difficult, if not impossible, for many. Given the extent to which sexual violence and harassment is chronically underreported, we know there is a whole lot of iceberg still below the surface. The only thing worse than these numbers is that they have hardly changed, for generations. If anything, the numbers get worse over time.[7] This is not new, although we may be newly alive to it.

Sexual violence can be ruinous. Sexual violence, sexual harassment, and negative sexual experiences carry significant health, social, and economic cost, and can have a devastating impact on individuals, their families, and communities. Long-term physical and emotional health, the capacity to undertake education, contribute to society, and otherwise lead a fulfilling life can be severely affected, and the incidence of premature death increases.

It is a very dark and dangerous thing, and yet it is a very ordinary thing. It is not overstating it to say sexual violence is ubiquitous. On every street, in every school, workplace, playground, train carriage, and bus, there are any number of survivors. Survivors of sexual violence are not some other people separate from us: they are us.

And so are their perpetrators.

By the time I was speaking to these Year 12 students, the public spotlight had been turned onto sexual violence and harassment with a new glare. Although survivors have been speaking up for generations — including First Nations people, people of colour, people with disabilities, and others whose stories are rarely given a platform — in 2021, Australia seemed to turn its full attention to the perpetration of sexual violence. It was colliding with our power structures in historic and symbolic ways.

In mid-2020, an explosive report revealed allegations that a former High Court judge had sexually harassed numerous women during his tenure. Between then and May 2021, a sexual abuse survivor had been named Australian of the Year, and a petition of current and recent students sharing their experiences of sexual violence — even before they left school, often at the hands of their schoolmates — and calling for better consent education had gone viral, collecting thousands of testimonies. There was widespread media coverage of the petition, with intense public interest in what it revealed about sexual violence in this country.

It felt like the community consciousness had — finally — been brought to a crossroads: how are we to answer the scourge of sexual violence?

On stage in that auditorium full of schoolkids, I squint in the hot lights, which add to my feeling of being scrutinised. I feel my hands wrap around the sides of the lectern, as is my involuntary habit, and I begin.

'Who thinks I'm here to scare you straight?'

Having heard that I'm a criminal lawyer who prosecutes alleged sex offenders, I know most of the students will expect me to deliver a sermon on the definition of consent and the legal consequences of sexual violence. They will have become accustomed to being treated to such an approach and are rightly wary, bored of being lectured at. So, I ask them: *Who thinks I'm here to scare you straight?*

I thought they might politely pretend otherwise, but hundreds of hands go up. I relax a bit at this, realising there is a shared spirit of frankness in the auditorium.

I tell them I do not intend to patronise or lecture them.

I have a narrow path to navigate here. I have been forewarned that there are students in the room who are angry — at the lack of education about sex and consent, at the fact it has taken a petition started by a former Sydney school student, Chanel Contos, through which thousands have told their stories of sexual violence for anyone to seemingly pay attention. There are others in the room who feel vilified, that they are being tarred as would-be perpetrators. I must hold on to both audiences without sugar-coating reality. I need to keep them with me if I am to sell them on their own empowerment.

So I start at a truth that my years in the justice system have revealed to me over and over again:

'If anyone is at fault, it is us. As the village that raises you, we have let you down.'

Some years ago, I was on the prosecution team for a trial in Canberra. It was a case about a young man at a university college who was accused of having sex with one of his classmates when she was passed out drunk and could not consent.

But this story is not just about the accused, nor is it about the victim.

This is a story about a young man who was in the common room that night, and what he saw.

Everyone else had gone out — a group of first-year friends who went to some bars in the city to drink and have fun. But not this boy; for whatever reason, he had stayed at the college. Later that night, he was up in the common room when he heard the door at the end of the hallway slam shut. He peered around the door, to see who it was.

His mate, one of the lads, was coming down the hallway with another of his friends — a young woman. She was obviously wasted: hardly able to stand, her eyes glazed over. His mate was physically assisting her, almost carrying her along.

He saw immediately that she was way too drunk.

His mate was propping her up, walking her towards the dorms. As they passed, the two young men made eye contact. The one who was later accused of sexual assault grinned. The witness would describe it as a knowing look, a kind of smirk.

Our witness felt deeply uneasy. Maybe his mate was just getting her to bed safe. Had he misread that look? Should he do something? What would he say? He stared after them with a gnawing in his gut, rooted to the spot in silence.

A year later he would sit in my office and explain that he had been struggling since his friend told him she had been sexually assaulted, dealing with the guilt he felt for not doing anything to stop it.

What he said next has stayed with me, all these years. He told me that after the incident, the college had organised consent and bystander intervention training. Lessons about how to intervene if you see something that doesn't seem right: what to say, how to look after yourself while looking after others. This is really common, for institutions to 'leap into action' once something has already happened.

I think I saw his chin wobble as he told me that if they had only had that session before the incident, he might have recognised what was happening and known how to stop it. His voice choked with regret and shame, and his wet eyes searched mine — for judgement, I think.

The trial came around, and he walked up the steps of the courthouse in painstakingly polished shoes. He swore an oath to tell the truth, and his hands shook when he reached for that small plastic cup of water — his only anchor in the loneliness of the witness box, where he sat and told the jury of what he had seen that night. Of what he had failed to do.

I am convinced to this day that his evidence was crucial to the outcome of the trial. I thought of him, as the jury foreperson's voice rang out with the verdict, and of that momentary encounter between three people, a shared look that lasted seconds.

It was chance that our witness had stayed home that evening. Chance that found him in the common room at that hour, peering around the door, curious. And it was chance that left him caught by uncertainty — his eyes following those two figures under the fluorescent lights, as they trod down the corridor towards their fate.

As the last person encountered by the victim and accused before both of their lives would be forever altered, this witness believed that he had been her last chance for the night to change course. And he'd missed it.

He was there, in the final steps of a journey that led to a sexual assault trial, and now he shoulders the guilt of not using those final moments, of not doing something he did not know how to do. I suspect he'll spend years wondering what might have been different if *he* had been different. If he had known or acted differently.

We should all wonder alongside him, because in one way or another, we are all that witness: if we could wind back time, would we only return to that moment of eye contact between two young people — time seeming to slow down as we hold our breath and hope that one person's courage will save the day?

Or would we go back further still, imagining a different journey entirely? One where we ensure that moment never even arrives?

'As the village that raises you, we have let you down,' I say to the auditorium of students in their final year of school. At the threshold of adulthood, no doubt most of them will go on to university and many will live at college when they do.

As I look out at this cavernous room, at the upturned faces full of hope for their own futures, that witness again appears in my mind. I manage to keep my own voice from cracking as I replay the scene in my imagination, for the hundredth time, of that chance encounter in a college corridor.

The truth is that we do not have to leave such things to chance. It is not fate that is responsible for the rates of sexual violence in our community; it is failure.

Our failure.

The rates of sexual violence are not some unchangeable constant, as inevitable as night following day. It's not enough to simply hope that it will not be so, for those we love or even for those we do not know. And, as someone who serves the institution charged with responding to sexual violence when it metes out its devastation, I know that it is not enough to put our faith in justice alone. File after file comes across my desk like a cruel conveyer belt: the damage is already done.

But there is another way, and those high rates of sexual violence need not be stubborn at all. It is within our power to create a different future, a brighter future. Sexual violence does not exist in a vacuum. It sits on a spectrum, kept alive by the apparently ordinary things we believe about sex, sexual behaviour, power, and violence. Kept alive by the attitudes and values we hold, sometimes unthinkingly, that contribute to an environment in which sexual violence, harassment, and unwanted sex happen frequently. Sexual violence does not exist in a vacuum, and it does not occur organically: it is a product of us.

None of us woke up one day with the ability to navigate sex and relationships. The knowledge and skills we needed didn't spontaneously manifest, like a reward for getting to the end of puberty. Reared in a culture that blushes and squirms at the mention of sex, a culture that believes 'boys will be boys', a culture that privileges entitlement to sexual pleasure for some but not others — many of us do not understand the nuances of consent. And many more who do not care to act in the best interests of another at the expense of our own desires. Or to even find out what those interests are.

We don't just hand young people the keys to a car with nothing but a wish and a prayer. How reckless, how negligent we would be if we did. We teach them how to drive, giving them all they need to stay safe on the roads as they use this new-found skill to pursue independence, employment, social lives.

We don't just throw kids into the swimming pool when they're little, hoping they won't drown. How culpable we would be if we did. We teach them how to swim. Not just so they can keep their head above water, but so they can experience the joy of going to the beach, of splashing in the local pool, of being confident in the water.

With these lessons, we give the gift of freedom. We recognise their right to it.

But when it comes to sex and relationships, we are ready to leave people to just figure it out themselves — even though the chances of getting it wrong might mean a traumatic experience for one person and the inside of a courtroom for another. Unfair would be a woeful understatement: reckless, negligent, culpable may be closer to the mark.

If we want people to have the knowledge, lexicon, skills, and values they need to navigate sex and relationships — healthily, happily, and ethically — we need to actually teach them. Otherwise, we leave their safety and wellbeing to chance: the safety and wellbeing we promise is their birthright. Young people know this, and have been calling for better sex education for many years now. Stephanie Liow, a then-Year 12 student in Victoria, Australia, said of her 2021 petition for holistic sex education in that state: 'Fighting for better sex education and support for survivors almost feels like a necessity, because I feel like I and most of my peers have been failed, and I do not want to see younger students go through the exact same thing. This has to change.' She went on to say: 'I know for a fact that my decisions would have been very different if I had received the proper relationship and sex education. I'm also aware that some people who put me in bad situations probably did not realise the impact they were having and would have acted differently if they had received the right education.'[8]

We can choose another way. There are communities all over the globe who imagine a society free from sexual violence, and who bring that imagination to life by harnessing the empowering qualities of education. In 2019, I travelled overseas to witness first-hand the use of age-appropriate, comprehensive relationships and sexuality education (RSE, for short) to safeguard sexual wellbeing. On a research fellowship, I stepped out of the justice system and into classrooms, parliaments, universities, offices, and parent groups — speaking to all the groups of people who are involved, in some way, in ensuring children and adolescents have access to comprehensive RSE, and all of whose roles we will explore in the chapters to come. I took a break from responding to sexual violence to explore how it might be prevented from happening in the first place.

For months I traipsed across borders, hauling overpacked suitcases onto trains and through airports, searching for answers. I wanted to find out how these communities have mobilised, taking up the fight for their young people's right to access comprehensive information and education that will empower them to pursue fulfilling lives.

Peering through this window into possibility, into what could be, has caused me to reflect on the cases I have worked on. On my own experiences, and those of my friends and family. The thousands of signatories to that petition. The students in that auditorium. I find myself imagining what could have been different for the victims, the perpetrators, the bystanders, and the families.

I marvel at those around the world who recognise that we all have a part to play in the solution and are making good on their promises of a brighter future.

So let us promise the same and chart a different course. Anything less is a betrayal.

Every Moment Counts

A few disclaimers, before we begin.

Terminology

In this book, I use the terms rape, sexual violence, and sexual harassment. I also use the term 'unwanted sex': for some, this is a contradiction in terms, on the basis that any sex that is unwanted ought to be understood as sexual violence or rape. However, research demonstrates that the language of unwanted sex is especially important for young people, many of whom do not recognise certain experiences as sexual violence or coercion, but rather as 'unwanted'. For example, the feeling of wanting to please a partner, or broader peer pressure to be sexually active. Indeed, this book explores a number of situations like this, with the express intention of demonstrating the importance of sex education in protecting against more than what might be legally understood as sexual violence. As Christopher Fisher, lead researcher at La Trobe University's Australian Research Centre in Sex, Health and Society, has pointed out: the research suggests that, in order to improve their sexual agency, 'we need to be more nuanced about the diverse ways young people experience unwanted sex and the different responses that are required'.

I use the terms sexuality education, sex-ed, and comprehensive relationships and sexuality education interchangeably. The term 'sexuality' is intended to have a broad meaning that captures sexual and intimate feelings, thoughts, and behaviours, as well as identity and attraction: 'Human sexuality encompasses the sexual knowledge, beliefs, attitudes, values, and behaviors of individuals. Its various dimensions involve the anatomy, physiology, and biochemistry of the sexual response system; identity, orientation, roles, and personality; and thoughts, feelings, and relationships. Sexuality is influenced by ethical, spiritual, cultural, and moral concerns. All persons are sexual, in the broadest sense of the word.'[1]

The presence and position of the word 'relationships' in the nomenclature is not intended to imply that sex and sexuality is only appropriate in the context of a traditional relationship, nor that education about those things should be taught through that lens. I use the word 'relationships' in this context to mean, very broadly, the means by which we relate to each other in various ways, to varying degrees of intimacy.

This book also uses both person-first and identity-first language.[2]

Below, you'll find a brief summary of the core principles and design features of comprehensive RSE, and it might look very different to the sex education you received. It is certainly a long way from what I got! And it is still very far from what many young people are getting today. Some of the things on the list may surprise you, or you may be unconvinced that all of it is necessary. You may even worry that some of it is inappropriate. If that's you, then I am so glad that you especially have picked up this book and am grateful for your curiosity. I warmly invite you to read on.

Format

Each chapter begins with a fictionalised vignette, before I explain something of RSE and my research. Some of these vignettes include descriptions of sexual violence and the trauma it inflicts. Others look at sexual experiences or encounters that are unwanted, or are negative or harmful in some way. Please take care when reading these vignettes, as some readers may find the content distressing.

At certain points, the vignettes slow right down to consider these experiences moment by moment. It may make for disquieting reading at times, but the reason for this is that when it comes to sexual violence and unwanted sex and sexual wellbeing, *every moment counts*. To understand what happens on these occasions — to see what forces are bearing down on the people in the room, what motivates them and what silences them — we need to linger a little. It is tempting to see these scenarios as black and white, or to wish that they were, but we need to reflect on the grey if we are to chart that different course.

It is important to note at the outset that the vignettes are silent on certain aspects of characters' identities: for example, race, ethnicity, faith, and, in the main, gender identity and ability/disability (although Chapter 9 focuses squarely on RSE for disabled and neurodivergent folk). This is not because racism, ableism, cis-normativity, and transphobia are not drivers of sexual violence, unwanted sex, and sexual harassment — they very much are. However, to write characters and their harmful experiences from some of those perspectives felt beyond the scope of my expertise, and certainly my lived experience. That said, the analysis that follows the vignettes does touch on some of these intersectional issues. All of this is to say that, while readers need not assume every character is white, cisgendered, able-bodied or neurotypical, I acknowledge that these chapters do not engage in a full intersectional analysis.

Any resemblance of the characters in the vignettes to people in real life is entirely coincidental, and no story is based on any particular case I have been involved in. Sadly, the rates of sexual violence and unwanted sex, and the commonality of the patterns and themes that run through those things like a dark thread, mean many of us will recognise our own experiences in these pages.

Limitations

With an honours thesis in the theory of sexual violence prevention versus response, followed by years at the coalface of the criminal justice system, I came to sex-ed an outsider, to some extent — I'm not a sexologist or a teacher, and I'm not a young person anymore, either. But this book speaks to what I can see from my position at an important crossroads: in one direction, the patterns of behaviour, the motivations, and the themes I have observed in sexual offence cases over the decade I've spent in criminal law; in the other direction, what I learned and observed overseas, and subsequently at home in Australia, about the implementation of comprehensive RSE.

One significant deficiency in my research is that my fellowship was Eurocentric: I went to Europe and North America, leaving out the leadership in sexual health and education that takes place elsewhere, like in Africa and Central and South America. Those I met with on my fellowship were all white, as I am, and I could be rightly criticised for contributing to an ongoing problem in sex research in this way. My research is the poorer for it, particularly given the importance of decolonising sex-ed to the relevance and efficacy of such education. For example, many of the concepts that comprehensive RSE endeavours to mitigate, such as shame around sex and sexuality, or hetero- and cis-normativity, are colonial and patriarchal concepts.[3]

This book focuses on sexual violence and unwanted sex between people who are old enough to consent to sexual activity with another person. It does not specifically deal with child sexual abuse, because while RSE is a protective factor against that type of offending as well, prevention efforts in that space carry an additional layer of expertise and nuance that is outside the scope of this book.

Although relationships and sexuality education ought to be lifelong, this book is about where that education journey starts — with young people — and how the lessons and information we do and don't get when we're young shape our experiences even as we get older, echoing throughout our lives.

This book is not only about the prevention of rape and sexual violence but also about the importance of ensuring sexual safety and wellbeing more broadly. It looks at the full spectrum of our expectations about sex, sexual experiences, intimacy, wellbeing, relationships, power, violence, and rights. We will consider the way we develop these expectations, learning social conventions, assumptions, ideas, and values about relationships, sex, and sexuality from a plethora of sources. From parents, families, faith, friends, peers, schools, teachers, coaches, and other people and places in our community to books, television programs, film, music, celebrities, role models, social media, pornography, and pop culture. We are inundated with messages about sex, relationships, consent, communication, respect, shame, pleasure, gender and sexuality, obligation, and entitlement. This book will interrogate how we think about all of those things, and how they work together to drive sexual violence as well as unwanted sex.

Of course, relationships and sexuality education is not a silver bullet for the scourge of sexual violence and harassment — nobody would say that RSE can prevent every rape. Nor will it inoculate against everything in those greyer areas of unwanted sex or negative sexual experiences. However, what the research tells us, what my travels overseas showed me, and what my work every day dealing with the result of refusing to talk to young people about healthy relationships and sex reveals is that while sex-ed may not be all we need, we will never get there without it.

This book will have a particular focus on the systemic, because the story of sexual violence and its prevention is a systemic one. Indeed, the story of RSE implementation ought to be a systemic one too. For this reason, I focus on the institutions of the settler-colonial state of Australia, such as its criminal justice system and its education system, because these are the institutions currently endowed with the relevant power, responsibilities, and resources when it comes to sexual violence prevention and redress.

Comprehensive Relationships and Sexuality Education

What do we mean by comprehensive RSE? There are some core principles and features of RSE recognised in the literature and, broadly, adopted by relevant peak bodies, educators, and advocates internationally. For children, it is not just learning about puberty and how babies are made. 'Prevention directed towards children serves to strengthen them, to further their independence, to expand their mobility, and to increase their freedom'; comprehensive, age-appropriate, and inclusive RSE for children includes themes of bodily autonomy, setting and observing limits, paying attention to feelings, getting help, differentiating between good and bad secrets, and gender roles and their diversity.[4]

And when it comes to adolescents, it is not just condoms on bananas and 'no means no'; it is not just about averting risk — risk of pregnancy, STIs, or sexual violence. Rather, comprehensive RSE is

> built on a framework of rights. It aims to provide adolescents with knowledge, skills, attitudes, and values that allow them to enjoy their physical and emotional sexuality on an individual level and in their relationships. [It] views sexuality in a holistic manner, as an integral part of adolescents' emotional and social development.[5]

RSE for adolescents focuses on areas such as gender, sexual and reproductive health, pleasure, violence, diversity and relationships. Such RSE has been 'associated with improved knowledge in sexual and reproductive health and fewer risky practices ... proper sexual education has been shown to delay sexual initiation, reduce the risk of teenage pregnancies, the frequency of sexual intercourse, the number of sexual partners, and increase the use of condoms and other contraceptive methods'.[6]

Indeed, comprehensive RSE approaches — that is, approaches 'that address a broad definition of sexual health and take positive, affirming, inclusive approaches to human sexuality' — have been shown to:

- Reduce homophobia and homophobic bullying;
- Improve recognition of gender equity, rights, and social justice;
- Decrease dating and interpersonal violence, including sexual violence;
- Improve knowledge and attitudes about healthy relationships and communication within them;

- Improve social-emotional learning (e.g. increased empathy, respect for others, improved communication, managing feelings, positive self-image, increased sense of self-control and safety, and establishing and maintaining positive relationships);
- A corollary of all the above is that such education improves academic outcomes as well.[7]

All of these things echo the core principles recognised in key international research — that RSE must:

- Be based on a human-rights approach;
- Be adapted for age and developmental stage and spread out over several years of education;
- Use a holistic concept of wellbeing (including health);
- Stress gender equality, the right to self-determination and acceptance of diversity;
- Promote a positive approach to human sexuality;
- Provide scientifically accurate information;
- Aim to increase knowledge, develop values and norms, and build behavioural skills.[8]

Comprehensive RSE in Australia must also be co-designed with First Nations people to ensure it is culturally appropriate. Such co-design has to be meaningful; as Lauren French, sexologist, sexuality educator, and First Nations woman, said to me 'Co-design can't be tokenistic.' Amanda Sibosado and Michelle Webb of Curtin University wrote, in March 2022, in respect of advancements in 'consent education' in Australia:

> Moving forward, the voices, experiences and expertise of Aboriginal and Torres Strait Islander peoples must be listened to. Historical and current colonial violence, as well as the strengths of culture, must be understood and incorporated. Engaging with First Nations people working in and for the community is where we need to start.[9]

1

All the Time in the World

Elliot and Amy

Amy noticed Elliot's hands were clammy as he fumbled across her skin in the dark. The moon was throwing enough light into his ute that she could see his face when he leaned over her in the passenger seat he'd hastily reclined.

She wanted to be anywhere else as Elliot clumsily pawed at her chest. She realised she was cold when she saw the goosebumps on her thighs as he pulled her leggings down. She wanted to ask him to wear protection if he was going to do this to her, but she couldn't make a sound. She felt like she was watching them from the back seat, him moving over her as she lay there, wide-eyed and unable to say a word. Her tongue felt welded to the bottom of her jaw, and her limbs were as heavy as lead.

She watched on until it was over, and he rolled back into the driver's seat and yanked up his jeans.

'This is our secret,' he said, driving them away from the empty carpark and towards her house. Towards her room where she had been only half an hour earlier. Towards her parents, watching the evening news with no idea who she was with.

If her voice ever decided to work again, Amy thought, she had no intention of telling a soul. After all, what would she say?

•

Cases like Elliot and Amy's are all too common. While this particular case is fictionalised, many of the elements frequently recur in cases that come across my desk, and I recognise them from my own and my friends' experiences as teenagers, too.

As the village who raised people like Elliot and Amy, in order to understand how they ended up where they did, we need to watch both their trajectories, to familiarise ourselves with their environments, their histories, if we are to understand the point of collision and have any hope of changing course.

At 23, Elliot was one of the oldest employees working Friday nights and weekends at the local cinema. He'd recently been made a manager, having worked there for several years since graduating from his Catholic high school.

The responsibility made him feel good about himself, and the team gave him a sense of belonging. He had never been particularly popular at school, especially not with girls.

But he could be different here.

Occasionally, an old classmate would come in to see a movie, and it would unsettle Elliot. He'd see the moment they recognised him, and he would feel small again: reduced by the unwelcome reminder that, no matter how much he sought to portray otherwise, he did not have the easy confidence of those who'd been blessed with the social currency of charisma.

When Elliot first started at the cinema, the other girls his age who worked there reminded him of the ones at school. They were polite, but they had no interest in him as anything other than a colleague. He was nothing but friendly, and still they seemed to look through him. One by one they left, off to study at uni or to work somewhere else.

As the years passed and he stayed at the cinema, he became one of the oldest there. Friday nights and weekends were ideal shifts for his younger colleagues, most of whom had school during the week, and he was rostered on as manager.

In this ecosystem, this new world order, Elliot was no longer at the bottom of the food chain. Being older became *his* currency. So too did his role as manager and the fact he could drive, and owned his own car. Now, he had something to offer. He would lean into those things when he felt insecure, telling the younger staff about whatever new trimming he was getting done to his ute or regaling them with stories of his night out at some new bar in the city.

His seniority, his car, his income became his claims to maturity and worth, and were carefully brought out at opportune moments. Sometimes he would even tell himself that those things mattered more than good looks or confidence. And yet, a girlfriend remained out of reach. Films where the awkward guy prevailed and got the hot girl gave him hope. So did the ones where the girl was attracted to the older guy — attracted to his maturity, his means. Elliot was more than a little confused that the girls in his life didn't always follow the same script.

When Elliot pined after a girl who didn't reciprocate his interest, his mum would say, 'They don't know what they're missing.'

He chose to believe her, brushing aside his nagging suspicion that in real life, nice guys come last. He couldn't say why, but he came to begrudge the friend zone and those who put him in it, frustrated that nobody seemed willing to give him a chance.

When he started hooking up with the girls at work, he began keeping a list. The number felt important to him — like his car and his pay cheque, it became another salve against the dull ache of insecurity.

If he was honest with himself, he might admit that the younger ones were an easier target. They didn't know better and that worked for him. After all, he wasn't doing anything wrong — it wasn't like they weren't legal. And didn't he deserve to be wanted?

Amy landed a job at the cinema just after she turned 18, towards the beginning of Year 12. Her parents hadn't wanted her to get a job before then, so this was her first, and it gave her a new-found independence. She loved being part of a new community that gave her new responsibilities.

Her manager, Elliot, was friendly, and after a while they developed a bantering rapport. He was patient with her and never made her feel stupid.

She didn't know many older guys, and this was her first time having a boss. Elliot was fairly informal and relaxed in their dealings, which suited her and, it seemed, everyone else. He seemed happy for the team to treat him more like a friend. They were all friends, getting together outside of work and, she learned, some of them even hooking up with each other.

So, when her phone vibrated one night with a notification that he had requested to follow her on social media, it was unexpected but not completely weird, given his work vibe. Besides, Amy found herself thinking, she was friends with the rest of the team on socials, her thumb hovering over the 'accept' button.

She'd only worked there a few weeks at this point, and would hate for him to think of her as rude. If she didn't accept, what if he asked her why on her next shift? She couldn't pretend she didn't use the app, as the others at work followed her on it. She shrugged to herself and accepted the request, before turning back to her homework.

He didn't message her immediately, and she forgot he'd added her until he sent her a joke a few days later. *Haha*, she replied reflexively — even though it wasn't that funny.

Gradually, the messages increased. Extensions of conversations they'd had at work, stories about funny regulars who had come in during the week, photos of antics at the cinema.

Then, one Thursday night, he told her about a couple who were hooking up in the back of Theatre 2. It felt a bit weird that he brought it up, and she didn't really know what to say when he told her he thought the girl was giving a blow job.

Gross, she wrote.

She seemed like she knew what she was doing 😉, he replied.

It was in that moment that Amy's feeling of unease began. Almost imperceptibly, like a tiny seed buried deep under soil, doubt took hold.

But she remembered that he was kind and helpful, and assured herself this was just banter. He always praised her maturity; he probably just forgot sometimes that she was younger. It's not like there wasn't sex chat sometimes at work, jokes between them all that she laughed along to.

She decided she'd been overthinking it when she heard him joking about the couple with the others the next day, and realised she wasn't the only one he'd told about the incident.

She relaxed again, the knot in her stomach easing slightly, and reminded herself they were friends, as he was always saying. He listened to her complain about exams and the girls at school and gave her good advice. And he confided in her about his brother, who was always getting in trouble and stressing his parents. They were friends.

Elliot started driving her home from work after the Friday shift, after one time she got stuck without a lift. Sometimes they would sit in the car talking for a while before she would walk up the driveway to her front door, turning to wave as he drove off. He thought they were becoming closer. She was pretty enough, and — reminding himself that she was mature for her age — Elliot found himself testing the waters, trying flirtation to gauge her response.

He was clumsy at it. One time, he asked if she'd ever had a boyfriend before. She had — one. Another time, he joked about her being a virgin and she protested, blushing, that of course she wasn't.

If ever she wasn't super chatty towards him at work, he'd ask her what was wrong. He seemed to take it personally, and Amy knew he was a sensitive guy.

For his part, he didn't think of himself as sensitive but he didn't like it when she seemed stand-offish. It made him anxious, reminding him of the girls at school who looked straight past him. He liked Amy, and he hoped she liked him back. Seeking to shun those high-school shadows, he would prompt her for reassurance. *Are you mad?* ☹, he would text, or sometimes, *Did I do something?* She never was upset with him, and although it was annoying that he always assumed she was, she was quick to reassure him.

One Sunday, he asked her if she wanted to hang out with him

after the shift finished. She was taken aback and, feeling his eyes on her as she swept up the popcorn from the aisle, she didn't know what to say. 'Maybe for a bit,' she said, buying time before she could come up with an excuse not to. 'I've got homework, though.'

'Yeah, just for a bit. I've got stuff to do, too.' He tried to sound casual, excited that she had agreed to spend time with him, even though she had homework to do.

He drove them to his place, and she felt more comfortable when she met his parents in the kitchen. He introduced her as 'Amy from work' and, when his folks seemed unfazed by it, Amy thought perhaps this wasn't that weird.

They watched YouTube on his laptop in his room, and she began to relax. Until, at some point, he asked if she knew two of their friends at work were hooking up. She shrugged and played on her phone. 'Mum's asking where I am,' she lied. 'Can you take me home?'

The next time he asked to hang out, Amy was in her bedroom upstairs on a school night.

I can come get you, he messaged.

I'm really tired haha, she sent back.

She watched with trepidation at the ellipsis blinking as he typed.

My brothers on his shit again. I need to get out of the house and talk to someone

Sitting on the edge of her bed, she chewed the inside of her lip as she hunched over her phone, trying to work out how to reply.

A few streets away, Elliot paced his bedroom, agitated and overwhelmed by slamming doors and raised voices between his parents and brother. Desperate to clear his head, he needed to see Amy. She always made him feel better. Why hadn't she responded? Hoping to avoid rejection, he texted again:

Don't you want to hang out with me? ☹

Amy rolled her eyes, anxious. That fucking sad face. What could she say to that?

Parents will ask where Im going

Tell them ur going for a walk

The feeling of unease in the pit of her stomach unfurled.

She felt confused. She couldn't tell where the lines were; they were so blurred.

She didn't want to disappoint him — Elliot was her friend. And he was her manager.

But it didn't seem like he was speaking as her manager.

What could she say — 'no'?

She knew any awkwardness in their exchange would just follow her into her next shift. Maybe all her next shifts.

She had to manage this.

Ok but I cant be long

He drove them to a carpark in a nearby industrial area, the grey streets empty and still after business had closed hours before. Pulling the nose of his ute up to a windowless brick wall, he was relieved at the privacy it afforded them.

By now, the unease had started to reach up into Amy's chest, like a jittery hand grabbing at her ribs.

Elliot sighed, turning off the ignition, feeling the tension in his shoulders slide away. Amy asked if he was all right, and he spoke for a time, while she listened attentively. He was awash with gratitude for her in that moment, reading her concern as something more. Suddenly, he was almost sure his feelings were reciprocated. Why else would she come out at night to console him?

Despite his list of conquests, he was still awkward in initiating anything. He took his cues from the world of film, where romantic moments are often depicted by a shared understanding of mutual feelings and a meaningful look. Characters simply gravitate towards each other, reaching out urgently, lustfully, without so much as a word.

Perhaps if he could just initiate some physical touch …

'Can I have a hug?' he asked.

Amy wavered. They'd hugged before, greeting each other at social events along with everyone else.

This time it felt different because they were alone.

As they embraced across the gear stick, she patted him awkwardly on the back.

She was looking over his shoulder at the empty carpark behind him when he kissed her neck. The car spaces seemed to stretch away from her as she stared at them, frozen. She could smell his deodorant; it was the same as her brother used. His breath tickled her neck uncomfortably.

Before she even noticed his hand had moved, he'd found the lever to recline the passenger seat, and suddenly she was looking at the roof of his car. There were flecks in the fabric, and she wondered what they were from. He clambered over the centre console and, in the moonlight, she saw him smile at her.

She stared back at him, and remembered that her parents didn't know where she was.

When I stepped off the train in Galway in May 2019, I misjudged the weight of my suitcases, and they rushed down the stairs behind me, clipping my ankles painfully — as impatient to leave the stuffy carriage as I was, it seemed. The air outside was crisp and biting, as if Australia's late autumn had followed me to Ireland. I looked around for my friend who was collecting me, with that unique thrill that comes from seeing someone you know from one place in an entirely different part of the world.

Galway sits on the River Corrib on the west coast of Ireland, a couple of hours by train from Dublin. The small city has been home to the National University of Ireland Galway (NUI Galway) since 1845, and I was there to interview one of its academics as part of my Churchill Fellowship.

A Churchill Fellowship is an annual grant for Australians to undertake international research, and I was one of the lucky cohort who went just before COVID-19 closed our borders. The motto of the Fellowship Trust is 'learn globally, inspire locally', and prospective Fellows propose a research project about any issue that warrants investigation overseas. And I do mean *any* issue: since the 1960s, Churchill Fellows have travelled to learn about such things as floristry, mid-century modern architecture, bias in police decision-making, public toilet design, restorative justice … If you can convince the Churchill Trust that Australia has something to learn from overseas, they will give you the means to go and research it.

I had been passionate about sex-ed since writing my honours thesis at the end of my law degree in 2012, arguing that education better protects against sexual violence than the criminal law. Despite writing page after page questioning the criminal justice system, I marched off to serve that institution as soon as I turned my thesis in. But my years at the coalface since then, as both a prosecutor and Legal Aid lawyer, only deepened my resolve, showing me the limits of the justice system in technicolour. Its capacity to react but not to prevent reminded me of a pawn on a chessboard, only able to advance in one direction.

In Australia, RSE has taken up residence in the too-hard basket: not important, not appropriate, not that easy. Dr Melissa Kang, a specialist in youth health, adolescent sexuality, and sexual health, spoke of the history of sex-ed in settler-colonial Australia during a symposium at the World Association of Sexual Health Congress 2021. She described it as telling a story of 'deficit and reactionaryism', with sex-ed policy decisions born of concerns about disease, dysfunction, or the protection of victims. The rise of diseases like syphilis and gonorrhoea after World War I, and the HIV pandemic in the 1980s, drove public discourse about sex education and shaped its content around safe sex. Teenage pregnancy prevention has long been the other twin focus of sex-ed. And then, by 2021, the overwhelming volume of disclosures of sexual violence and harassment by young people had put consent at the heart of sex-ed discourse in Australia, giving it a harm-prevention focus.

The Australian national curriculum provides some guidance for the states and territories, and those responsible for it have recently increased the focus on respectful relationships and consent. Lack of clarity means that Australian students have wildly varying and inconsistent experiences of RSE — but the guidance of the national curriculum can only do so much in any event, when each jurisdiction, and each school therein, has the autonomy to determine sex-ed content and delivery. Schools may feel that it is a matter for the home, or may consider sex-ed to be less important than academic and sporting achievements — even though research has shown 'less truancy and an improvement in academic performance in those who have taken sexuality education courses'.[1] Schools often don't know where to start, or how to navigate what is a nuanced and specialised area. There are no regulated standards to ensure educators are appropriately qualified to deliver RSE, and many teachers report feeling unconfident in teaching this subject.[2]

Importantly, surveys of young people's experience of sex-ed routinely reveal that they want more information on relationships, intimacy, sexual pleasure, and love — not just on 'bodies, bugs, and babies', as Curtin University sexologist and academic Dr Jacqui Hendriks has quipped.[3] I've been advocating in this space for years now, and it saddens me that so many young Australians' experience of sex-ed today is similar to mine decades ago: puberty picture books and condoms on bananas the high watermark, scare tactics and shaming polemics the low point.

Don't get me wrong — there are excellent RSE resources, providers, and educators out there, in every state and territory. It is just that young people's *access* to sex-ed in Australia is a lottery, one where the odds are not good.

So, in 2018, surer than ever that our justice system is little more than an ambulance at the bottom of the cliff and frustrated by Australia's apparent apathy towards sexual-violence prevention efforts, I convinced the Churchill Trust to send me to Europe and North America to find out how other countries do sex-ed. To see what other chess pieces they deploy against the adversary of sexual violence.

Galway was my first stop. Sarah and her boyfriend, nicknamed Shaggy for his mop of hair, found me outside the station and helped me load my luggage into the boot. I had met Sarah twice before, but never in her home country. Serendipitously, she worked at NUI Galway in the same department as the academic I wanted to interview, and she had put us in touch.

I was to meet Dr Siobhán O'Higgins the following day, but on this afternoon, Sarah and Shaggy told me they were taking me to the Cliffs of Moher. The stunning and imposing cliff faces that look out over the North Atlantic are only revealed on a clear day, and apparently you are quite lucky to get one. My friends must have brought me some of their Irish luck as a welcome gift, because the sun was high and there was not a cloud to be seen. Gazing at the monumental formation stretching away from us, as far as we could see, I hoped it was a good omen for the months of travel and enquiry ahead.

The next day also started out sunny, and Sarah walked me to NUI Galway, to the School of Psychology, to introduce me to Dr O'Higgins. The campus is old and beautiful and green, and I had a moment to take it in before heading into a campus café with my interviewee.

When Dr O'Higgins introduced herself, I was immediately intimidated, as I always am by women I admire. I had read about her work developing sexual health and consent workshops, including the Active* Consent programme (then the SMART Consent programme) and the West of Ireland Sex Education Resource. We sat next to the window and got off to a faltering start. This was my first fellowship interview, and everything I had planned to ask simply fell out of my head. I suddenly realised how little I knew, that I didn't even know what I didn't know, and I had no idea where to begin.

Lucky for me, Dr O'Higgins did. She spoke quickly and directly, and I struggled to keep pace, my pen flying over the pages of my notebook as I took notes. She started with what she considers the natural jumping-off point, as a researcher and sexuality educator: parents.

'I work with parents first. If parents are educated well, they feel empowered to talk to kids. I say to them, "If you don't talk to your children about sex at all, they will find out about it anyway and miss out on things you want them to know".'

This is a sound strategy. We know that parents and caregivers are the first educators of kids and young people. They are often the first port of call for young people when it comes to the subject of relationships and sex, and ideally they would feel able to fulfil that role. But parents and caregivers can also be the most reluctant to talk to their kids about sex, whether out of embarrassment, shame, uncertainty about what to say, or fear that doing so might encourage their kids to engage in sexual behaviour.

And this is not necessarily their fault. When I think about cases like Elliot and Amy's, I can't help but wonder what Elliot's parents would have wanted him to know about sex, and how much — if at all — they had spoken to him about it. Did they feel confident to speak freely with him about sex and relationships? Did they know what to say? Had *their* parents ever talked to them about it, or did they grow up with storks bringing babies and the 'birds and bees' chat? Our collective shame around sex runs deep, and we pass it down through the generations, relying on euphemisms and make-believe so we don't have to say the words.

When Elliot's mum said to him 'They don't know what they're missing', hoping to quell his insecurity, she may not have understood that it could suggest to Elliot he was being hard-done by girls who weren't giving him the time of day. What if instead she had said 'You won't always be liked by everyone, and you need to respect that, but when someone does really want to be with you, it is a wonderful feeling and is worth the wait'? Could that have equipped Elliot with a mindset that ensured he cared more about whether Amy really, actually liked him, rather than just hoping that she would if she got to know him better?

And when Elliot brought Amy home that day, did his parents wonder what was going on between them? Did they ask him how he felt about Amy? Did they notice Amy was younger, and talk to Elliot about what that meant in terms of power imbalance? Did they explain to him that the age difference and his role as her supervisor meant she may feel less able to voice her boundaries?

If they didn't, perhaps it's because they did not feel comfortable or did not know how. This is why Dr O'Higgins spends hours with parents first, digging into the subject matter, unafraid and unembarrassed, answering their questions and assuaging their concerns. She is their ally, not their adversary.

This is an important point, because when it comes to RSE, I have noticed a divide: there are some who want it to be taught in schools because they are uncertain how to do it themselves, and others who believe it should be reserved for the home. The latter group often fear that the effort to improve RSE in schools seeks to exclude parents from that discussion. In fact, the answer to both these perspectives is one of partnership: between school and home and community. Research shows 'encouraging results of sex education interventions that … involve teachers, adolescents, and parents'.[4] Robert van der Gaag, a municipal government RSE implementation officer I met with in Leiden, Holland, described a 'triangle of education': education of children, education of parents, and education of teachers, and we will consider all three points on this triangle (and a few others that might make it a square or a pentagon) as we move through the book. In any event, experts and advocates in every country I visited prioritised engaging with parents, caregivers, and community first and foremost.

Those professionals recognise that if parents like Elliot's feel empowered to talk to their kids about sex and relationships, they are more likely to have constructive, healthy conversations around the kitchen table, and the values taught in sex-ed lessons at school are more likely to be reinforced at home.

With more information and greater literacy themselves, Elliot's parents, and the community around him — his extended family, his colleagues at the cinema, his mates at the gym, perhaps — may have been able to set the record straight about some things. And with that kind of input, Elliot may not have believed that his masculinity could be measured by the number of sexual conquests he'd had, or that his carefully kept list was more important than Amy's wishes.

And if the village that raised him had been more comfortable talking openly about sex and relationships, and communication and cues in those contexts, he may not have found initiating things so difficult that he felt it necessary to launch straight into kissing Amy without asking. He may not have bought into the myth that talking, in the moment, would kill the mood. He may not have been left to take his cues from films in which characters understand each other's lust and enthusiasm with no more than a look.

Telepathy in lust or romance is not confined to the silver screen. It enters our interactions via our discomfort to openly discuss what we want in bed, or to ask what the other person likes. What they want to do. Where to touch, where not to venture. In a heteronormative world, it is in the scornful jokes about men being clueless in finding the clitoris, and in the anxiety not to offend by offering direction. It turns up in our fear of 'killing the mood', and in our elevation of sex to a plane where emotions, desires, and needs are unspoken.

Is there any other social interaction where we rely so wholly on reading another's mind, especially when it involves touching them? Intimately? By the time Dr O'Higgins was talking about ambiguity in sex, the grey stone of the quadrangle outside had started to blend with the sky as clouds gathered, scurrying across the sun and bringing with them a light drizzle. She was telling me about the Active* Consent Workshops she helped develop, which include sessions and workshops for university students, and others for secondary students in schools. The sessions for university students have them responding to short scenarios about intimacy and sex, discussing the 'grey areas' that can arise in that context. Different participants read the scenarios differently, based on their own perspectives — powerfully demonstrating the obvious reality that people will see the same event with completely diverging views of what occurred. How many bystander witnesses have I called to give evidence who report different, sometimes completely opposing, versions of the same incident, even when they both saw the whole thing?

The Active* Consent Workshops encourage participants to consider such ambiguities in the sexual context, and equip them with the skills to communicate effectively in that context. A report about the program describes how, before the workshops, students 'spoke about the difficulty of inferring intentions and of choosing between multiple possible interpretations of events'.[5] Afterwards, however, participants felt better about establishing and asking for consent, and put greater emphasis on verbal and nonverbal consent rather than passive consent. Those discussions helped them feel more confident about navigating those ambiguities with communication.

I can't imagine Elliot would have had any such workshops at his Catholic high school. If he had, would he have assumed that Amy's agreement to come over the first time he asked, 'even though she had homework', meant she really wanted to spend time with him? Or might he have considered that she, put on the spot by the request from her older boss, felt compelled to agree? That the mention of homework was actually an effort to say no, couched in an unassailable excuse. And when she came out at his request the second time, when he needed someone to talk to, would he have been so sure that it was because she reciprocated his feelings of desire, or might he have considered that she did not want to offend? Or just wanted to be there for her friend and colleague who needed someone to listen? If Elliot had been in some of the sessions delivered by Dr O'Higgins, he might have been taught about how power imbalances can impact our ability to communicate freely, to advocate for what we want.

And he might have learned that people may freeze when they are afraid. This is an instinctual physical response that we can't control; our nervous system taking over, like a mouse in a field going still to avoid detection by the eagle circling above. He might have recognised that Amy's stillness, her apparent acquiescence to him touching her, was not acquiescence at all — let alone encouragement. Would the teachers at his Catholic high school have talked about how someone might react to sexual touch? Would they have spoken about sex at all?

The Active* Consent workshop results showed that most students were dissatisfied with the sex-ed they'd received at school. I was quickly reminded that most of those students would have been Catholic educated when Dr O'Higgins chuckled about being kicked out of two schools decades ago, by the bishops in charge. 'How many schools in Ireland are Catholic?' I asked.

An old memory stirred, and I had to focus to catch it before it eluded me. I was a small child, peering through the breeze bricks in a wall that separated my school playground from the garden of a house where nuns lived, feeling naughty as I tried to spy on them. I had forgotten about the close relationship between my Catholic primary school and the church whose grounds we backed onto. That was a school where I received no sex education, and where traditional, binary gender roles were still embraced: my teacher offering toy cars to the boys, while the girls played 'house' at the back of the oval, sweeping dirt and inviting guests for 'tea'. That was a school where I wrote a love note to someone I liked, nervously leaving it for them to find at their desk, and everyone laughed at me. That day, thanks to my precocious but naive daring, we all learned that expressing feelings might be met with ridicule. The teacher did nothing to correct that lesson. Our relationship with the church, whose steeple we could see from behind our desks, saw me memorising Catholic prayers in class, but not learning about my own body, my own feelings.

Evidently my Australian experience of Catholic education was not a unique one; with a wry laugh, Dr O'Higgins brought me out of my reverie. 'How many schools are Catholic? This is Ireland. It's easier to say how many are not.' That's when I learned 90 per cent of schools in Ireland are Catholic run, even the state schools.

It turns out the students in her study were not the only ones dissatisfied with sex-ed in Ireland. Later that week, I would find myself in the richly carpeted halls of the Oireachtas Éireann — the Irish Parliament — meeting with the Clerk of the Joint Committee on Education and Skills, to find out about the national review of RSE that had just taken place. Notwithstanding Ireland's Catholic roots, the influence of the Church in Irish schools had dwindled over the past couple of decades, and parents had — according to Dr O'Higgins — come around to RSE. With the national review, this small country with a strong religious history had decided that its kids deserved sex-ed that wasn't governed by, as it was expressed in one document I saw, 'outdated morals'. The clerk told me that, while younger and more liberal politicians had contributed to the review, there had been an organic cultural shift, and even more conservative folk had acknowledged the need for it.

So, if a Catholic country like Ireland can do it, Catholic Education in Australia — my primary school, Elliot's high school — can do it too. In fact, I would learn that one of the most effective programs in Ireland was in a Catholic boys' school. I know there are similar examples in Australia, of faith-based schools bucking stereotype and trying to equip their students with the information they need. I have been approached by dedicated staff of Catholic Education institutions in this country who are, with open hearts and open minds, endeavouring to genuinely improve relationships and sexuality education for their students while upholding the pillars of their faith.

If only Elliot's school had balanced the values of its faith with the importance of accurate and age-appropriate information about sex and relationships. Information that would have given Elliot — and Amy — a much better chance.

•

In a faith system that says sex is for reproduction only, it's hard to imagine sexual pleasure on the lesson plan, in classrooms that have Jesus hanging on a crucifix next to the clock. But: 'If you don't talk about pleasure, you get objectification of the act,' Dr O'Higgins said to me. 'I'm trying to bring the loveliness back to sex.'

And so Dr O'Higgins had arrived, inevitably, at what is the stickiest point in sex-ed — and not just for the Catholics. Sticky because, as we have already considered, it can feel impossible to discuss sex even while we're actually doing it with someone we want to be doing it with. But talking about sexual pleasure in the abstract, in polite company? Mortifying. And speaking about it to young people? Disgusting. Corrupting, even.

There is a fear that, upon learning about their bodies and sex, young people will run off and engage in sexual activity. As if giving them accurate, age-appropriate information will be construed as some sort of encouragement. That it will flick a switch in their brains and they'll no longer be able to contain themselves. In fact, the opposite is true: the more you speak to young people about sex, their bodies, and their rights, the later they will have their first sexual experience and the less likely they are to have negative sexual experiences. School-based sexuality education can improve adolescent sexual health outcomes. The evidence bears that out time and again.[6]

Young people deserve our honesty. At the age and stage that it's appropriate, they deserve to hear us speak openly about sex in a positive, healthy, respectful way. Including the truth that people have sex because it feels good. Leaving this part out may be the most damaging, dangerous thing we do. Because consent and intimacy, even pleasure, are — or should be — completely intertwined. The standard of consent to sexual activity should be that everyone present is really into it, wants to be there, is getting a lot out of the experience. Otherwise, too much sexual activity occurs in those grey areas. That ambiguous zone, the risky margin, becomes the playing field — where consent is mere permission to access, rather than active participation.

The danger in that is realised in cases like Elliot and Amy's. What did Elliot know about sexual pleasure? What did he know about Amy's right to it? Had he been taught to care about it? In his school biology lesson, learning about reproduction, had he been given anything more than diagrams of the penis, the scrotum, the uterus, and the fallopian tubes? Erections and ejaculation in the spotlight, everybody else erased. Leaving his frame of reference about sex to be defined only by his own desires. His own wants. Something he got to do to someone, if they would let him. Rather than something they wanted to do *with* him, because he turned them on, made them feel good, excited. Perhaps he'd internalised all the messages from film, social media, pop culture, that women aren't as into sex as men anyway, that girls will be more demure about their desires than guys.

Because if he had been watching for enthusiasm, excitement, from Amy, he may not have seen her stillness as a green light. He may have recognised in her wide-eyed face that she was afraid. All he was looking for was permission to access, and he took her silence and stillness to mean he had it. As though she had all the time in the world to tell him she wasn't up for it. As if permission was there until expressly rescinded, with no duty to ask first.

Didn't she have the right to be asked? The right to want or not to want? To expect that everyone she encountered would recognise and respect her autonomy as a person, not just as a vessel for someone else's pursuit of sexual gratification?

This is why it is imperative that we make active participation in sex, autonomy, rights, and pleasure the standard. The status quo. But to do that we need to admit it, to talk about it, to teach young people to expect it.

If Elliot had truly cared about Amy's enthusiasm, her pleasure, would he have tried it on with her in the first place? Would he have realised she wasn't into it and stopped? Could she have been spared the trauma of those frozen moments? Was she destined to flinch every time she smelled that brand of deodorant, to feel her heart rate quicken and her mouth go dry every time she saw a ute? Didn't she have the right to be spared all that?

What could have been different, had his village raised him differently?

2

In the Dark

Max and Bec

'Can you give me head?' Max whispered hoarsely. They had been making out for ages on his bed with the lights off, shy in the newness of each other.

His mum was watching television down the hall, and occasionally they could hear her moving around the kitchen. The sound of cutlery clinking and the tap gushing would tug at Bec's attention, pulling her out of the heady fog of lust. She craned her neck towards the door, peering at the light coming under the crack and waiting for it to fling open at any moment. Even though she was 17, there was no way her parents would let her have a boy in her room with the door shut. 'She won't bother us,' Max said, cupping her jaw in his hand and turning her face back to his. He kissed her again and the butterflies in her stomach went wild.

Bec liked Max a lot. They'd first met on the bus back from an athletics carnival where a few different schools had competed, the only passengers remaining by the time the bus route terminated at the interchange. They caught each other's eye and he asked her what events she'd competed in. Wanting to appear nonchalant, Bec didn't admit to having noticed him throughout the day. She had, of course — his confident air and easy smile stood out. She had seen him flirting with Anna Thomas, one of the popular girls from her school: tall and pretty, Anna always managed to look good in their frumpy, itchy uniform. The way the pair had been interacting made Bec think they were a couple, but later, as the bus lurched into its station and Max asked Bec if he could add her on social media, she assumed she must have read that wrong. The memory of him and Anna flew clean out of her mind when he winked at her as they parted ways. She almost skipped home.

They arranged to meet in a local park one night after a few weeks of messaging each other. They lay under the stars and, with nobody around and the uneven turf no impediment, they kissed. Bec was hooked. Max took up residence in her mind — unable to stop thinking about him since, she wandered through the clothing racks at her weekend retail job in a daze, remembering every moment over and over again.

So when he invited her over to his place the Friday after their grass-stained adventure, she was excited at the chance. Kissing him in the park had been momentous for her. A revelation. Every touch had been exhilarating, like when she was little and used to leap off the highest diving board at the pool, arms freewheeling and squealing with delight. And now, just like when she would hit the water and the adrenaline would rush in, she wanted to chase that high again.

Before Max, her crushes — and there were lots of them — had been unrequited. She was painfully aware that she was not attractive to her peers, for whatever reason. She didn't think she was ugly, just nothing special. She felt stupid and boring. Sometimes she cried to her mum about it, her anguish spilling out of her eyes and onto her pillowcase. Bec's mum despaired that she could offer no explanation, the memories of her own lonely high school years holding no useful lessons for her daughter's plight.

But now she, boring Bec, had been invited over to a guy's place. Not just any guy, someone genuinely charismatic and popular. She had told her parents they were studying, worried they would quiz her about him if she said more. The question she was avoiding was why Max had asked her over rather than out — the honest answer to which was that he might not want anyone to see them together.

As she drove through the suburbs in the rain, newly minted

P-plates on her dad's sedan, she was practically light-headed with anticipation. But something was nagging at her. Something underneath the excitement, another emotion that she couldn't quite put her finger on.

Her conscious mind tried to suppress it, wanting to stay with the effervescent glee that was fizzing all over her, replaying the scenes from the park like a kind of amuse-bouche for the events of the night to come. But her gut feeling wouldn't be silenced, and suddenly Anna Thomas rushed into her mind. Bec remembered how Max had been flirting with her at the carnival, how he had leaned in to speak to her, how his eyes had followed her as she walked away with her friends. He'd watched her with a look on his face that now seemed familiar. What did it remind her of? Bec wondered, scrunching her nose in concentration as she waited at the intersection to turn into his street, the indicator clicking like a metronome to her thoughts.

Click.

Click.

Click.

Ah.

It occurred to her: what she saw in Max's face that day at the carnival was something she recognised in herself. A longing, a yearning. Max looked at Anna the way Bec looked at him.

When she knocked at Max's front door, his mum answered. Bec hoped her palms weren't sweating too much as they shook hands. She felt herself blushing when Max came into the room, the heat crawling up her face at his lazy grin. *How could someone so effortlessly cool be interested in someone so … disappointing.*

After some polite conversation, Max made an excuse for the two of them to disappear down the hall into his room, where he shut the door behind them. The only place to sit was on his bed, so she lowered herself onto it, and they had a stilted conversation about English Lit and poetry. She told him her favourite poet was Sylvia Plath, hoping he would think her interesting.

•

Max *did* think she was interesting. He was pleasantly surprised to discover they had shared interests, and he found that he enjoyed talking with her. And he thought she was pretty cute. Not a stunner, but cute enough. Plus he could tell she liked him, and he enjoyed feeling admired.

As a rule, he loved getting attention from girls. It made him feel really good to know that they thought he was attractive, and he would often chase the stroke to his ego. Because he was genuinely nice as well as charming, he had lots of opportunities to practise flirting, and it became one of his favourite pastimes.

With big eyes and dimples, he'd been a cute kid, and cheeky. The adults around him seemed to find his cheek endearing, even while they were scolding him for it. His aunties would pinch his face and dote on him, even when he was being a little shit. They told him he'd grow up to be a heartbreaker — something he didn't understand when he was little. What he did understand from a young age, though, was that he would be indulged. The lady who ran the shop down the street would affectionately chide him for being a rascal when he acted up, and his coach would laugh along as he played the clown, holding court with his under-12 soccer team. Max's name was also on heavy rotation in the classic primary school anthem about sitting in a tree.

He grew up knowing he was lovable.

As an extrovert, he drew energy from social situations, one of those people for whom human interaction is a lifeblood. As he got older, being a flirt became a natural extension of that, an outlet for his quick wit and easy confidence — with the added ingredient of attraction, or at least its promise. It made the other person feel good, and it made him feel good: *win-win*, he figured.

So while he didn't really want to *be* with Bec, as her boyfriend, he honestly liked talking with her and had fun hooking up with her. If he was going to be anybody's boyfriend, though, it would be Anna Thomas's — his mate's sister, who he'd crushed on for years.

The one girl his charm didn't seem to work on.

The afternoon he met Bec, he was feeling deflated: he'd seen Anna at the athletics carnival that day and, despite some of his best work, she seemed immune to his attention. He was mystified and frustrated: he was not accustomed to being slighted and he didn't like it. He sat at the back of the bus, scrolling on his phone in an effort to distract himself, but it wasn't really working. He didn't like feeling agitated — it was an uncommon emotion for him and he wanted to shake it off.

He noticed a girl sitting a few rows in front of him and caught her looking at him shyly. In that moment, with his ego outside its comfort zone, he saw an opportunity to scurry back to what he knew. Her glances were a siren call to his pride, and he threw her that cheeky grin that had served him faithfully all his life. She blushed and smiled back and, as with the first tug on a fishing line that signals a catch, he got the shot of dopamine he was after.

He took out his headphones and struck up a conversation, noting her barely disguised astonishment that he was talking to her. Even though they were alone on the bus, she practically looked over her shoulder to see if he was talking to someone else. She giggled just a little too much at all his jokes, and when he winked at her as they said goodbye he could have sworn her pupils dilated. *Still got it*, he thought as he strode home, feeling reassured that he always had options.

They talked in the following weeks, and one night, feeling restless and bored, and seeing Bec was online, he asked if she wanted to meet at the park. They hooked up, and it was fun. He felt she could be a reliable friend-with-benefits, and while he hadn't discussed that arrangement with her yet, he would. At some point. A bit later maybe, once they'd got to know each other more and he had a better sense of her. Hopefully he wouldn't have to, though, and it would just kind of … evolve. As it had with plenty of other girls in the past few years. He had mostly managed to avoid having 'the talk' when he would have to expressly tell someone he didn't want to be their boyfriend. He hated hurting people's feelings and would dodge it studiously, not wanting to be thought of as anything but a good guy.

The next Friday it was raining and all his mates had plans, so he invited Bec over to his place. They couldn't hook up at the park in the wet, but he knew they'd have privacy in his bedroom, where they could cash in on those benefits.

Perched on the edge of his bed, Bec was nervous, babbling about Plath and not knowing where to put her hands. Her breath had already quickened when Max leaned in to kiss her. He reached over to turn off the bedside lamp and Bec was relieved he wouldn't be able to see all her imperfections.

She wondered what he thought of her, as his hands explored her small breasts, her waist, her hips. His fingers moved into her underwear, and her first thought was to hope that he wasn't expecting a full Brazilian. She had tried to wax herself earlier but couldn't bear the pain. Now, feeling self-conscious, she regretted not pushing through — what if he preferred no hair? Is that what he was used to? Bec thought of Anna Thomas's perfectly smooth skin, wondering if Max was comparing the two of them. She squashed her suspicion, deciding she was reading way too much into that one interaction she had seen at the carnival.

Unfortunately, her instinct was close to the mark — Anna had his heart and so was never far from his mind. It wasn't that he was actively comparing Bec to her, just that a part of him wished he could do this with Anna instead.

But, unpractised at identifying red flags and craving his attention and his touch, Bec ignored the nagging sense that it was too good to be true. After all, feeling wanted is a potent drug. Realising he was aroused when he pressed his hips against hers, she was amazed that she was responsible for it. It made her feel less inadequate, stoking her own desire and proving it wasn't destined to go unanswered forever. Finally, she was desired. She hadn't been rejected. It gave her a sense of agency — power, even.

And it was all the more thrilling knowing he had clearly

done this before with other girls. The confidence in his touch, his assurance that they wouldn't be disturbed, that he looked the way he did — obviously he was well experienced. And still she turned him on. He could have anyone, and yet he wanted to kiss *her*, to have *her* in his bed. Drunk on his touch, she couldn't imagine ever tiring of it.

But then he asked her to give him head and she came crashing out of her haze. She hesitated, suddenly anxious.

She didn't know if she wanted to do that. It had crossed her mind that he might ask, but she had hoped he wouldn't because she didn't know how to arrange it so they could stay where she was comfortable. Faced with the question, she felt uneasy without understanding why. She liked Max. She was attracted to him. But she felt uncertain: was this too fast? What was the deal with STIs and oral sex again? She had never done it before; what if she was terrible? What if his mum did walk in? It felt so … personal and intimate. Did she even know Max well enough? Did he even really like her the way she liked him? Or was she just the one in his bed right now?

'No,' she answered eventually, her voice low.

As soon as the word left her mouth she wanted to snatch it back. But it was too late — the syllable hung in the air, filling up the darkened room. The mood changed immediately, like when you feel the temperature drop and the air pressure shift right before a storm opens up. He was still, and the silence seemed to stretch on for an age. 'I'm not sure,' she blurted, desperate to recover the moment — worried she had disappointed him or hurt his feelings and unable to gauge his expression in the dark. What if he did actually like her and she had made him feel rejected? She knew how much that could sting. She didn't know how to tell him she liked him, and was really attracted to him, but that she was content to just do the other stuff for now.

For his part, any shyness he had felt when they first started undressing in the dark was drowned by lust. No thoughts were clamouring for his attention; this felt good, and he knew it would feel even better in her mouth, so he asked. But he wasn't troubled when she had said no: it was awkward, and he didn't know quite how to recover, but he wasn't going to hold it against her. It was still early in their friendship. Of course he would prefer it to her hand, but he wasn't about to make her do something she didn't want to.

But then she said 'I'm not sure', and to him that sounded like she was considering it. It was what his parents said sometimes when he asked them for something. It meant negotiation, an invitation to persuade. It meant: *I'm weighing this up.*

And so, he engaged. 'I can go down on you first, if you want.' He didn't mean it as a quid pro quo, he was just trying to show he wasn't selfish.

Still, Bec was unsure. It felt like a vulnerable bridge too far. But if she said no to this as well, her sexual naiveté would be embarrassingly obvious. She was already worried he was comparing her to others; why add frigid to the list of her inadequacies?

She wanted him to like her, to want her. And why would he want her if she was not as adventurous as other girls? Not as mature? He was a guy, he had needs that could be met elsewhere. Deep down, she felt lucky that he wanted to do anything with her: beggars couldn't be choosers, could they? She'd gone this far with him — she may as well try it. She couldn't articulate to herself why she felt uneasy, hesitant. So maybe she should just give it a go. Saying no had felt awkward and awful, so maybe that meant she should say yes?

She flinched when he first put his tongue on her. She felt embarrassed — this was the closest anyone had ever been to her vagina, and she was worried he would find it gross. What if she tasted bad? She didn't feel more turned on or anything by it, so she supposed it must just not be her thing. She let it go on for a few minutes so as not to offend him, but eventually she reached down to touch his head and whispered, 'Come back up here,' pretending she just really wanted to kiss him, so he wouldn't feel bad.

Unsure what to do next, they lay there hugging each other, and Bec was worried she had made a mess of this. There seemed to be an expectant air in the room and, still tense and confused, Bec thought she might be able to fix it if she returned the favour.

'Your turn,' Bec said.

'Oh. Are you sure?' he asked.

Bec untangled herself from his arms and kissed him, before wriggling her way down his torso.

Afterwards, she felt almost proud of herself, remembering how his body had shuddered, the guttural sound in his throat — she had done that. For a brief moment she felt the power had shifted between them and, feeling in control in the aftermath of that intimacy, she let herself believe he would ask to see her again.

But he didn't, and later, as she went to leave, there was something in the way he kissed her forehead that felt ostentatiously platonic. The alarm bells she had kept muffled up until then wailed in her head, and she felt compelled to ask.

'Do you like someone else?'

Her directness caught him off guard, and his pause said it all. He rushed to reassure Bec that he thought she was a great girl and that he had a lot of fun with her. She tried to seem unbothered, but he could tell she was crestfallen, and he felt like a prick. She immediately wished she hadn't given him head, feeling used and self-conscious that he had gone down on her.

A taxi dropped me off at The Loopy Shrew, a quaint inn sitting at the bottom of a hill in the town of Shrewsbury, flanked by a cobblestone lane on one side and facing the town centre on the other. Behind it was a sprawling park on the bank of the River Severn, where scores of locals gathered every day to play football, walk their dogs, and sunbake.

Shrewsbury is an idyllic town in Shropshire, England, and I was charmed as I took in the view from the window of my tiny but comfortable room above the pub. The town is home to the award-winning 'Respect Yourself' RSE program, chiefly developed by Alice Cruttwell, the then Shropshire Council's health development officer and public health curriculum advisor. In the UK, county councils provide the majority of public services for that area, including education and social care. I had taken the train to Shropshire from London to learn the secrets of the program's success.

Respect Yourself is a 'coordinated, county-wide approach' to RSE that was developed by the county council public health team and is delivered in a number of schools across the Shropshire county. While geographically large, Shropshire is sparsely populated, with fewer than one million residents. Shropshire schools can opt in to implement the Respect Yourself program, which includes lesson plans, resources, and guidance for teachers.

Cruttwell picked me up outside the Loopy the next day, and gave me a short tour of the town. We would spend a lot of time in each other's company that week: visiting council offices, attending local community meetings, sitting in classrooms, and sharing meals.

She even took me on a day trip with her sweet mum, driving us down winding, bucolic roads near the Welsh border to see some nearby ruins. We stopped in a small village, which seemed quintessentially English to me — perhaps because of the scones and tea and bookshops we enjoyed. It was also the day of then prime minister Scott Morrison's 'miracle' re-election in 2019. The week before, I had made my way to Australia House in London to cast my vote, disappointed that the democracy sausage was not a tradition carried over for expats abroad. Days later, as the results came in when I was with Cruttwell and her mother, my friends texted me updates as it happened, all of us in shock, given it had been so confidently predicted his conservative party would lose.

For me, the utopian bubble of sex-ed positivity that I had been happily ensconced in for the past few weeks burst. Talking to RSE experts and advocates day after day, I had allowed myself to hope that Australia could do better. That there was a future where we would give young people the information they need — that they deserve — to safeguard their wellbeing.

But then came the news that we had re-elected the man who agreed that a particular sexuality education program made his 'skin curl', and who confessed to sending his own girls to a private school where they would avoid such programs. In 2018, then prime minister Scott Morrison had gone on talkback radio station 2GB, discussing with Australian broadcaster and shock jock host Alan Jones a 'respectful relationships' program developed by the Victorian government. Jones claimed the program included content about sexuality and would have students in classrooms role-playing characters who were bisexual or who thought they might be a lesbian. Jones asked the prime minister if that made his 'skin curl' [sic], and Morrison agreed that it did, saying:

> I don't want the values of others being imposed on my children in my school and I don't think that should be happening in a public school or a private school. That's why I want to protect the independent schools to ensure they can continue on providing at least that choice. When it comes to public schools [...] how about we just have state schools that focus on things like learning maths [and] learning science [...] It's not happening in the school I send my kids to, and that's one of the reasons I send them there.[1]

My phone was vibrating non-stop with notifications about the election result. An apparent RSE-sceptic had secured power for another three years, declaring in his victory speech that night: 'I've always believed in miracles.'

I told Cruttwell what had happened back home, and she patted me on the arm. 'This work takes bloody-mindedness,' she said to me. 'Individual, pioneering bloody-mindedness.'

The people I spoke with on my fellowship had been working in this space for decades, often at a grassroots level: quietly, determinedly persisting. Individuals who made all the difference for a single community, a single school, even a single class, because of their commitment to giving young people the very best chance. Individuals who recognise that condoms on bananas is not enough. That *no means no* is dangerously inadequate — like putting your kid behind the wheel for the first time and only pointing out where the handbrake is.

There is one particular teacher I remember from my time in Shrewsbury: the Deputy Principal of Shrewsbury School — an impossibly posh private school and Charles Darwin's alma mater. Prioritising RSE, and thanks to Cruttwell's persistent advocacy, she implemented the Respect Yourself program, and created a dedicated department of teachers who demonstrated both an interest in and an aptitude for the subject — not just 'Bob from geography because he has a spare period', as Cruttwell was fond of saying. The Deputy Principal leveraged her position in the school leadership to ensure their students got quality RSE from dedicated and qualified teachers. Cruttwell told me that once other schools in the area heard that Shrewsbury School had adopted this RSE program, more followed suit. In this way, one teacher at one school had contributed to the uptake of RSE in the wider community.

And resources. When RSE is seen as the purview of individual schools, its success is hitched to the whim and budget of those institutions. When either will or resources, or both, are in short supply, we cannot fulfil our duty to all young people and we risk their safety. Remember the athletics carnival Max and Bec attended, with different schools competing? Imagine some of those students had received excellent RSE in their schooling lives. Maybe they had one teacher who was brilliant on this subject, or there was a parent on the P&C Association who pressed the school to adopt a strong RSE curriculum, or they had a principal who recognised the importance of it and had the funds to bring in some of the fantastic specialist providers that exist in this country. How wonderful for those students that, due to the personality or attitude or capacity of some individuals in their lives, or due to a privilege and access to resources, they had information and answers. But what about kids like Max and Bec? By luck of the draw, they missed out. Dr Christopher Fisher, who leads the National Survey of Secondary Students and Sexual Health (a five-yearly survey since 1992), told the ABC: 'Some young people told us how amazing they found sex-ed, that they learned so much. But then down the street, someone else maybe isn't getting as good of an education.'[2] Access to this information cannot be a lottery, it should be a guarantee.

When Cruttwell designed the Respect Yourself program, she drew from research, national data, and consultation with the local community — including its youth — to ensure it was age- and stage-appropriate, evidence-based, and informed by what young people want to know. It is imperative that RSE is co-designed with young people. Lauren French, sexologist, sexuality educator, and First Nations woman, said to me, 'We cannot, as adults, decide what young people's issues are and how those issues are to be fixed without having the conversation with young people. We live in hierarchies that do not value young people the same as adults.' This is consistent with the UNESCO 'International Technical Guidance on Sexuality Education' principle that young people must be involved in RSE design, alongside other stakeholders. The guidance is a key international resource that provides an evidence base for comprehensive RSE, and outlines the necessary characteristics of effective RSE, key topics and learning objectives, as well as how to plan, deliver, and monitor it.[3]

If young people are involved in RSE design, we will be more effective in giving them information they need, in a way that makes sense for them. In Shropshire, I asked Cruttwell whether she thought teaching young people about consent was enough. 'You cannot divorce consent from the other aspects of RSE — you can't do it without explaining what is a good friendship, a good intimate relationship.' She described teaching about consent and violence prevention as a 'deficit model', and 'backwards reasoning'. 'If you do consent in isolation it might be ineffective, artificial, and won't build transferable skills,' she told me. Young people already know that you can't force somebody to drink a milkshake if they don't want to, or pour a cup of tea down someone's throat if they decline it[4] — the problem is that we treat sex as a unique social setting that appears to have its own set of rules, as we will see in later chapters.

Perhaps Bec knew enough to recognise that rapists were not just strangers in dark alleys; maybe she had been taught that she should not be pressured or cajoled to engage in sexual activity. Maybe she had been told to *just say no*. Meanwhile, Max had been taught that *no means no*, and he knew he would respect that word when he heard it.

But, as Jan Hargrave, a specialist in relationships and sexuality education for disabled and neurodivergent people, with whom I would meet later in Lincolnshire, said to me: We teach young people that to be good is to be compliant. *Do as your father asked, be good for Mum, be polite and give your grandfather a kiss otherwise you'll hurt his feelings*. Gold stars for sitting up straight in kindergarten, awards for attendance, punishment for talking back to the teacher. Kids grow up in a world where good behaviour is celebrated, and disruptive behaviour is reprimanded. Where they are expected to behave as others want them to.

And then, we ask them to say no. No to drugs, no to sex, no to peer pressure. Without ever teaching them how, when even for adults 'no' can be the hardest word — for all manner of reasons, in all manner of circumstances. Most of us prefer to avoid conflict, some of us desperately so. There is a whole self-help genre on the power of NO and how to use it. We reach for platitudes in the romantic context — 'it's not you, it's me' — to avoid saying *I'm not into it*. To avoid that awful task of rejecting somebody.

These are not skills we innately possess: we are social creatures, and the idea of rejecting someone, of disappointing them, of asserting your boundaries at the expense of their desires can feel overwhelmingly hard. Terry Humphreys, an academic in human sexuality at Trent University in Ontario, put it this way: 'Our society treats sexual rejection as a fate worse than death.' We learn that sexual rejection means we are undesirable and unworthy, and if we think of sexual rejection as confronting to our sense of self-worth, why would we want to inflict that on someone else? How many times, when I was a young woman, did guys especially access my personal space or make me feel uncomfortable, and take my silence as permission when actually I just didn't know how to assert my boundaries? Or the horror of rejecting them felt worse than simply putting up with the experience until it was over?

Just say no assumes several things: that people always know exactly what they want; that we will always use the word 'no'; and that it is an easy word to use. Yet our desires don't just sit on a binary of want/don't want, and our feelings don't pop up with labels telling us what they are. Bec's uncertainty came from her mixed feelings — she liked Max and was enjoying exploring a sexual side to their relationship. She hoped that he liked her the way she liked him, but she wasn't convinced, and that had a bearing on how she felt about going further with him. She was unsure if she would like oral sex because she had never tried it and hadn't considered doing so. Bec struggled to identify the source of her uncertainty and hesitation, and was confused by the dissonance between that and the powerful feelings of desire that she felt towards Max generally. She could hardly articulate that to herself, trying to sift through these confusing emotions rapidly while he waited for her answer in the darkness, let alone articulate it out loud and risk hurting his feelings and losing the chance to be with someone she really liked.

At Coleham Primary School in Shropshire, I sat on a kid-sized chair in a classroom of 8- or 9-year-olds to watch one of the Respect Yourself lessons in action. The teacher asked if the class remembered the exercise from last week, where they had split into pairs and walked towards each other gradually, getting closer and closer, before identifying when they felt uncomfortable and articulating why. The morning I was in class with them, their teacher handed out worksheets that described different scenarios like *Your friend wants to hold your hand, but you don't want to* and *You said a friend could borrow your toy, but then you changed your mind.*

In pairs the kids were asked to imagine what they might say in those scenarios, and I watched as they wrote out things like 'I wouldn't feel comfortable', and 'You can say no even if you think your friend will feel sad'. They even imagined how they would respond as the other party: 'Okay, we will just walk without holding hands', and 'If they say no, don't keep asking them'.

They were good with uncertainty, too: *You ask your friend to do something and she nods but you aren't so sure that she really wants to* elicited responses like 'Hey, it's fine if you don't want to', and 'If they don't answer, don't just take it as a yes'.

I would be reminded of this a couple of weeks later in the Netherlands, when I learned of the Spring Fever RSE program, which includes an activity where students touch different materials against their skin — like sponges and feathers — before expressing how it makes them feel. These exercises recognise that identifying our own feelings and articulating them — as well as listening for and respecting others' feelings — is a skill we need to practise. Giving younger kids these foundational building blocks means that, when they get to the age when it's appropriate to do so, we can start teaching them how those skills translate into the context of an intimate relationship. We don't teach kids maths by starting with algebra when they're 15: we start earlier with numbers, sums, problem-solving, and build from there.

Perhaps if she'd had such lessons, Bec would have been better equipped to identify how she was feeling and give expression to it in the moment. She may have recognised that she had conflicting emotions and that, in this context, she ought to defer to the feelings that pointed to uncertainty and hesitation. To recognise that although she felt buzzed on the power of Max's attraction to her, it was still worth engaging with the alarm bells she was hearing and that she had a right to listen to those alarm bells. If she had even been able to articulate that she was feeling alarm bells she couldn't further describe, it might have helped. And perhaps if she had been taught that rejection is not the worst thing a person can suffer, the situation may have felt less delicate, and she may have felt freer to express her feelings respectfully but honestly.

Just as we teach young people that you can't force someone to play with you in the sandpit, you can't force someone to be your friend or to invite you to their birthday party, we must teach them that they are not entitled to someone romantically or sexually. We must teach them that respectful rejection is an ordinary part of life, that when one person doesn't desire you sexually, it does not mean you are undesirable, unlovable, unworthy.

If we teach young people that rejection is something to lament and fear, it becomes a bogeyman. Bec wasn't the only one struggling with the task of rejection: Max also dreaded hurting Bec's feelings. This meant that he put off being open with Bec about how he felt about her, hoping she would organically arrive at the same conclusion he had — that they were friends who hooked up occasionally. This was also manipulative: he anticipated that Bec might say no if he was forthright about his feelings, and because he saw hooking up with her as something he could get *from* her, an experience she could give *him* as opposed to one to be shared mutually on open terms, he put his desire above her feelings. It meant Bec was unaware of the terms of their relationship and the things they were doing. As a result, they had vastly different perspectives of the event, because they both spent a lot of time guessing how the other felt and avoiding finding out explicitly, in case the truth was disappointing. The gap between those perspectives is where the margin for damage yawns open.

Just say no is unhelpful when we can't properly identify what we want — do we want to say no? — and it doesn't work if using the word is hard to do. As Bec did, we regularly try to soften the blow by resorting to other language, like 'I don't know', or 'I'm not sure', hoping the equivocation will send enough of a signal. But if Max has only been taught to listen out for *No*, he may not recognise or respect *I'm not sure* as the brake light that it was.

Max saw himself as a lovable scamp, someone who knew how to use his charm to get what he wanted. If he had been taught that he was not always entitled to have his cake and eat it too, he might have learned how to deal with the discomfort that comes when someone rebuffs you. He may not have felt the need to self-soothe when he experienced Anna's rejection by using Bec's attention to mollify his smarting ego. And he may not have interpreted 'I'm not sure' in the way most favourable to him, reading it as an invitation to persuade instead of recognising that his desire had to take a back seat to Bec's uncertainty. Instead of offering to go down on her, he might have asked 'Is there something else you'd like to do instead?' or said 'I'm really enjoying just doing this if you are'.

This scenario challenges our assumptions that the dynamics in sexual encounters are black and white. It's tempting to think of them that way, but to do so leaves no room for grey, and renders us ill-equipped to anticipate and then navigate the grey when it inevitably appears.

And even if Max and Bec had both been taught it was not okay to pressure or be pressured for sex, how would that have helped them in this scenario? Max did not overtly pressure Bec, or at least did not recognise how his actions and words may have contributed to Bec *feeling* pressured. Max did the right thing in asking the question before moving ahead, and Bec felt safe enough to use the word 'no' at first, although the discomfort that followed saw her try to dilute it. Nevertheless, several other forces acted as a source of pressure for Bec that night, although neither of them may have recognised those forces. As we have already considered, she did not want to offend or embarrass Max, and he did nothing to neutralise that fear — for example, verbalising that he was fine with her initial 'no'.

Bec was also uncertain about what she wanted, and part of that arose from her own expectations of the encounter. Bec did not go into that situation thinking about her own physical desires and pleasures as much as Max did his: her first thought was about what he made of her grooming efforts. She worried about what he thought of her body. She was anxious about his experience of her vagina when he went down on her, and experienced no pleasure from it. All her reference points, the metric she used to judge the occasion, were more about his experience than hers. She focused on what he wanted, believing she needed to meet his needs if she was to keep his interest. In later chapters, we will look more closely at the danger in creating expectations that prioritise 'male' desire. In this situation, Bec's pleasure and participation took a derivative form. She felt that to enjoy sex was to enjoy the act of service, of meeting Max's wants. That she had to compete with other young women for Max's affection.

Compounding this was Bec's sense of an air of expectation in the room. Indeed, they both would have been under the impression that the activities they had enjoyed up to that point — kissing, touching — were a lesser form of sexual activity. We have entrenched sexual scripts that tell us these things precede 'home base', mere stepping stones in a linear trajectory to the main event. Understanding sexual activity as goal-oriented means that kissing and touching are a means to another end, carrying with them a sense of anticipation for a *next*, not equally joyful activities to be enjoyed in their own right. Bec worried that Max had a legitimate expectation that they would progress to that coveted *next*, and that her desire to move more slowly was depriving him of something that he was entitled to.

So this pressure on Bec grew and grew, in a dark room and in a context where Max had deliberately avoided giving her all the information about how he felt. Where neither of them knew how to have a useful conversation about what they wanted. If they had been taught how to have those difficult but honest conversations, to navigate conflict and not be governed by the fear of rejection, Bec may not have been left feeling so hurt by the experience.

I remember a counsellor at a boys' school in Sydney telling me that she sees kids seeking help on how to raise their hand in class and contribute. Communicating when we're nervous, or worried about saying something that will have negative consequences, can feel impossible even in non-sexual situations. Communicating through conflict, or at the very least different interests, and navigating the minefield of rejection (as either rejecter or rejectee) is not something that comes easily to us. The social, emotional, and communication skills required to navigate intimate moments and relationships are more like learning to hold a pen and write with it, or learning to tie your shoelaces, learning to drive or play the piano. We were none of us born knowing these things, and they are complex enough that we can't learn by mimicking — we have to be taught. The same is true of the skills necessary to develop emotional intelligence, to communicate openly and respectfully, to deal with rejection ourselves and to navigate the task of rejecting another assertively.

And perhaps if both Max and Bec had been taught to expect that Bec should truly enjoy every sexual experience, that her pleasure was not a derivative one, she may have understood that the way she felt about the kissing — that pure joy and unadulterated excitement — was how she should expect to feel about every single sexual moment. And perhaps Max would have watched and worked for that, too.

To achieve that, we need to talk to young people honestly and articulate a standard they should expect for their sexual experiences: a standard of feeling safe, excited, joyful. Surely that is what we want for all our kids — that their experiences will be ones that aren't just free from violence, but are *far* from violent. We don't want them to feel hurt and exploited like Bec; we want them to feel respect and agency. But to want that for them without teaching them what it looks like is an exercise in hope. Rather than just telling them to rely on the word 'no', to use only the avoidance of overt violence and coercion as their northern star, we need to show them what the alternative is. Otherwise, we leave them to fumble around in the dark.

Teaching young people about green flags as well as red flags means speaking to them openly about healthy relationships and sex in a positive way. However, like me on that day in a village near Wales, many will feel that Australia is just not ready to have this conversation. 'Imagine the tabloids!' people say to me when I want to talk about educating for sexual wellbeing and not just violence prevention. Thanks to past experience, many of us remain nervous about the media's reaction to any progress in sex-ed that involves talking to young people about relationships, sex, and sexuality in positive terms. The 2018 discussion between Morrison and Jones on 2GB talkback radio about 'skin curling' sex-ed is but one example of many of a political hostility towards RSE that has been stoked by the media. We will take a closer look at some other examples in a later chapter, when we look at the role of politicians, opposition, and the media machine.

But as I travelled, I came to learn that the countries I visited were not utopias where everyone universally agreed on sex-ed. It's not like politicians, schools, teachers, and communities in these countries did not experience backlash. Media scrutiny. Protests. Campaigns of lies about what was actually being taught (if I had a dollar for every false claim that a sex-ed program was teaching kids how to have anal sex ...). They did and still do experience resistance. But these communities allowed themselves to be led by the evidence. These communities stood up for their young people and their right to pursue fulfilling lives, refusing to condemn them to the likelihood they will experience sexual violence, sexual harassment, and unwanted, hurtful sexual experiences.

Australia is no different. All we need is a dash of courage: both personal and political. Cruttwell reminded me of something significant that had taken place in the UK shortly before I landed in London. After decades of advocacy by the bloody-minded, the UK government had just introduced laws which, broadly speaking, mandated that all young Britons have access to RSE. 'It surprised us all that it was a conservative government that finally did it,' she said — proving progressive politics do not and need not have a monopoly on courage in these quarters.

Or perhaps proving that, at the very least, politicians of every stripe may act when the politics are such that they don't need much courage at all. In the UK, the legislative mandate was introduced by a conservative government after the rates of sexual abuse and sexual violence among young people became too great (and too public) for any political party to ignore. Politicians had no choice but to act on the evidence that RSE is protective not corrupting. I had the impression that the community sentiment at the time, not to mention the decades of work by RSE advocates that preceded this moment, had softened the ground considerably, and consequently the move was not so politically risky.

Australia's own conservative government — the same one elected when I was with Cruttwell — would make a similar move, and in similar circumstances. In Australia, education remains the constitutional purview of the states. However, the federal government is still a significant player, not least due to its purse strings. Australia also has a national curriculum, designed to improve consistency in education across the Federation. In early 2022, when the Morrison government was still at the helm, before the federal election in May of that year, a revised Australian Curriculum, which includes increased content on 'consent' from foundation grade to Year 10, had the support of all education ministers around Australia. Although it was quietly announced in the Senate Education and Employment Legislation Committee, it received some media attention due to the increased public interest in the issue, arising in part from the Contos petition and her advocacy for the inclusion of consent in the curriculum. In other words, education ministers of various political leanings were on board with this step, at least.

But it is a step that is more baby than giant leap. Greater inclusion of 'consent' in the national curriculum is an achievement, insofar as it recognises that the topic of 'consent' is an important part of every young Australian's schooling life. It also demonstrates the power of youth advocacy in this space: young people drive these conversations, which we will see more of in later chapters. What I am about to say is not to detract from that achievement, nor to diminish the advocacy that led to it. However, like the UK legislative mandate, the greater inclusion of 'consent' in the national curriculum, which was already under review at the time, was not a politically risky move, given the community sentiment at the time. Sentiment stoked, in part, by advocates who made a lot of timely and compelling noise about the issue, and a receptive media that kept it in the public consciousness. Faced with sustained public anger at the rates of sexual violence and the need to do something about the culture that drives it, the government agreeing to consent in the curriculum is a bit of a political gimme, for two main reasons.

First, 'consent' is more palatable politically than comprehensive RSE that takes a positive and inclusive approach to sexuality and sexual wellbeing. Consent education is far less likely to make anybody's 'skin curl' — it doesn't even have the word sex in the name. This is, unfortunately, a danger to the efficacy of RSE, even if the prevention of sexual violence is your goal, as we will see in later chapters. This is what Cruttwell meant when she described teaching the stuff of RSE in terms of 'consent' as a 'deficit model'. I asked Cruttwell and others about the adequacy of teaching 'consent' alone specifically because, even back in 2019 at the start of my fellowship, before I knew much of anything about RSE and its implementation, I suspected that this was how it could so easily go. Like many other advocates in this space, I saw it coming, saying when I appeared on *60 Minutes* in April 2021, in an episode about the relationship between education and sexual safety: 'We can't just fix the curriculum and add in a couple of extra lessons on consent and say, "job done".' I was nervous that, in an effort to be seen to be doing *something* without being too contentious, there would be an emphasis on that magical, all-powerful notion of consent. If only sexual violence and unwanted sex, and their drivers, were so straightforward.

The second reason consent in the curriculum is political low-hanging fruit is that, while it reflects a political concession, it does not represent much more than that in practical terms. The national curriculum provides guidance to states and territories, with some adopting it and others adapting it, and gives general direction to schools and teachers. But jurisdictions and the schools within them are vested with a significant degree of autonomy as to how the curriculum is in fact implemented, and how it translates into classrooms. Emily Ross, a lecturer of Curriculum and Pedagogy at the University of the Sunshine Coast, wrote in *The Conversation* in November 2021:

> Imagine the Australian Curriculum is a map — a broad picture of all the learning a teacher covers in each year of education for

> each particular subject. Using the map, teachers charter a course for each unit to ensure the territory is covered across the year and then plan the route they will take with their students.
>
> When using a map to travel a particular route to your destination, you may take a detour along the way. It's the same when travelling using the curriculum. A student may ask an interesting question, and that might take the class in a different direction for a bit. But that just adds to the journey.[5]

We will see why this discretion and these detours matter so much when it comes to the sensitive, nuanced subject of RSE, described by La Trobe University sexual health academic Christopher Fisher as a 'patchwork' approach, resulting in a 'mixed bag' of sex-ed delivery in Australia.[6] We will also see why a new curriculum does not answer the need for schools and teachers to be properly equipped and qualified in delivery. Nor does it change school or community cultures more broadly, with policies designed to reinforce those messages outside of the lessons themselves. Nor does the curriculum give parents the confidence and skills to carry on these conversations at home. It does not even tell us whether, and to what extent, schools will prioritise or even deliver this part of the curriculum, in a climate that still says mathematics, science, and assessable outcomes are more important.

These were similar criticisms of the legislative mandate in the UK: essentially that it is the starting block, not the finish line. In February 2022, well after the legislative mandate was introduced in the UK, a survey of more than a thousand 16–17-year-old Britons revealed RSE was still being delivered inconsistently, important topics were being neglected, and young people's opinion about RSE was rarely sought.[7] While politicians and government support is absolutely critical to RSE, their true power lies not in announcements or concessions, but in implementation — something far more complex, resource-intensive, and contentious, as we will see.

3

Windows of Opportunity

Nadia and Leon

Nadia woke to a pounding in her head. She realised she was sweating, warily opening one eye to see the sun streaming onto her face because she'd forgotten to close the blinds last night. *Damn*, she thought as she rubbed her eyes and felt yesterday's mascara under her fingertips. *Didn't take off my makeup.*

She frowned, trying to remember why she had failed to abide by her cardinal routine of nightly skincare, which she always honoured — even if she was stumbling at her basin and trying not to throw up, she would still get in there with the cleanser and moisturiser.

The mystery would have to wait, though, because her body was screaming for water. Peeling her tongue from where it had stuck to the roof of her mouth, she felt that if she didn't hydrate immediately, she might die. She navigated the seesawing floorboards to get to the kitchen, steadying herself on the sink as she turned on the tap and gulped down water so fast it spilled down her chin and onto her dress.

Wait, her dress? Oh god, she hadn't even taken off her clothes from the night before. Her bra felt tight, underwire digging into soft tissue where it had twisted as she slept. She got to the toilet, hitching up her dress to pull down her underwear as she sat down — but her thumbs found no purchase, sliding over bare hips. Confused for a second time this morning, Nadia looked down and saw her underpants were gone.

The night before came back to her in pieces, like vignettes of a mortifying show.

It was the first time Nadia had gone out since she'd split up with her ex. She was still sad, finding it hard to be around people. She tried to wash the loneliness away with booze that evening, having met up with friends at a local pub. It was a venue popular with uni students for its cheap drinks, and the dancefloor became stickier, and the patrons less aware of that, as the evening wore on.

Leon was there, an old friend in their circle who was also recently heartbroken. Everybody liked Leon: he was affable and popular, the life of the party. Nadia had once had a thing for him, which was common knowledge — the timing hadn't been right, though, and it was ages ago now.

They sat together for much of the night, the house vodka giving her a brittle cheer that she hoped would last. Later, though, when she became teary and declared herself sad, Leon put his arm around her comfortingly. 'Nobody wants me,' she sobbed into his shoulder.

Every round seemed to be Leon's shout — Nadia lost track of how many times she saw him coming back to their booth with fresh vodka sodas for the table or, when the others had disappeared on the dancefloor, for just the two of them. At one point their friend Angie insisted that Nadia drink some water, and Nadia saw her raise an eyebrow at Leon. 'Don't be mad at him!' she implored, grabbing Angie's hands and slurring, 'He's taking care of me,' before flinging her arms around him affectionately. Angie smiled and shook her head at the two of them. 'Maybe slow down a bit on the drinks, yeah?' she threw over her shoulder before melting back into the throng.

'I love this song!' Nadia exclaimed, pulling Leon to his feet and unsteadily to the dancefloor. Nadia wanted to dance, closing her eyes to lose herself for just a few moments, feeling nothing but the music as she swayed. She opened them to see Leon reaching his arms around her shoulders to sway with her, and she smiled to herself, glad she had chosen to be out with friends tonight.

Now they were hugging, and Nadia noticed they had moved to the wall at the side of the dancefloor. Nadia's back was against it, and she realised Leon was looking at her intently, and leaning in towards her. Too late, she realised he was kissing her. He pushed her against the wall as he did so. 'Ow!' she said, pulling her face away from his and rubbing the back of her head. He was taller than her, and he was being quite rough. She could tell he was drunk, but not as drunk as her.

She was too sad for this. There was just no room in her to want it. She started dancing again, trying to close off that moment and leave no window for Leon to try again. She even took his hands in hers, swinging their arms to the beat and avoiding eye contact, lest he take it as some kind of invitation. She made her body language say *platonic platonic platonic* as she searched for their friends in the crowd.

Eventually, she found them back at the booth and announced the next round was on her. She was still terrified of sobering up, desperate not to go home, where her loneliness was inescapable, like the stale smell of cigarettes in a hotel room. Later, her mood turning on a dime, she found she couldn't bear to be around her friends a moment longer. She told the group she was leaving, and Leon said he would, too. They lived near each other and shared the same train station. 'You don't need to leave!' she protested, but he insisted he was tired and ready to go, setting his jaw and holding out her coat. They bade their friends goodbye, and Angie cocked her head as she watched them go, wondering if she should say something. 'Let me know when you get home safe,' she called out to Nadia's retreating back.

'Maybe those two will finally hook up,' one of the others said, wriggling their eyebrows.

'I don't know if that would be a good idea.' Angie frowned. 'She's sad.'

'And wasted,' someone else replied.

•

They left the bar and Leon put his arm around Nadia as they walked. Part of her was grateful, because she needed steadying, but as they began to cross the road, he picked her up playfully, carrying her across. She laughed along at first, but then his grip on her arms started to hurt, and she could feel her dress riding up, exposing her bum to the cars waiting at the intersection.

'Put me down,' she said. 'I'm serious!' when he wouldn't.

She tried to wriggle free but was surprised at how strong he was. She felt her frustration rising. 'Leon, put me down, you're hurting me!'

Eventually he did and they walked the rest of the way to the station, where instead of taking the stairs down to the platform Leon pulled Nadia into the elevator. As they were waiting for it to make its slow descent, he picked her up and sat her on the handrail, wrapping her legs around him and kissing her. Again it was rough, and Nadia was at the mercy of his strength. She felt like her brain and her limbs were moving through molasses — as soon as she realised what was happening, it had already stopped.

He had been interrupted by their arrival at the platform, where a few late-night stragglers were milling about. He put her down and she followed him out of the elevator, feeling ashamed in her drunken state as she tugged down on her dress, looking at the ground so she wouldn't see the judgemental glances of those who had noticed.

She felt confused, but relieved the night was coming to an end. They were both drunk and would laugh this off in the morning, no doubt. As the train rocked on the tracks, she felt those last couple of drinks catch up to her. She could hardly keep her eyes open.

When they got off at their station, he insisted on walking her home to make sure she got there safely. As they weaved down one particular dark stretch that always gave her the creeps, she was glad not to be alone. When the pair reached her door, she let herself in and turned to say goodbye only to find her nose at his chest. He was following her in: 'I really need a piss before I go,' he said.

Too drunk to suggest her friend relieve himself in the alley if he was so desperate, she stumbled through the door and kicked off her heels, gesturing in the direction of the toilet as she moved towards her room. She threw herself onto the bed, seeking respite from her spinning head.

She was so tired, and her eyes were so heavy. She could hear him urinating in the bathroom and called out, 'Just lock the door when you leave,' before her mind slipped into blackness.

Leon hadn't planned on kissing Nadia when he went out that night. Studying his reflection before he left his housemates at home on the couch, he had wondered if he would pick up. As he slapped on some aftershave, he decided he was ready to have sex with someone else, for the first time since his ex had dumped him and trampled his heart. It had been ages since his last fuck, and it was well overdue. He felt like he'd arrived at the next stage of recovery: getting laid.

When he arrived at the pub, though, the idea of making small talk with a stranger felt exhausting. He ended up sitting in the booth with his friends for most of the night, particularly Nadia. They'd always had a thing for each other, but the timing had never worked out — now they were both single. And ready to drown their sorrows.

They talked scathingly of their exes and admitted they were sad. A few drinks in, there were brave declarations of being ready to move on. Another round, and they were reassuring each other, at volume, that their exes were missing out, that they were both *fucking hot*. Then she was weeping on his shoulder and the curtain of bravado was pulled back, Leon glimpsing just how fragile Nadia's self-confidence was.

As the night wore on and she got drunker, he thought something could happen here. She was feeling low, and they could both do with getting laid, it seemed. He would be doing her a service, really — finally consummating the chemistry they'd always felt and making her feel wanted. Given the right opportunity, it would probably be on.

•

You make your own luck, he resolved, as he caught the bartender's eye and ordered the umpteenth round of vodka sodas. His chances would improve the more relaxed she was, and he asked the bartender to make this one a double. Shit, he was spending a lot on this girl tonight. *It's an investment*, he laughed to himself drunkenly.

He almost rolled his eyes when Angie got all maternal and insisted Nadia have some water, looking at him sceptically. But then Nadia cuddled up to him and he felt smug, vindicated: it's a truth universally acknowledged that if a girl is touching you more, she's flirting with you. Then she pulled him to the dancefloor, and he figured she probably did it so they had an excuse to be close.

He saw her smile, felt her lean into him, as he put his arms around her shoulders. *Yeah, this is happening*, he thought. He shuffled them towards the side of the dancefloor, trying to create a bit of privacy, where they wouldn't be interrupted by the likes of Angie. Women like a man who takes charge, so as he kissed her he pushed Nadia back against the wall in a way that was meant to be sexy, but then she seemed to hit her head. *Oops.*

She took his hands and they kept dancing. *A slow build-up kind of night, that's cool.* She probably didn't want to do this in public, so he just had to see if they could be alone at some point. Then she announced she was leaving, and Leon switched on the chivalry — insisting it wasn't safe for her to travel home by herself.

He pretended not to hear the serious tone in her voice when she asked him to put her down as he carried her across the road — she was probably just doing that thing girls do where they act coy, pretending they're not *that* into it so you keep chasing them. Girls love being chased. She was never going to initiate anything, even though she seemed like she'd be into it: he'd have to create the right conditions for it to happen.

He walked her to her front door, but didn't want the night to end yet. He thought himself still in with a chance, if only he could land it. Maybe if he just got inside, the opportunity would present itself.

•

In her bathroom Leon zipped up his fly, hoping it would be coming back down again shortly. So confident was he that something was about to happen between them, he felt himself start to get hard. He heard her mumble something from another room, but didn't catch what it was. He found his way to her bedroom where she was already lying on the bed, and he smirked. Her dress was riding up and he could see a hint of underwear. She looked like she'd passed out.

He stood in the doorway, hesitating. Having come this far, he was reluctant to give up now. He had really thought it was going to happen — and even now he wasn't ready to abandon this shot, to lose his window. She'd left the light on, after all.

Fuck it, just one last go. Might as well make sure. He went over to her bed — maybe she wasn't fully asleep yet. 'Nadia,' he whispered in a sing-song. There was a sound from her throat that Leon decided was a moan, seeing her eyes moving under her eyelids. *Not asleep, then*, he thought. He leaned over her, watching her face and stroking her arm. Her eyes fluttered open and briefly focused on his. He took it as his cue and kissed her, and although she didn't kiss him back immediately, she didn't pull away as she had at the bar.

She just sort of lay there, and then her eyes were closed again — but who keeps their eyes open when kissing? She was obviously a bit out of it, but all she needed was the right inspiration. When you're trying to start a fire, you need to blow air on it for a bit before it catches alight. He was itching to touch her, her body was *right there* and she wasn't saying no. Then he was touching her everywhere and he couldn't stop — it was too tempting and he was a red-blooded man after all. She was offering no resistance and occasionally making noises that he told himself were moans of pleasure. He lifted up her skirt and it was just so easy to pull her underwear down.

He stopped after a while, deciding she wasn't going to warm up and was too drunk or tired or both. He wasn't going to actually have sex with her — he wasn't some kind of *rapist*.

What a shit session, though. Leon felt frustrated — why did she lead him on if it was going to end up like this? He could have tried it on with a stranger, if he had known. If she hadn't let him think otherwise.

Nadia stared at her underwear on the floor next to her bed the following morning, dizzy with hangover and dread.

In starts, she remembered. His tongue on her clitoris. His fingers in her vagina.

She remembered trying to speak, but, thwarted by fatigue and intoxication, her brain refused to do her bidding and the best she'd been able to do was grunt. She heard his voice whispering, *it's okay, you're okay, just relax*, and it sounded so sinister.

Her phone chimed, breaking her trance as she saw his name flash up on the screen with a message:

Good to see you last night, hope you're not feeling too dusty? xx

The vomit she'd been holding down came up her throat in a violent rush.

Doncaster is a fairly central city in South Yorkshire, a main stop on most of the train lines that snake out to the surrounding towns and villages. I was there to learn from Big Talk Education, a social enterprise with its headquarters in the Midlands, which now delivers RSE in 210 schools all over England (it was 170 when I was there — the legislative mandate has them busier than ever!). Big Talk has lessons and resources for both primary and secondary levels, and a modest-sized team of staff, which is mostly made up of educators. Unlike Shropshire's 'Respect Yourself' program, which was a package of resources and training to equip schools and their staff to deliver RSE, Big Talk staff deliver their in-house designed classes themselves. As a social enterprise rather than a private organisation, Big Talk is reliant on funding and school budgets; they are, as they would humbly tell me, 'In it to make a difference, not a million.'

I met with Big Talk Education's founder and director, Lynnette Smith, on my first afternoon there. She drove us to a fancy hotel for afternoon tea in its posh dining rooms. Our lively conversation of sex and genitals and the orgasm gap seemed to clash with the pristine tablecloth and the polished silverware. Among the tables of stiff upper lips, ours were loose, and I felt our words ricochet off the fine china and ring around the room of otherwise hushed and civil conversation. I was very aware of those turning to look, perhaps disapprovingly or at the very least curiously. I wanted to tell them to spare their blushes.

Because of the subject matter of my research, over the course of my travels I found myself having countless discussions in public spaces about sex — not just with people I was interviewing for my fellowship, but with bartenders, fellow patrons, taxi drivers, and any number of strangers I struck up conversation with. I've come to expect the pricking ears and side eyes from those nearby when I refuse to whisper words like 'sex' and 'vagina' and 'penis'. Yet that refusal is often a mindful choice: I am not immune to feeling self-conscious about having these discussions in 'polite company'.

But I feel more self-conscious about even tacitly endorsing the notion that talking about sex is always, by nature, impolite. So I actively work to overcome the ingrained feeling of shame or discomfort about this topic that we were all given at a young age, and I do not drop my voice. Censoring respectful, consensual discourse about sex and sexual wellbeing keeps alive the idea that those things are somehow shameful. That talking about them is dirty, uncomfortable, awkward.

This is why we need courage in the fight for sex-ed: this shame and discomfort and fear of *talking* about bodies and sex and intimate relationships is incredibly powerful, even as adults — no wonder we baulk at the idea of talking about it to children and young people! No wonder we're wary of comprehensive RSE for little ones. No wonder we fret about what the tabloids will say, worrying that, as a community, we're not 'ready for this conversation'.

But ignorance is not the same thing as innocence, and if we continue to cover our kids' ears, we leave their safety and wellbeing to chance. If we continue to cultivate this taboo, if young people grow up seeing us embarrassed at the subject matter or, worse, their curiosity about it, then we have no right to be surprised when they struggle to communicate about sex at an older age, even in their private lives. Even with someone they want to have sex with. Even about their own wishes. Even about their own body parts. When we refuse to talk about it, when we make it shameful, it is as though young people have no right to their own bodies.

Most of us grow up rarely hearing the adults in our lives speak openly and respectfully about this topic, and if it ever does come up, we see the squirming. We feel the acute embarrassment when a sex scene comes on the television in the family living room, so potent someone has to leave. We were taught to feel that way. We were taught that sex is a big unmentionable, that talking about it is embarrassing and difficult. And as long as we never make it easier to talk about, we can expect the continued deference to euphemisms, to body language, to unspoken assumptions, to sexual scripts that we presume everyone adheres to.

The danger in this is twofold: we make it hard for people to talk about sex and consent when they would benefit from doing so (as we saw with Max and Bec in Chapter 2), and we make it easy for people to avoid talking about sex and consent when they benefit from this avoidance . We will come back to the latter when we look at Leon's decisions.

Recall that, in Chapter 2, we considered how the skills required to navigate different interests and to communicate in an intimate context do not come easily to us. In order to teach the necessary social, emotional, and communication skills to navigate intimate moments and relationships, not only must we first recognise the need to do so, to recognise that we don't just learn these things by osmosis, but we must also overcome powerful barriers of shame, embarrassment, and taboo.

My time in Doncaster showed me just how early we learn that the stuff of sex-ed is something to blush about, something hard to talk about. I attended several Big Talk classes in primary schools in the area, across different age groups. In some schools, Big Talk starts with the pre-school children, as young as three or four years old. One of the first activities they do is have the kids identify the parts of their body that no one can look at or touch if the young person doesn't want them to. They start by asking the young people to put their science hats on, and we all pull on imaginary hats, reminding them we are talking sensibly about our bodies, before having the kids repeat a chant that includes the words mouth, chest, penis, vagina, and bottom.

In the youngest age group the kids had no qualms, enthusiastically repeating the words penis and vagina (or, often, peanuts and bagina). However, after we shuffled around the corner to the very next class up — five- or six-year-olds — those words were met with giggles, sheepish grins, and a reluctance to repeat the words. I saw this over and over again, from that age group up. The educators dealt with it deftly every time, asking the kids if any of them thought penis and vagina are naughty words. Without fail, hands went up.

Just imagine that: a group of five-year-olds telling us that the mere names of their genitals are *naughty*. Kids understand naughty as something bad, disobedient, wicked — something deserving of punishment. This is the value being ascribed to their genitals even as they are still learning to read. And there is an extremely thin line between the names being naughty and the body parts themselves being naughty: what does that mean for the feelings and sensations associated with our genitals as we get older? Are they naughty, too? And if, deep down, we imbue those feelings and sensations with shame, how comfortable can we feel giving voice to them — whether to ourselves or to another person? Even when we really need to?

In the face of these raised hands, the educators asked the kids whether they thought their teachers would let the Big Talk staff come in to teach them bad words. This question would be met with a shaking of heads and a chorus of 'no'. The educators then pointed to their nose, chin, elbow and asked the kids to name them, before saying 'nose, chin, elbow, penis, vagina — these are just the names of our body parts'. Then they do the chant again and usually the giggles die down this time, and most kids participate (nobody is forced to say the words, of course).

What the Big Talk staff are doing here is encouraging young people to think and speak about their bodies in a healthy, appropriate way and in appropriate circumstances; for example, they remind the kids there is no need to yell the words penis and vagina in the playground just for the sake of being silly. They do this *without* using shame as the method for instilling that lesson.

Significantly, in the schools where Big Talk had been delivering their sessions year on year, the giggles and embarrassment were far less pronounced, because the students had been exposed to positive language about their bodies from an early age. Big Talk only started going into primary schools after realising their sessions in secondary schools were coming far too late: Smith told me sometimes people say to her, 'You can't teach consent at 13 years old!' (I imagine a strand of pearls being gripped.) And she replies, 'That's right, you can't. It's about ten years too late.'

Indeed, data 'strongly indicate that [topics often deemed inappropriate or premature for young children] are developmentally appropriate and produce positive outcomes … not only are younger children able to discuss sexuality-related issues [but] the early grades may, in fact, be the best time to introduce [such] topics.'[1] The importance of introducing these lessons from infancy cannot be overstated, for we only have a small window of opportunity in every young person's life to give them this information before they need it. Although I have said this book does not specifically deal with child sexual abuse, one thing I will say is that the research suggests knowledgeable children are less likely to be targeted by predators: knowledge is, after all, power.

One of the justifications Smith cites for doing this activity at such a young age is that, in the awful event that there is any abuse, young people need to be able to accurately talk about their body parts if they disclose. Indeed, in my experience of the criminal justice system, even adults will use expressions like 'down there' when reporting sexual assault. Such is the power of shame.

While that may be an important reason for these early lessons, another critical one is the need to teach young people that their bodies are not a source of shame or embarrassment. Not just for clarity in the event of harm, but so that young people don't grow up feeling dirty about themselves. So they don't grow up thinking the words are hard to utter. So they know their right to their own bodies doesn't come with a shame caveat.

Normalising the simple act of speaking about our bodies in a healthy, respectful, confident way can have a profound impact. A longitudinal study of fourth-graders who had participated in a Mexican program called *Yo Quiero Yo Puedo*, 'which focused on the importance of talking about taboo and difficult subjects, demonstrated improved communication skills in these subjects and increased self-efficacy and intentions to discuss difficult subjects, including romance, sexuality, and threatening or unpleasant topics'.[2] Setting a standard of positive communication about sex and sexuality, not just in classrooms but more broadly, can help break down our reliance on the unspoken, and dismantle our taboos.

There is another danger in our fidelity to silence here. We've looked at how the social consensus that we don't talk about our bodies and sex can make it hard for people to communicate when they need to. Now let's consider how that same standard makes it easier for people to avoid communicating when they don't want to.

Leon engages in all of his conduct towards Nadia without asking a single question. In Chapter 2, Max asked the question but didn't really engage with the answer beyond face value. Here, Leon barely says a thing: he has an internal monologue and if he suspects Nadia of not working to the same script as his, he allows himself plausible deniability. Unfortunately, we have not created a world where that is socially inconceivable — instead we have created one where it is quite normal.

Notice how many times the word *probably* appeared in Leon's internal monologue when he was assessing Nadia's behaviour. None of Nadia's actions — being affectionate towards Leon, dancing with him, permitting him access to her toilet at the end of the night — were explicitly communicating *I want to hook up with you.* Leon was interpreting them in that way because it was the interpretation most favourable to the result he was hoping for. And when Nadia said and did things that challenged or upset that interpretation, Leon found ways to explain them: for example, deciding that her signs of disinterest meant she wanted a slow build-up, or that she was being coy, when it was more likely, and in this case actually, those signs indicated that Nadia was not interested.

Without ever clarifying, Leon felt able to rely on unspoken 'signals' to divine what Nadia was thinking or wanting. In this scenario, as in many, Leon assessed Nadia's conduct and actions against sexual scripts that he learned from a young age: that an increase in tactility means flirtation; that women don't pursue sex and prefer to be chased; that women like it when men are domineering and take the lead in sexual experiences; that she somehow led him on because she hugged him and danced with him and let him into her house. Even more seriously, Leon interprets her lack of resistance as consent — as with Elliot (Chapter 1), the assumption is that permission is there until it is rescinded.

Given the multiple possible inferences Leon could draw from Nadia's words and actions, wouldn't he want to be sure? Why not just ask?

Here is why he doesn't want to ask: the answer might be no. So long as he stays on this side of a hard no, he gives himself permission to interpret Nadia's 'signals' to mean that she's up for it. Whilst ever it's not a red light, he can treat it as a green light.

Leon is taking advantage of the social consensus that when it comes to sex, we don't communicate about it explicitly. We rely on assumed cues, signals, and scripts, and we use the sexual activity itself as the question. Until or unless we get an answer in the negative, we carry on. He sees the opportunity as existing until it is expressly shut down, rather than the other way around: the window is open until somebody closes it.

Leon is doing this a little more wilfully, more nefariously, than Max (Chapter 2) was. Not only does Leon assume the window is open, he *actively seeks to keep it that way* by lowering Nadia's inhibitions with alcohol. In doing so, he tells himself the 'opportunity' is more likely, as though it is an independent event that will simply transpire if he is lucky enough. Maybe that's why we call it 'getting lucky', and Leon certainly thinks about it in those terms. By plying her with alcohol, he is deliberately trying to make her more malleable, hoping an intoxicated Nadia will be more likely to think it's a good idea to have sex with him.

Although drink spiking tends to conjure images of strange men slipping roofies into cocktails, in fact alcohol is a common spiking agent and — where the spiking incident involves sexual assault — the perpetrator is more likely to be known to the victim.[3] When Leon orders a double without telling Nadia that he's done so, he is trying to render her more vulnerable without her knowledge.

Let me divert for a moment to clarify that I'm not saying *all* sex where someone is affected by alcohol is unethical and wrong. And I'm not saying that the moment someone buys you a cocktail it renders any later sexual activity problematic. However, in the context of this scenario, Leon was clearly doing it to lower Nadia's inhibitions and even her capacity — to increase his chances of doing something with (and later, to) Nadia, and to decrease the likelihood that she would refuse him.

This scenario shows that there is no formula: every sexual encounter is made up of many different factors. Just as I cannot say intoxication in and of itself always makes a sexual encounter problematic, it cannot be said that touching another person is never a sign of flirtation, or that allowing someone into your house is never an invitation to stay.

In the past I have run workshops with university students alongside my colleague and friend, Nina Funnell, the award-winning journalist, founder of #LetHerSpeak, and long-time advocate for sexual violence survivors. We have facilitated sessions where we ask students to identify things that someone might do or say that indicate they are enjoying sex, compared with things they might do or say that indicate they are not. We get answers like: *eye contact, laughing, increased heart rate, trembling, crying, closed eyes, moaning, saying nothing*. If you hadn't guessed which column those answers appear in, it's both.

The point, of course, is that relying on assumed cues alone, to divine what another person is feeling about a sexual experience, is risky business. Just as in the scenario with Nadia and Leon, each ingredient on its own doesn't render a situation problematic. For example, touching could mean flirtation. Leon may have had many other consensual sexual experiences in the past where the other party touched him as a means of flirting with him. But in this context, Nadia was sad and craving affection from her friends. Of course, it could have been that Nadia asking Leon to put her down as he carried her across the road was playful banter, or — as was the case — she wanted to be put down. Perhaps allowing someone into your house and leaving the light on in your room may signal an invitation to stay, but in this context, Nadia was drunk and out of it. All of this could have been clarified with communication, a consideration of the circumstances, and a sense of responsibility on Leon's part to do so.

We can't hand out a sex rule book that says *x will always mean y*. What we can do is teach people that it is incumbent on them to enquire what *x* means in each encounter, to listen to the answer, and to consider the context in which the answer is given. It requires a nuance that I refuse to believe we are incapable of. The only universal truth is that it is incumbent on everybody to ensure that there is true, enthusiastic consent from all parties to a sexual experience before proceeding.

So why didn't Leon feel that sense of responsibility?

•

To illustrate the answer to that question, it is helpful to return to Nadia's intoxication.

Some may wonder at what point it becomes her responsibility to slow down, to stay sober enough to keep herself safe. And some may consider that Leon's own state of intoxication reduced his moral culpability. Indeed, many institutions consider that reducing alcohol consumption is a solution to sexual violence, but it is a Band-Aid on a gaping wound. We still hold people accountable if they get really drunk and king-hit someone, recognising that it was their *decision* to assault someone that was to blame — not the victim for being out on the town and drunk themselves.

Yet when it comes to sexual violence, we are ready and apparently eager to examine how the victim-survivor got themselves in that vulnerable position. We accept as a given that there will always be potential perpetrators, and so the solution must be to limit the vulnerability of the victims.

So let's consider the role Nadia's intoxication might have played in the events of that evening, in terms of cause and effect. Nadia was sexually assaulted at the end of the night — was it her state of intoxication that caused it, or was it Leon's decision to engage in sexual activity with her when she could not consent?

Let's imagine Nadia got completely plastered to the same extent, and went home alone. Intoxicated Nadia would not have been sexually assaulted. Or perhaps Leon didn't come out that night at all. Intoxicated Nadia would not have been sexually assaulted. Or perhaps Leon walked her home but chose to leave her at her door. Intoxicated Nadia would not have been sexually assaulted. And if Leon followed her inside still hoping to have sex with her, but chose to leave once he saw that she was completely out of it on her bed, she would not have been sexually assaulted.

Unless we believe Leon had no agency in that situation, it cannot be the case that Nadia's state of intoxication *caused* the sexual assault. Leon may have exploited her intoxication to facilitate his choice to sexually assault her, but the cause was still that choice of his.

We are not so ready to blame the intoxication of either victim or perpetrator when it comes to other types of crime. People get really, really drunk and still abide by some of our strongest social conventions: most people don't go out and murder someone, no matter their state of intoxication. And if they did — or if they drove a car drunk, and caused someone's death — we would still hold them accountable.

The problem lies not in the vulnerability of individuals, but in the vulnerability of our social conventions around sexual behaviour and sexual violence. Our expectations about what, and how wrong, sexual violence is are simply not as clear and strong as *thou shalt not kill.*

I would wager most people are intrinsically motivated not to murder. Most people would believe, from a young age, that even property offences like theft are morally wrong. But, for many, that intrinsic motivation is not the same when it comes to sexual violence, and I think this is for two related reasons. First, not everybody understands the full spectrum of what sexual violence looks like: I'll return to this in the next chapter, but it's why Leon figures he's not a rapist so long as he doesn't penetrate Nadia with his penis.

Second, we don't do enough to make sexual violence, or the pursuit of personal sexual gratification without regard for another's wants, so unthinkable.

Leon grew up looking at the world around him, only to see that we would forgive him this behaviour. That we would minimise it, because he was Nadia's friend, and he didn't even put his penis in her, and maybe she just regrets it. Because it's not like she was attacked by a stranger in an alleyway who violently raped her. Leon saw that we would excuse his behaviour, on account of his being a 'red-blooded man', at the mercy of his own sex drive and urges. Allow it, because some of Nadia's actions were 'leading him on', and he was therefore owed something. Facilitate it, by creating and perpetuating the scripts that he relied on: the idea that women don't like sex as much as guys, that they won't be the ones to pursue it, that Nadia's affectionate touch meant he could touch her in any way he pleased.

And he grew up looking at the world around him, only to see that we would never challenge any of those things, because we do not, will not, talk about it.

This is a world we have created, and unless we get more comfortable talking openly about sex and intimate relationships, how can we ever reshape it?

As recently as 2017, a third of Australians still believed that rape results from men's inability to control their desire for sex.[4] But the very fact that there are plenty of people, plenty of men, who don't buy into these assumptions and scripts and who do not, would not, behave this way, is all the evidence we need that these things are not rooted in nature. This is not 'the way things are'. What is it that those people have that Leon does not?

I think the answer is revealed by the moment when Leon says to Nadia *it's okay, you're okay, just relax.* It is a moment I have seen time and time again, in the cases I've dealt with — shushes, assurances, placating words at the moment of violation. I always wonder: who are they trying to convince? The other person or themselves? Why this vain effort to recast the mood, even when the other person is out of it or frozen or protesting or crying or saying it hurts?

Having sex with someone who is passed out, who is not consenting, even someone who is not that enthusiastic, should be deeply undesirable and unarousing. When people like Leon offer those reassurances, those words of 'it's okay, you're okay', it's as though they hope that uttering the words will make it so. Funnell says that in these moments, many people treat orange-light signals as a reason to speed up rather than slow down — to get through before the red light illuminates. So they try to control the narrative, for themselves as much as anyone else.

I think this is also why they often check in the next day, as Leon did by texting Nadia. He was trying to rescue the situation, because he knew that, on some level, what he did was wrong — even if he doesn't think of it as *rape.* He knows that Nadia's response was not what enthusiasm looks like, but he tells himself he's still on this side of consent — even as, I suspect, he knows that Nadia was not consenting, was not able to.

The problem is, he does not care.

Not truly, sincerely, in his bones, does Leon care that Nadia does not and cannot want this. Certainly he does not care about it more than his own wants and 'needs'. He's not interested in her desires, her agency — he's interested only in what he can get from her. If he gave a damn, he would not see orange and red lights as something to find a loophole for.

We live in a world where sex is something that is 'for' men, or at least more than it is for anyone else. Leon looks at Nadia and, when it comes to sex, he thinks, *We are not the same.* I doubt he would be able to articulate it like this, but deep down his desires feel more important than hers. His desires feel like something he has a right to pursue all the way up to the line of 'no', and even beyond if he can just turn it into a 'yes', through persuasion, nagging, convincing, guilting. Anything more than not-no — interest, passion, pleasure — is a mere bonus.

Leon thinks of sexual gratification in terms of his own experience — a solo event, in one sense. And he gets to experience that event through contact and access to another body, some sort of living, breathing sex toy — not from the mutual desire for each other, the feeling of knowing he turns someone else on. What a lonely experience that must be; but he thinks of sex as a prize to be won, something almost separate from the person he does it with, something you get *from* someone or do *to* someone. 'I fucked her', rather than 'we fucked'. She is the gatekeeper of *his* sexual experience, and the harder it may be to win that prize, the more he has to work for it, the sweeter the victory.

We taught him that. He knew what we expected of him and what we expected of Nadia. We taught him that when we told him his worth lies in his bedroom conquests. When we taught him that men are biologically wired to want sex, that they are driven by that desire and are unable to control it. When we taught him that women and sexual access to them are a prize to be won, a feather for his cap, rather than a person with the full gamut of rights, just like him — that unless he thinks of them as his daughter/sister/mother, he cannot empathise with women. When we taught him that men are supposed to be strong, and that to be strong is to be tough and unemotional and rarely empathetic. When we taught him that he was entitled to sex, that it was something he was owed in the power structures that privilege him above everyone else. We normalised all this in our language, in our stories, our songs, films, shows, even in our jokes.

So is it any surprise that, having imagined a sexual encounter going a particular way, he feels indignant (perhaps even rageful) when the other person refuses to follow that script? Is it surprising that he feels he has the right to push for what he wants, to pursue his desires? In his mind, he is pursuing sex, not rape: he is not the same as the violent attacker leaping out of a dark alleyway to rape a strange woman. He does not understand, as so many don't, that the harm of sexual violence is the violation of autonomy. That losing control of what happens to your body is terrifying: even in your own bed, even at the hands of someone you trust. That having no choice, not knowing what may come next, is traumatic.

And in a space where the other person is not expected to enjoy sex as much anyway, where sex is not as much for her as it is for him, where a violation like this isn't really that bad, where his position at the top of society's food chain entitles him to this, of course Leon doesn't care what Nadia actually wants. He only cares what he can get away with.

He does not feel responsible because he has never been expected to feel responsible. And unless we change that, we will only ever look to blame things like Nadia's actions, her vulnerability, her intoxication, Angie's failure to intervene. If we don't get more comfortable talking about sexual violence, we will never strengthen the social convention that Leon's behaviour was wrong. If we don't get comfortable talking about what positive, healthy, respectful sex and intimate relationships look like, if we don't get comfortable expressly challenging gender norms and inequalities, and if we don't get comfortable talking explicitly about what our standard for sex and intimate relationships *should* be, Leon will never consider his actions unthinkable.

Because he will never learn to care, or even that he should.

4

What Do You Expect?

Xavier and Ashley

Xavier eased himself from under the bedsheet, holding his breath and willing the springs in the mattress not to give him away as he shifted his weight. From here to the door seemed an excruciating distance. It was still dark, so he used his phone screen to illuminate a path around discarded clothes and shoes, hoping Ashley was not a light sleeper.

He knew this was the coward's retreat, but he saw no other option. He hadn't been able to find words at the start of this encounter, and he didn't imagine that had improved in the hour he'd since spent paralysed with indecision. He stubbed his toe on a pile of textbooks and had to swallow an expletive. Grimacing, he closed the door behind him, pausing to listen for her deep breathing, satisfying himself she had not stirred.

On her stoop he pulled on his shoes before hastening into the night. When he got home, he showered, despite his exhaustion, hoping the hot water drumming on his bowed head would cleanse him of this unease, and the queasiness in the pit of his stomach would melt away.

He found her number under 'Recently Added', from when she'd saved it in his phone earlier. His anxiety churned as he typed out a message:

Sorry, had to get home. Couldn't sleep, and I've got training later. Talk soon.

That evening, Xavier had been pre-gaming with his teammates before heading to a house party in a suburb near campus. The theme was 'monochrome', and he'd dressed in pink, wearing his shirt open at the lads' bidding, because they were all doing it. *So the girlies get a load of these abs! Give the people what they want, mate,* Tommo cackled. Xavier felt like a bit of a twat, but he went along with it, not knowing how to resist the full force of his friends' group-think. Maybe people would get that he was doing it ironically? Probably not, but after a few beers he cared less.

He was used to their group getting a fair amount of attention from the ladies. They were the footy boys — tall, fit, and confident, they filled every room they entered as if they owned it. People seemed to believe it, too: everyone treated them like alphas, even though Xavier didn't really feel like one. He never felt completely at home with the showboating, chest-beating antics that screamed *look at us,* but he loved his mates and the fun he had with them. Where he did feel at home was in the sense of belonging they gave him. They were family.

And even though he was more shy than his mates, he wasn't complaining about his new-found popularity with girls. Since moving to college from his regional town, he had gained a lot of sexual experience and a reputation to match. He was good-looking, to be sure, but his sudden desirability was also a perk of being associated with the guys at the top of the food chain. It created a kind of symbiosis between them: a shared enterprise in which they were greater than the sum of their parts. Xavier noticed girls noticing him, backs straightening as they glanced over at him in class, fingers combing through their hair. Mostly he loved it.

Sometimes, though, especially if he was stressed, the attention irritated him. In those moments, he wasn't able to put his finger on what annoyed him. His tendency to shyness didn't entirely explain it. Maybe it was the weight of expectation it seemed to carry — the sense that he would always fit this mould that people had carved out for him in their minds. He felt as if he had an unrelenting audience to perform for.

He wanted to join study groups and learn, not just be flirted with — or at. That was if people even included him in their study groups, often assuming he was a pretty jock who would be an anchor to their diligence. He sometimes got so anxious about failing an exam that he wanted to weep, right there in the library. He would find himself lying awake in his college dorm feeling homesick, missing his mum and fantasising about getting on the next flight home to give her a hug. As much as his friends felt like family, he couldn't confide in them about these moments of weakness. Easier to endure until the moment passed or he was sufficiently distracted. When he and his mates showed each other affection, someone always had to say *no homo,* and, god, it was exhausting.

Deep down, even if he didn't know what to call it, Xavier craved intimacy. He found himself unable to enjoy the company of female friends without hooking up with them, sometimes unsure if that's what he really wanted. He never disliked sex, but if he was honest, sometimes he was left feeling dissatisfied, and not in a physical sense.

Everyone assumed he cared about two things: footy and getting laid. And while they *were* two of his favourite things, sometimes he wanted to scream that just because he was friends with dickheads didn't mean he was one. Little did he know, his friends sometimes felt the same.

Ashley and her housemates were throwing a party, the first in their new place since moving out of college. Renting a place made them feel mature and independent, more worldly. It made Ashley feel more self-confident, and when she saw one of the hot jocks in her Economics tutorial looking at her as she discussed the party with her friends, she felt emboldened to suggest he come along and bring his mates. As she walked out of the room, she couldn't believe she'd been so bold, and she felt exhilarated.

Now the night had arrived, and she was in a frisky mood. She shaved her legs and wore her lacy black underwear in the hope she might hook up with someone. 'Have we made enough jelly shots?' she yelled out to her housemates as she swiped on red lipstick, looking at herself approvingly in the mirror on the back of her bedroom door.

For the first few hours there was absolutely no talent, and she began to feel exasperated. Every time the door opened she would survey the new guests and consider whether she would go for any of them, and for ages the answer was no, no, no. *What is the point of looking this good and having your own place if you can't capitalise on it?* She felt her social battery starting to wane.

And just then, as if the gods themselves had heard her prayer, a group of guys walked in. Her interest piqued, Ashley's eyes followed the one in pink.

They encountered each other over the Esky in the kitchen. Ashley had seen Xavier go in there, and thought this was as good a chance as any to make herself known to him. She knew of him from uni, and was aware of his reputation as a ladies' man. Ashley fancied her chances with him — he was obviously fond of a bit of fun, and she herself had a near perfect strike rate.

Almost immediately they found a sweet spot of banter, and Ashley was on song —witty, charming, and confident. 'That red lipstick isn't technically monochrome,' Xavier said to her, gesturing at her otherwise all-black outfit.

'I'm the host! I made the rules, so I can break them,' Ashley replied, raising an eyebrow coquettishly. She turned on her stiletto and strutted off, feeling his eyes on her. At the door she turned: 'I'm Ashley, by the way. Help yourself to anything,' she said. With a wink, she left the room.

'Mate, she is up for it! You gotta get that, she is a nine at worst, brother,' Jared howled, wrapping his arm around Xavier's neck. A couple of the other lads came over and Jared gleefully relayed the exchange. Collectively, the boys crowed, reminding Xavier of a pack-animal ritual you might see on a David Attenborough special. All of a sudden, he felt tired. The boys seemed so triumphant about this development, like they were proud of him or something, as if his success was a success shared. 'I dunno,' was all he could manage. 'Is your dick broken, what's the matter with you?' Tommo said scornfully.

Xavier didn't know how to say he wasn't really into Ashley. She was hot, but he just wasn't feeling it. He was anxious about an essay he'd been procrastinating on that was due the next day. How could he voice that, though? He didn't want to field an interrogation or, as odd as it was, to feel like he was letting the boys down: boring behaviour wasn't part of their brand. Back claps and rounds for the boys were reserved for scores on the field or in the sack, not for those written in red pen. He wanted to avoid their derision. He was confident they wouldn't get it, and he felt like his reputation as one of the lads was on the line.

He couldn't even begin to imagine what else he might say to them, so it was easier to say nothing. Maybe he could just avoid her for the rest of the evening.

Playing host, Ashley surreptitiously looked around for the guy in pink. She had walked away from him, intending to play it cool and hoping he would follow her. She knew she looked good, and thought she'd detected some interest in his eyes as he regarded her; yet he hadn't come to find her. Maybe he didn't chase.

Eventually, they ended up in the same room again, and then they were standing near each other, and his friends seemed to melt away. They talked for a while, and she asked for his name. She gave her best performance, making suggestive comments and batting her eyelashes. Her confidence fuelled by shots of cheap alcohol, she laid it on thick, figuring he would find her audacity sexy.

Dropping her voice, she asked if he wanted to see her vinyl collection. What could Xavier say? This was her house, her party, and he didn't want to be rude. He felt his mates' eyes on him from across the room. Why did this feel like a test? Ugh, maybe there *was* something wrong with him if he didn't want this; the idea that he might not be up for sex seemed … signficant. It made him feel a bit panicky. He probably just needed to get out of his head.

He decided to go along with it because he couldn't think of anything else to do.

When they got to her room, she lay on the bed in a way that was meant to appear casual, but Xavier could tell she wanted him to see the way her waist dipped in before her hip curved back up like a ski-jump. To see her lacy bra where the collar of her shirt fell open. Her body was banging; why was he still not up for it? She was practically throwing herself at him. Now he was in a spiral, monitoring his own confusion so closely that he felt disoriented.

'Aren't you going to kiss me?' she asked.

Ashley's experience of guys was that they were invariably thrilled to get some action; when she deigned to offer it up to a guy, he was at the mercy of his constant desire. Growing up, she'd been told over and over that 'guys are only after one thing', so she thought their readiness for sex was a permanent state, like those power points that don't even have a switch — just plug into the electrical current and away you go. It was *her* willingness to participate that was the deciding factor.

By the time he had agreed to come to her room, the idea that Xavier wouldn't be up for it had not even crossed her mind. It was a fait accompli, and she was already calculating when to have the discussion about using protection, hoping he wouldn't be one of those dudes who complain about condoms.

So when she asked if he was going to kiss her, it was purely rhetorical.

'Um,' Xavier said, hesitating. She could hear the trepidation in his voice and Ashley was blindsided, immediately self-conscious and reeling, wondering if she had made a fool of herself.

Even in that mere moment, Xavier could see the incredulity gathering on her face. He could almost hear the wheels turning. *Fuck.* What if she started crying? What if she got defensive and told everyone he didn't, wouldn't, *couldn't* perform? His mates were still here. The panic rose in his chest like a king tide. The very last thing Xavier wanted to do was make this gorgeous girl feel bad about herself, or for his mates to find out he'd passed up this trophy they seemed so stoked about, but he had no idea what to say.

Years before he came to college, Xavier's school organised for some cops to come in and talk to the students about sexual violence and consent. They split the class into boys and girls, sending them to different rooms. The boys heard from a retired police officer, a gruff man with a gravelly voice who had, so he declared, 'seen it all'. Anything Xavier might have learned in that single hour wasn't coming to mind now, though. In fact, if anyone had asked him about it right there in Ashley's room, he would have struggled to recall the lesson at all. If he did, it wouldn't help him here: the former sergeant spent most of the time telling the boys about rape cases he'd worked on, barking at them that *no means no* and that drinking too much leads to bad decisions all round. There was much discussion among the boys afterwards about how terrifying it would be, to be accused of rape.

No, Xavier had nothing to draw on. He felt trapped — if he left the room, his mates would see him; if he stayed, what would he say to Ashley?

So he kissed her. What was the worst that could happen? Maybe fooling around with her would make him feel *less* anxious. Distract him from his own thoughts. As her hands moved into his shirt, and she moaned softly into his mouth, he started to get hard. She reached into his shorts and started stroking his cock, and eventually he was erect. It felt fine when she started to give him head, and he decided, for what felt like the millionth time this evening, to just go along with it. It felt more bearable than fully having sex with her, like he was a little more removed from it or something. Like she was doing something to him, so all he had to do was lay back and enjoy it.

And yet, he couldn't really enjoy it. The truth was he just wasn't that attracted to her, as attractive as she was. Yet he could practically feel his mates in the room with him. He was petrified he would lose his erection, and he couldn't have people thinking his gear didn't work. After what seemed like an age, a lot of enthusiasm from Ashley, and a concerted effort to mentally play out every porn clip he'd ever watched, he got there.

By way of hitting pause, Xavier hugged Ashley to him and kissed her forehead, caressing her back. His stomach twisting, he wanted so badly to be at home in his own bed. 'I just need a little rest,' he said. They lay there for an age and eventually fell asleep. A short while later he stirred, uneasy, and realised they had rolled away from each other. Checking his phone, he saw the guys had messaged him when they'd gone home.

He could tell Ashley was asleep and, even though it felt unkind, he decided to leave. Once he made it outside into the cool night air, he took what felt like his first full breath since he had gone into her room hours before. He jogged home, and with every stride he tried to put more distance between himself and what had just happened.

It was raining when I arrived in Amsterdam, emerging from the train station into a moody afternoon. I find rainy days comforting, as though I'm being embraced, and that's how this city greeted me: in just a short cab ride down wet streets, the clouds sitting low and cosy, it stole my heart completely.

The Netherlands is home to Rutgers, a not-for-profit, government-funded 'international centre of expertise on Sexual and Reproductive Health and Rights'. Rutgers has dedicated departments for sex education, sexuality, and sexual violence, with a qualified workforce of around a hundred people. The institute develops interventions, evaluates programs, conducts research, and advocates for reproductive and sexual rights in the Netherlands and internationally. It also assists organisations (including schools) to implement the interventions and programs it develops. Remember the Spring Fever program mentioned in Chapter 2, the RSE program for primary school children with the feathers and sponges? That is a Rutgers brainchild, which has been implemented in Holland for over 15 years and adapted internationally.

It would rain again the day I went to the Rutgers headquarters in Utrecht, to meet with Elsbeth Reitzema, the lead for Rutgers' primary school work. I hurried into the foyer completely soaked, managing to just keep my balance as I skidded through the doors on a floor slick with water from boot soles and shaken umbrellas.

My discomfort was drowned out by my enthusiasm to meet Reitzema. Sitting across from this softly spoken woman, I would soon discover the wealth of knowledge and expertise that sat behind her eyes, and the weight that it carried.

In most of the cities I visited during my fellowship, I made an effort to meet people socially, but I was so infatuated with Amsterdam I had no need of any company here except my own. I would stroll alongside the canals for hours each evening, stopping at bars when I was thirsty or hungry or seeking refuge from the weather.

One night I was walking home alone through a busy strip, when a man approached me and asked if I was single, and could he have my number. I demurred, and he wished me well before going on his way with an amiable smile. I can't deny that one of the emotions I felt as he walked away from me was relief — in that brief encounter, something in my amygdala had stirred. I'd had a few drinks, was alone at night in an unfamiliar city, and was being approached by a man I did not know: all the hallmarks of risk. These are the very scenarios we warn and are warned about, the ones we are taught to recognise as dangerous.

So, our efforts to prevent sexual violence often come in the form of urging people (women especially, and others we consider vulnerable) to avoid this kind of situation. Not only does that absolve us of responsibility to deal with the true source of the risk, but it also blinkers us from the myriad other forms that sexual violence may take. This narrow understanding of what sexual violence looks like allowed Leon (Chapter 3) to act as he did without holding himself accountable or recognising his conduct as sexual violence. Statistically, I was far less likely to be sexually assaulted by that man in Amsterdam than Nadia was at the hands of a friend who was purporting to get her home safe when she was drunk.[1]

This picture of sexual violence that we continue to paint, of the armed stranger who jumps out of a dark alley and overpowers a struggling woman, leaves out so much — I could count on one hand the number of sexual assault cases I've been involved in that looked like that. This means we don't learn to recognise other situations that are dangerous, or unethical, or unwanted, or uncomfortable, as situations that we have a right not to experience.

Teaching young people about this narrow picture of rape would be like teaching them that the only danger in the ocean is a shark, and failing to teach them how to swim, and to stay between the flags, and how to recognise a riptide. I sometimes wonder if this is why some defendants seem so incredulous that they are accused of sexual assault, because if whatever they did doesn't fit that construct of rape, they struggle to comprehend why they are in the dock. Like Leon, they might understand what they did as wrong, but not as rape.

Certainly the former sergeant that came to talk to Xavier and his classmates about consent, by encouraging those young men to respect the word 'no', was doing a little better than just warning young women to avoid strangers in dark alleys at night — but not by much. He had zoomed out slightly, but still left out most of the picture. He didn't even capture the Leons in the room, perpetuating the idea that the word 'no' is all that matters. When we leave things out, when we are not holistic or comprehensive and rely on a narrow risk-aversion model, we are not just ineffective but counterproductive. We don't just fail to prevent all forms of sexual violence, we help perpetuate it, and other kinds of negative sexual experiences.

Because it had never occurred to him that men might be the ones who want to say no, Xavier was unequipped to navigate that very situation. Not only did he not know how to navigate it, he believed he *shouldn't* want to say no. And both of those things saw him engaging in sexual activity that he did not want.

There may be some readers of this chapter who wonder how plausible it is that a young man, faced with an attractive young woman who wants to sleep with him, would really say no. I can understand that scepticism: we are constantly inundated with the message that men are always, always, always up for sex. That it's all they think about. That they don't even care who it is, so insatiable are they.

But it is this very assumption that saw Xavier in strife, and it's a dangerous assumption for us to maintain. I have lost count of the number of times young men have approached Nina Funnell and me, after one of our university sessions, to express gratitude to us for touching on this stereotype. I have been struck by the emotion it evokes, the palpable relief that someone has even named it. Many young, and not so young, men have disclosed to me occasions they had sex when they didn't want to, and how deeply it impacted them. The 2018 Australian National Survey of Secondary Students and Sexual Health reported that almost 16 per cent of male students had engaged in sex when they didn't want to, with 53 per cent of them reporting that it was because 'My partner thought I should' — a similar percentage to female and trans and gender-diverse respondents of the same question (although trans and gender-diverse respondents were far more likely to have engaged in sex when they did not want to, compared to male and female students). However, male students were significantly more likely to indicate perceived peer pressure as the reason for their unwanted sexual experience than female and trans and gender-diverse students.[2]

The influence of this assumption, this expectation, can be seen in the way Xavier's sex-ed class was divided by gender. By separating the class, Xavier's school and the cops who came to talk to them assumed that the 'boys and girls' needed different information. Chances are the young women got a completely different session — one that encouraged them to say no, that taught them how to defend themselves, how to hold their keys between their fingers, warned them not to get too drunk and to keep an eye out for their friends. In a piece for *The Monthly* about relationships and sexuality education called 'Ill-informed Consent', author of *Eggshell Skull* Bri Lee wrote about visiting a co-ed school to speak to the students about consent, only to find the school had arranged for her to speak only to the girls — the boys instead hearing from a male presenter about mental health and financial planning. This is a common practice.

When we do this, not only do we reinforce the idea that sexual violence will always look a particular way, we also suggest to young people that the parties to a sexual encounter will act in particular ways based on whether they are man or woman, boy or girl, male or female. And we are teaching them that their responsibilities in that encounter are therefore different, creating a kind of 'us and them' dynamic. This assumes that all sexual experiences will be heterosexual ones, and that everyone is readily categorised as male or female, man or woman. These assumptions are unrealistic and they don't reflect the complexity of human experience, leaving our kids grasping anytime they are faced with something that does not fit that narrow expectation.

When we teach mathematics, we don't give students one equation to rote learn: we give them the skills to solve any number of equations they may face, including those they will encounter in real life. When we teach English, we don't ask them to memorise an essay response to one particular text: we give them the analytical and communication tools to engage with a world of books, articles, films, art.

Yet when it comes to sex and relationships, we teach young people how to confront one single kind of scenario (if we even do that). That scenario is one where a guy, driven by an insatiable sex drive that he has little control over, pursues a girl who doesn't want sex as much as he does. It's up to her to stop him, and to stay invulnerable to his advances. At best, we teach that he ought to respect her wishes (provided she has expressed them).

The number of sexual encounters that fall outside that scenario is immeasurable, as is the weight of those expectations we create.

•

In Chapter 3, Leon relied on the expectation that he was a 'red-blooded man' to permit his sexual violence, rationalising his conduct by some innate biological drive. Here, that same expectation saw Xavier experience a sexual encounter he did not want.

Xavier was left feeling bewildered by his disinterest in sleeping with Ashley. He felt a pressure to perform — to prove his qualifications as a man, as one of the lads. Ashley hadn't contemplated that he might not be up for it, believing that whether or not they had sex was entirely contingent on her desire to do so, because his could be assumed.

And just like that, Ashley and Xavier were not the only ones in the room. The expectations about Xavier's motivations and how he would behave had followed them in, like an invisible force with a life of its own, wrapping itself around them and compelling Xavier to 'go along with it', assuring Ashley that he was up for it.

Where have we seen this before? Not just the expectations of masculinity, but of how people will interact in sexual encounters? Expectations of behaviour and the meaning behind it? Expectations about what people want out of a sexual opportunity, and how they can get it? Those expectations followed Elliot and Amy into his ute, Max and Bec into his room, and they followed Nadia and Leon around the bar, accompanying them to the train station and up into her apartment. We will see them join Dominic and Jeremy in the next chapter, and in every chapter to come.

These expectations are the invisible forces that operate on us all in sexual encounters. They create a pressure that is hard to identify, and not solely referable to the other person involved. They drive and shape our sexual experiences, and they create the environments in which sexual violence and unwanted sex not only are permitted but can flourish.

So long as we keep those forces invisible, so long as we never name those expectations and assumptions, we will never be free to make the choices we want in sex and relationships, or to voice them. We won't even recognise them as something that *can* be challenged.

Instead, they will continue to feel like incontrovertible truths: laws of nature that govern us.

These expectations are layered, complex and systemic: we grow up seeing them all around us, and they are planted in our minds from a young age. In Chapter 3, we reflected on how early we teach kids to feel shame about their genitals. Do you remember when you first learned that feeling? I don't.

This is why *no means no* is so desperately inadequate. The messages young people receive about relationships and sex and their bodies, and the way they ought to perform masculinity or femininity, are so pervasive and ubiquitous that they are unquantifiable. And they do not just come from the usual suspects (or scapegoats) of music and television and social media and pornography: some of the most powerful messages come from the most innocuous places. They are the ones we unthinkingly pass on in our off-hand comments, the relationships we model, our unremarkable reactions to things we see and hear. When we rush to pull our little girls' skirts down on the playground; when we make kids give us or anyone else a hug; when they're told that the boy who is pulling their hair and pushing them off the slide is doing it because he likes them; when we say catcalling is a compliment, that being desired is the same as being respected; when they hear us whinge about our boss and call her a bitch or a dumb slut; when they hear us remark about a rape or sexual harassment case in the news: 'Well, what did she expect?'

Comprehensive relationships and sexuality education helps young people make sense of those messages, and challenge the habitual and the apparently unremarkable. This is why we need to start young, why the window of opportunity closes so early — we need to interrupt those messages before they set in, before they become 'how it is'.

Nothing in Xavier's sex-ed, nor Ashley's, it seems, equipped them to recognise this encounter as one that Xavier did not want to experience, and one which he had a right not to. Neither of them recognised that Ashley had a responsibility not to assume he was consenting just because he was a man. Nothing in Xavier's sex-ed interrogated the idea that his value as a man, his worth to his mates, was dependent on his desire and ability to bed women.

I reflected on the kind of cultural bonding experience around sexual success that we have created for straight men as I wandered around the Red-Light District in Amsterdam. Groups of men were taking up so much space with their alpha pageantry: posturing, geeing each other up and cheering each other on as they celebrated their sexual achievements with the women in those windows. Like when you turn to your friends at the football to cheer together when your team kicks a goal — maybe that's why we call it *scoring*. This dark camaraderie is a mighty force and, at its extreme, you see it in gang rape.

Xavier's sex-ed assumed and reinforced that he would only ever be the one pursuing sex, that he would find it ever-interesting, ever-valuable. The fidelity to these expectations of manhood is powerful: as well as Xavier, it is what drove Elliot in Chapter 1 and Leon in Chapter 3. Were any of them taught to question that? To question the role models they saw in films, shows, music, podcasts, social media, sport, celebrities or even in their own lives? Or were they told boys will be boys, that they would only ever be after one thing? Never told to expect nuanced feelings, never given permission to feel vulnerable.

It is not just gender roles and norms that must be challenged. As we have already seen, and will see in the chapters to come, there are so many insidious messages and expectations about sex and relationships that must be unlearned, reshaped. To do that is going to take more than simply telling some young people not to rape, and others to make sure they don't get raped.

Sitting across from me, Reitzema was quietly commanding as she told me about Rutgers' success with its RSE programs. It's a product that has been delivered for long enough now that she and her team have been able to test its efficacy: they know that it results in later first sexual experiences, and a reduced likelihood of negative sexual experiences.

This success wasn't born of chance. Curricula, lesson plans, picture books, contributions to television programs — the Rutgers work is based on rigorous research and is designed by people whose entire expertise is RSE, evaluated for quality assurance. Reitzema herself is an expert in RSE, with 20 years of experience in the field.

And, like any good specialty product, the Rutgers model is no click and collect: Rutgers works by engaging with municipal health departments to improve RSE in schools, training teachers and engaging with parent communities. The Rutgers' Long Live Love program (a school-based sex-ed program for adolescents in secondary schools) is 'one of the most successful, evidence-based programs in the field of school-based sex education in the Netherlands' and its effectiveness 'has been largely accredited to the quality and extent of its implementation'.[3]

Their collaboration with health departments is significant. It is curious to me, the choice to use police officers or some other representative of the criminal justice system to educate in this space. I suppose, however, that if your focus is only on avoiding the crime of sexual violence, you may be so inclined. In Australia, we do seem to see the work of sexual violence prevention as sitting at an intersection of criminal justice and education.

In most of the other countries I visited on my fellowship, safeguarding sexual wellbeing can be found just a few streets away, at an intersection of education, health, and human rights. You arrive at this intersection if you let RSE expertise and evidence guide you. Expertise and evidence that reveals teaching RSE from a risk-avoidance perspective is less effective — it is like educating into negative space. Is there any other area where we educate solely by reference to what *not* to do? Did we ever learn to tie our shoelaces with our parents showing us only how *not* to do it? Did we learn our ABCs by being taught what each letter does not sound like? Scare tactics like 'don't rape or you'll end up in jail' are about as effective as what someone described to me as 'health terrorism', where you try to shock young people into using condoms by showing them grim photographs of genital herpes. Recent research out of Oxford shows that emphasising eroticism and fun in condom-use messaging was more effective at increasing people's uptake of condoms than other approaches, such as those that focus on messages about negative health outcomes.[4] The same has been argued in respect of preventing sexual violence and unwanted sex: focusing on scare tactics and negative outcomes is less effective than taking a positive approach.[5] Perpetrator-focused strategies may backfire, because 'the very attitudes and behaviours at odds with ethical sexual behaviour can be exacerbated by the "quick-fix" workshop approach to rape prevention education'.[6] Perhaps this is why Xavier and his peers found themselves preoccupied with being *accused* of rape, rather than thinking how they might approach sexual encounters.

By contrast, the Rutgers approach is full of life: bright, joyous, playful — the primary school program even has a theme song, and during Spring Fever week the kids decorate the school with hearts to celebrate love and friendship. The Rutgers high school program takes a similarly positive approach to healthy, safe, and respectful sex and relationships. Even if the prevention of pregnancies, STIs, and sexual violence is your only goal, every RSE expert would still endorse a positive, comprehensive approach as critical to achieving that, and we will see why in the next few chapters.

Expertise in RSE matters. Having high expectations for who designs and delivers it, who is sufficiently qualified, makes all the difference. Reaching adulthood does not automatically qualify us, otherwise we would not have the rates of adult sexual violence that we do. Even being a teacher does not qualify us, for many feel ill-equipped and under-resourced to deliver this education in a way that is effective, or to answer the many questions that students ask.

Something all RSE experts are clear about is that getting it wrong is not just ineffective — it can actually perpetuate harm. Things like phrasing and demeanour matter — kids are highly attuned to subliminal messaging, and teachers who aren't comfortable with the material, or equipped to answer the more difficult questions, can end up reinforcing problematic attitudes. As someone in Canada said to me: 'Even a well-meaning teacher is very likely to end up giving abstinence messaging because it is difficult to get over the cultural taboo of talking about sex.' I observed this first-hand in one school, where a teacher was unsure about the law in relation to image-sharing and resorted to saying, 'Just don't do it.' In one study, Swedish teachers 'described a sense of taboo around sexuality, which hindered them from comfortably talking about the issue. They reported a possible clash between teachers' personal experiences and values and learners' cultural and religious beliefs, requiring a delicate balance between teachers' ideas of right and wrong and the learners' personal values.'[7]

This risk extends to external educators or speakers too, no matter how they bill themselves. Speakers like the former sergeant who came to Xavier's school. For that same piece in *The Monthly*, Bri Lee spoke to Chanel Contos, who told her about one such speaker who came to her high school:

> He's an ex-cop. And he's really good at teaching what sexual assault is and the criminal punishments for it, but … it's very victim-blaming. It's telling the girls to not get sexually assaulted. It was enough for me to realise that I'd been sexually assaulted, but it didn't address opportunistic rapists, because it didn't address toxic masculinity. It didn't address sexual coercion. It didn't address all the societal pressures that create that environment. And I'm sure there's still a lot of girls who had been sexually assaulted that probably couldn't pinpoint it from that [talk].

This is why we must treat RSE like the specialist area that it is. This is what places like Rutgers show us, and Dr O'Higgins in Galway, Alice Cruttwell in Shropshire, and the Big Talk Education team in Yorkshire. I would see it again in Germany and Canada, and you can find it in many other parts of the world.[8] The UNESCO 'International Technical Guidance on Sexuality Education' includes the involvement of experts on human sexuality, behaviour change, and pedagogical theory as a key principle of RSE development.

•

If we acknowledge that this is a specialist subject matter, a thing of experts, does that mean we should expect only specialist providers at the front of classrooms, delivering sex-ed? Not necessarily.

Although Rutgers is the powerhouse behind the design and implementation of quality RSE in the Netherlands, they do not actually send Rutgers staff, arguably the country's sex-ed specialists, into schools to deliver the lessons. Instead, they focus on equipping schools and teachers to do it themselves.

The reason for this is simple: if we are to normalise talking about sex and relationships, if we are to eschew the shame and embarrassment, if we are to dismantle the expectations that come from the most innocuous of places, it is critical for young people to see the adults in their everyday lives talking about it. Young people must see this as something normal, part of their ordinary classroom experience — not something unusual or special or mysterious that is only ever taught by somebody external who parachutes in before disappearing again, like a Mary Poppins of sex-ed. And, given the nuance required, school staff may also be better attuned to the needs of individual students, and can tailor sex-ed classes to those needs, provided they meet the fundamental principles of comprehensive RSE.

Treating RSE as a specialist subject matter and relying on everyday teachers to deliver it are not mutually exclusive. Rather, we are compelled to build up the requisite expertise in everyone. If we are to take this up as a community-wide effort, it should be incumbent on all teachers to become sufficiently expert in this subject matter, even at the qualification stage. Some universities in Australia endeavour to equip their pre-service teachers with training to deliver RSE, but it is not a core requirement. A 2021 study of teacher training about sexuality education in Australia found that 'all Australian pre-service teachers are potential sexuality education teachers, and some minimal level of sexuality education training should be provided to all pre-service teachers regardless of teaching specialty'.[9] We must provide professional development opportunities and resources to upskill teachers, and to maintain their professional knowledge: as an interviewee in Ireland said to me, 'Capacity is a state not a trait.' Research has shown that 'school training interventions that improve teachers' skills in sexual health maximise the effectiveness of interactions with their students'.[10]

> A wealth of research shows teachers, and similar professionals, who receive training to develop the skills and knowledge to teach sexuality education are more likely to feel comfortable with, and have more self-efficacy regarding the delivery of this content, which thereby increases their likelihood of adhering to high-quality sexuality education curricula.[11]

In Australia, as well as countries such as Canada, the United Kingdom, and the United States, teacher preparation has been lacking.[12] Dr Michael Davies, a lecturer in Health and Physical Education at the University of Canberra, is committed to improving pre-service teacher training in RSE for his students. He told me:

> I believe all teachers should get this training, not just for their future teaching but also for personal growth as an individual. People mature physically, mentally, emotionally, spiritually, and sexually at different stages, so I believe tertiary institutions have an important role to play.
>
> From a teacher perspective, I want to ensure we provide Australia's future teachers with the pedagogical content, knowledge, and confidence to address the various sensitive health topics to create generational change within the school curriculum. From a school-aged student's perspective: I believe it is the right of all students to receive holistic RSE so they can make their own informed decisions.

Importantly, the 'train the trainer' model only works for teachers if they get adequate support from school leadership as well, as we will see later.

That said, there *are* arguments in favour of external specialist providers too, if they are the right kind of specialist. Part of the reason Big Talk Education in the UK is so successful is that *all* they do is RSE, so they are able to ensure a deeper level of expertise than can be expected of classroom teachers. They can be more flexible to adapt content to address topical issues because of that expertise, which may make them better equipped to respond to questions or sensitivities that arise compared to classroom teachers. Their expertise comes through the practitioners, rather than just the curriculum. Everyday teachers who sit in on such sessions can learn from them, too.

External agencies are also less likely to be affected by prejudgements of particular groups of students or individuals, which can in turn affect lesson delivery. Furthermore, as explored above, the demonstrated attitudes and values of those delivering the subject matter is critical, and quality control of those elements is more easily attained in a specialist agency. Perhaps most importantly, not all teachers will feel comfortable delivering this subject matter, particularly if they have a personal history of sexualised violence or abuse.

Thankfully, we need not choose between well-trained classroom teachers and external providers: when it comes to RSE, more is more. Young people deserve to learn about RSE from the everyday adults in their lives as well as the expert external providers.

When I say 'more is more', I don't just mean ideally. For relationships and sexuality education to work, for it to do what we want it to do, it must be repeated, consistent, and lifelong. A review of three decades of research about comprehensive RSE showed that its efficacy is dependent on 'instructional scaffolding over a period, and not just one session', providing 'substantial evidence that sexuality education is most effective when begun early and before sexual activity begins' and that 'building an early foundation and scaffolding learning with developmentally appropriate content and teaching are key to long-term development of knowledge, attitudes, and skills that support healthy sexuality'.[13] The stuff of sex-ed is nuanced, detailed, wide-ranging: it cannot be dealt with in one hour, or even in one week. The opportunities for conversations with young people about relationships, sexuality, and sex will come up in all sorts of unexpected ways — and we need to be prepared to meet those opportunities even (perhaps especially) when they arise outside of the class lesson plan.

In Holland, Spring Fever week alone is still considered inadequate. I spoke to the person responsible for RSE implementation in a municipality of the Netherlands, at the municipal health department there. He described Spring Fever week as 'agenda setting and awareness raising', cautioning that if it is only taught once a year it is ineffective and will not change behaviour. He explained how enthusiastic schools integrate it into their curriculum, helping to normalise the subject matter and increase the children's skills to recognise situations that are not okay, asking for help, talking about it. Research supports this: the topics of RSE can and should be addressed across the curriculum, and such an approach 'offers much-needed flexibility to schools, both in terms of available time and talented teachers to tackle difficult and important topics'.[14]

This is one of the reasons schools are so important to relationships and sexuality education. Not at the expense of parents and community, but in partnership; as a central site of intervention, rather than the sole site. If we treat RSE as a specialist subject matter that demands expertise and quality assurance, both in design and delivery, then existing education systems are key to ensuring that the lessons, curricula, and materials are helpful, not harmful. To ensuring that the lessons can build consistently, year after year. That those who deliver RSE are appropriately qualified and confident to do so. That it is normalised, integrated into one of the main parts of a young person's life, so that they learn about it alongside literature, maths, art, history, and sport — and even within those subjects.

It is important for young people to learn about relationships and sexuality alongside their peers; this means they see that everyone learns the same things, and is subject to the same expectations. The values and standards of behaviour expected are not simply a matter of personal belief, but rather something we all strive for.

Which brings me to another reason schools are so important to sex-ed. As an interviewee in Germany said to me: 'How do you reach every kid?'

5

On Our Watch

Dominic and Jeremy

'Will you text me when you land?'

'Yes, Mum.'

'Don't forget.'

'I won't!'

'Okay, but sometimes you do. I'll be worried.'

'You're always worried,' Dominic said as he kissed the top of her head, having been tall enough to do so for years now.

Dominic was moving to one of the country's biggest cities to go to university, and his mum's nerves about it had nothing on his. He was excited for the opportunities it would bring, but secretly he feared that the city would be too big for him, that he didn't have what it would take.

Leaving home behind him, everything he knew 30,000 feet below, for a moment Dominic felt a sense of calm. He had heard once that, before they fly, pilots sign for the souls on board. He thought about that as they floated down to land over the blue, blue harbour — carried into this next stage of his life by inexorable momentum and complete trust in a stranger.

There was a flurry of welcome activities for the new residents at the college, designed to help them get to know each other and the city itself, for almost all of them were not from here. They were assigned nicknames by the senior residents, and they had to refer to each other accordingly. Some of them would wear that nickname for the rest of their lives.

With stunning originality, Dominic got 'Curly' on account of his hair. 'Curls get the girls!' someone whooped, clapping him on the back as it was read out. He smiled along.

They got buddied up with an older student, a resident who had been there for a few years. Dominic's buddy was Sam, a friendly dude who was studying engineering. He showed Dominic to his room, down corridors with carpet that was threadbare in spots, past wooden doors that had been scratched and worn down over generations. This was an old and prestigious place, where tradition, camaraderie, and the college 'way' were gospel.

As he helped bring Dominic's stuff into his room, Sam saw the photo on his phone's home screen of Dominic and his best friend Millie at the Year 12 formal last year. 'Girlfriend back home?' Sam said affably. 'You're allowed to have visitors, you just need to tell the staff and get the okay first.'

Dominic smiled. 'Thanks.' He thought about correcting Sam's assumption, but this place was still too new, too unfamiliar for him to do it. He didn't have the energy to field the reaction, to do the dance where Sam got all self-conscious about his mistake, and Dominic had to make him feel better about it.

Later in the week, before the toga party, the freshers were summoned to a brief lecture from the college leadership about not drinking too much and upholding the college reputation. They had to watch a video that was played on a screen at the front of the room: 'You can't force someone to have sex with you, just like you can't force them to eat a slice of cake if they aren't hungry,' the voiceover intoned. People fidgeted in their bedsheet togas.

'You can't have sex with someone if they are asleep. That's rape.' *Obviously,* Dominic thought, along with almost everyone else in the room. God, this was all so patronising, but the staff were being so earnest about it, standing there with solemn expressions.

And, as a parting word of wisdom, the head of college chided:

'Treat the girls with respect, lads. Don't be upskirting them or sending photos of your junk, okay? We take that very seriously, so don't be stupid.' By this point, Dominic had tuned out.

Despite the welcome events, Dominic hadn't made many friends by the time tutorials kicked off a few weeks later. He was beginning to wonder if he'd made the right decision, moving so far from his comfort zone. Even though he was tall enough to kiss his mum on the top of her head, he felt too small for here. Too sheltered, too unsophisticated. He found uni life at once underwhelming and overwhelming; it was the most crowded place he'd ever been, and yet he had never felt so isolated.

For his first tutorial, he found the right building on campus, but the layout was confusing and he couldn't figure out where the room was. He wandered around, trying to look like he had some idea of where he was going. He neared a doorway with a group of people gathered outside, but someone was leaning on the wall covering the room number, and he didn't want to ask them to move or if he was in the right place. He worried he would be late for his tutorial if it was somewhere further away, so he panicked and kept walking.

As he moved down the corridor he could see from the sequence of numbers that the right room had been the one with the people outside. He couldn't turn on his heel now — they'd all see and realise his mistake. No, he was not about to draw attention to himself. So he kept going, until he got around the corner, where he pulled out his phone and scrolled for long enough to make it seem he had gone to the bathroom or something, before making his way back. Damn, why was he so awkward?

The tutor had opened the door by now, and the small crowd shuffled forward and began to move inside as Dominic walked towards them.

And then, as if the students parted like the seas, Dominic saw him. The most beautiful boy he'd ever laid eyes on. He had a magnetism to him that made everything else go dull, like white noise. He seemed glamorous, too, with a leather jacket and nose piercing. Dominic suddenly realised he was gawking, and he blushed, looking at his feet.

Once inside, Dominic sat down and fought the urge to stare. They went around the class to introduce themselves, and Dominic had to be asked to repeat himself, he said it so softly. When it got to the beautiful one, he said his name was Jeremy. He said it with ease and confidence, as if everyone would be waiting to hear it, wanting to know it.

As the tutorial went on, Jeremy answered the tutor's questions using words like *reductive* and *obsolete*, which seemed to roll off his tongue. Dominic didn't notice that it was a little obnoxious — he was impressed, even as it drew into sharp relief how inadequate he felt. Soon it transpired that this tutor favoured the Socratic method — *shit, shit, shit* — and then, the worst, the dreaded, she called on Dominic. He managed to get something out, sweat beading on the back of his neck as he felt everyone's eyes on him, but he stumbled over his words and basic syntax seemed to escape him.

Afterwards, Dominic tried to scurry off with his head down, to recover from his own awkwardness and figure out whether it was too late to change tutorials.

'Hey!' he heard behind him. He turned, surprised to see Jeremy striding to catch up to him. 'I liked what you said back there.' Dominic wasn't sure if he was teasing, but he didn't seem to be. 'What was your name again?' Jeremy said with a devastating smile.

'Dominic.'

'Jeremy.'

'I know,' Dominic said before he could stop himself.

'Do you want to get coffee?'

Fireworks went off in Dominic's heart.

Over the following weeks and months, Dominic fell hard for Jeremy: he was sophisticated and mature, and the chemistry between them was incredible. Jeremy made him feel seen, like he was something special. This city was his hometown, and he took Dominic out to great bars and introduced him to all his friends. He came with a social circle that Dominic could slip right into. At a time when he felt all at sea, Jeremy was a lighthouse.

And Jeremy adored Dominic: his thoughtful and shy nature, his quiet intelligence. He loved how wholesome and sweet he was, this boy from the outback. He was funny, too, although he didn't know it — Jeremy would often find himself clutching his sides with laughter at something Dominic said off-hand.

One night, Jeremy took Dominic out on a fancy date. They went to a nice bar in the city, and Jeremy paid for their eye-wateringly pricey cocktails and perfectly cooked steak.

They gazed at each other in the amber lighting. 'Why are you so good to me?' Dominic asked. Jeremy laughed and shrugged lightly. 'Because I'm obsessed with you.'

They went back to Dominic's dorm, where they lay on his bed and kissed. Dominic had never felt this kind of lust with his previous boyfriends, this shared rhythm of ecstasy. He was sure he would never get over the feeling of their limbs entwined.

He began kissing down Jeremy's perfect body, moving to give him head as he usually did, when Jeremy stopped him, cupping his hands around Dominic's face.

'I want to sleep with you.'

Dominic paused, nerves exploding in his stomach. 'Like, go all the way?'

'You're so cute. Yes, I want to go *all the way*,' Jeremy said with a laugh.

The thrill Dominic felt was intense. He was nervous, but in a good way. He had never done it before, but neither had he felt this way about anyone else. He felt ready.

'I want that, too,' he said. 'I have condoms.'

'You're so cute, babe,' Jeremy said again.

As Dominic leaned over to the drawer beside his bed, he thought he detected a hint of condescension in Jeremy's voice. He paused, his hand outstretched.

'What?' he asked, defensiveness creeping into his tone to cover his self-consciousness.

'Well, I'm not seeing anyone else — we don't need to use a condom.'

The nerves suddenly shifted, feeling sharper. 'I just feel like we should be safe, you know?'

'You're safe with me. I've never felt this way about someone, and I really want to feel close to you. I get that you haven't done this before, but you can trust me,' Jeremy said in a soothing tone.

Dominic suddenly felt immature and naive. He already believed deep down that he didn't deserve Jeremy, like he was punching well above his weight, and he spent so much time trying to disguise his inadequacy. Now he had given himself away.

His best friend Millie had told him about guys doing this to her, pushing her to do it without a condom, and he remembered scoffing, confident that he would always insist on protection when he got to that stage with someone.

But now here he was, faced with the same situation, and he didn't know how to be insistent. He couldn't comprehend what Jeremy saw in him and he didn't want the glass to shatter. He didn't know what to say, and could only hope Jeremy would stop pushing it.

Jeremy hated wearing a condom during sex; it just didn't feel the same. He used to wear them, but now, with experience and PrEP, he didn't see the need. And he especially didn't want to wear one with Dominic — this could be the greatest sex of his life, and he wanted to completely lose himself in the experience. He knew he posed no risk to Dominic, and he didn't really get what the big deal was. He could tell Dominic had never had anal sex before, but didn't he trust him?

'I didn't expect you to be such a baby about it. I can't keep it up with a condom on. Besides, don't we have something special?' Jeremy was sulking now. Dominic felt guilty, as if he were letting Jeremy down, and betraying the strength of their connection. If he pressed the issue, it would be like admitting he didn't believe Jeremy when he said he wasn't seeing anyone else. It had been such a special evening, too, and Dominic didn't want to be the one to ruin it. Jeremy did have more experience after all, so maybe he was right, and Dominic was just being silly. He could trust Jeremy, couldn't he?

'I want you so bad,' Jeremy said, kissing Dominic's neck.

Finally, Dominic capitulated.

Afterwards, he felt unsettled. While he had enjoyed aspects of the sex, he'd felt a constant anxiety about being unsafe. If he was honest with himself, there was also a rupture in how he felt about Jeremy. He didn't want to admit that he felt disrespected, that Jeremy had put his own wants first. It seemed to confirm his deepest fear — that Jeremy didn't love him as much — and now their trust felt tarnished. He was also annoyed at himself for giving in.

Dominic found himself growing impatient with Jeremy, anytime he suggested what they should do, where they should go, who they should see. 'Don't you ever wonder what I want to do?' he snapped one day.

Jeremy was taken aback: 'Of course I do! It's just that you're not from here, so it's easier for me to suggest stuff for us to do.'

'You think I'm just some parochial, small-town boy,' Dominic said accusingly, before stomping back to college, flinging himself on his bed to stare at the ceiling.

He wasn't sure why this was affecting him so, but as much as he willed himself to get over it, he couldn't. He didn't know what to do, who to tell. All his friends here were Jeremy's, and everyone would probably think he was silly and naive for being upset about this.

Who else? His 'buddy' Sam? As if. The head of college? Imagine telling that old goat that he was sad because his boyfriend had fucked him in the arse without a condom. Dominic almost laughed at the thought. This place treated the queer experience as an afterthought; a rainbow box they had to tick. They would probably act like he'd been the victim of some kind of homosexual depravity, and he wasn't about to give them any fodder for that dangerous old chestnut. Or he would just get in trouble for having a visitor in his room and bringing it on himself.

Besides, he loved Jeremy, and he didn't want him to get in trouble — and it's not like he had done anything that bad, because Dominic had agreed to it in the end. He didn't want to tell his mum or Millie, because he didn't want them to think poorly of his boyfriend.

So he called Millie to talk about anything else, and when she answered, tears caught in his throat: it was the sound of home and her voice was so close, yet so very, very far away.

The sandstone bricks of the cathedral in Koln have been blackened by years of acid rain and pollution spewing from the central train station just below. An imposing show of Gothic architecture, it is the first thing you see when you climb the station steps, and one of the only buildings that survived World War II in a city that was otherwise flattened by aerial raids. I went on a walking tour on one of my first days there, the guide telling us of the theories that emerged afterwards about why it had survived. Apparently, some said it was the will of God, while others claimed citizens of the city extinguished any flames that threatened it, rushing to protect this monument of faith. 'The real reason,' the guide said, raising his voice to be heard above the nearby buskers and the wind whipping around us, 'was a bit more confronting, and had nothing to do with fate. The twin spires served as a landmark for the bombers. It was deliberately spared.'

Deliberately spared. Those words would ring in my ears the next day when it came time to meet with representatives of Germany's Bundeszentrale für gesundheitliche Aufklärung (BZgA): the Federal Centre for Health Education.

Every time I address university students about sex-ed, or deliver workshops with Nina Funnell about sex, consent, and bystander behaviour, at least one person will say afterwards, 'I wish we had learned this at school.' Without fail.

This is wholly unsurprising: young people do not suddenly become confident and knowledgeable about sex and relationships the moment they graduate from high school. No matter how many times I hear this comment, every time it breaks my heart, because what that person is really saying is that they already needed this information. They are remembering an occasion when they were left wanting, perhaps with devastating results. The 2018 National Survey of Secondary Students and Sexual Health found that 46 per cent of students in years 10–12 had engaged in sexual intercourse (that is, vaginal or anal intercourse), and in Year 12 alone, that percentage rose to 55.8 per cent.

The reality is that Dominic and his peers would have had wildly varying experiences of sex-ed by the time they got to uni. Some would have had the style we saw with Xavier in Chapter 4 — a bit of *no means no*, be careful when you're drunk — and some would have been warned only to avoid STIs and pregnancy. Others still would have been told that abstinence was all they needed to know. If they were lucky, some would have got the kind of comprehensive RSE that we know is effective.

RSE in Australia is enormously inconsistent. As we considered in Chapter 2, the national curriculum (even the 2022-revised one that includes more about consent) provides some guidance, but it is just that — guidance. A good curriculum is like having a life-saving vaccine in a pandemic: without the means to store it, transport it, and get it into people's arms consistently, it will spoil on the shelf. So too, even the best sex-ed curriculum, designed by the best experts, means little if it is not being delivered effectively. Or at all.

Not only are states, territories, and the schools within them vested with a huge amount of autonomy but, as we explored in prior chapters, their sex-ed choices are at the whim of budgets, resources, and the capacity of individual teachers. Teachers are already asked to carry so much, and on the list of things they need to achieve each year, sex-ed may easily fall to the bottom. Fear plays a significant part, too: fear of not getting it right, fear of criticism. Many schools may not know how to best deliver sex-ed, or will play it extremely 'safe' to avoid opposition and backlash. Jane Corcoran, an Australian teacher of 14 years who has published articles about the need for improved sex-ed, told me how patchy it is. She told me that, intrinsically, she understands that teaching sex-ed 'makes sense, but I have no idea where to start and it makes me feel nervous, anxious, and vulnerable.'

'Vulnerable — tell me more about that,' I said. She rubbed her forehead and fidgeted as she began to answer:

> I've grown up in a culture where sex and sexuality is a private thing and I haven't even had conversations with the people closest to me about pleasure and sex; it's not in my everyday lived experience, to talk about those things. To think about having to stand up in my job in my role as a teacher and openly talk about sex as a natural part of a wonderful life makes me feel fearful. I'm a 40-year-old woman who is also a mum, I'm in the safest demographic as a teacher to talk about these things to students. What if I was in my twenties? Or a male? I would feel vulnerable on a whole other level.
>
> I also feel vulnerable to being misinterpreted and criticised by parents, by students who aren't comfortable, by the principal. What if I get a question about an orgasm? Having to think on the spot, where to draw the line … education is all about boundaries and making sure you are the teacher in that authoritative role … this feels like you're crossing over to a grey area. I don't even know how to approach it. Do I be jovial? I think it would take a special kind of person to deliver it well.

Perhaps a special kind of person, but at the very least a trained person: 'The absence of compulsory sexuality education training may leave teachers not knowing how to cover sensitive or controversial topics in the classroom, often meaning these topics are not covered.'[1] As Dr Jacqui Hendriks, Courses Coordinator of the Sexology Program based at Curtin University, has said: 'Schools can get away with doing the bare minimum.'[2]

It is easy in this country to do sex-ed poorly.

For the purposes of this scenario, neither Dominic nor Jeremy was lucky enough to get lessons at school that taught them about navigating sex and relationships. Imagine, though, if they'd learned that just because you love and trust someone does not mean you have to do something with them if you're uncomfortable. That someone you love and trust, and who otherwise treats you very well, may still try to coerce, manipulate, or guilt you into doing something you don't want to do — and that that is not justified by all the other good stuff in the relationship. That harmful sexualised behaviour is not limited to strange men jumping out of bushes to attack women, or to people taking advantage of someone who is drunk.

Imagine if they'd been given the skills and the comfort to communicate openly in that situation, to feel confident that such a conversation did not present a risk to their relationship — or the knowledge that if it did, then perhaps the relationship was not a good one. Dominic had a right to assert his boundaries, and Jeremy had a responsibility to respect them. You never 'owe' someone sex, no matter the circumstances or the sense of obligation. It's not okay to lean on someone to do something you want when they are uncomfortable, even if you think they *should* feel comfortable.

Imagine if they had learned all that before they started their first year of university, where they would meet.

Sexual violence and harassment at universities is prevalent, and a significant proportion of the sexual assault cases I deal with occur in that context. Students in their first year, their first weeks, even in their first days — and beyond. Students in relationships, or just hooking up with someone they met at a party, or in a class or club or society. Cases that occur in college dorms, in share-houses, on ovals.

And, as ever, those are only the ones that make it to my desk.

The 2021 National Students Safety Survey, which 'collected data on the scale and nature of university student experiences of sexual harassment and sexual assault' from across the university sector, found that one in six Australian university students have been sexually harassed, and one in 20 sexually assaulted, since beginning their degree. Almost half of the incidents occurred in general campus areas, and only one in 30 made a formal complaint, and one in six sought support.[3]

Young people arrive at university embarking on a life of greater freedom and independence, starting or continuing their sexual lives with perhaps greater liberty than before. Universities could and should do a lot, in terms of giving their students (who are often also their residents) RSE once they get there. Some universities and their colleges try, as Dominic's did: but how much can be achieved before or during O-week? A week of partying and abandon to introduce young students to their new world, many of whom will have had little or no comprehensive RSE. And, if an hour from a police sergeant was not enough for Xavier at school, as we saw in Chapter 4, why would a single lecture, a video using food metaphors, an online module, be enough for anyone at uni, or anywhere else post-school?

When I speak to student leaders at university colleges, I say to them: there are people in your colleges who will have had next to no sex-ed. This is the context for many of the students who will be under your leadership at college. You cannot assume a level of understanding, knowledge, and skills about relationships and sex and consent, nor that everyone will come to university with the same values about those things that you may have, or may expect them to have. It takes work, and time, to set that standard.

As we saw in the last chapter, comprehensive RSE cannot be achieved in one-off sessions, and it needs to start much, much younger than the cusp of adulthood. When I asked Lynnette Smith of Big Talk Education in Doncaster if this was something you could just teach at uni, she said, 'You may as well wait until they start having kids.' In other words, it is too late. Now, while I would say it's never too late, it certainly is if you want sex-ed to do its *best* work. It certainly is if you want to give young people what they need before they first need it: *I wish we'd learned this at school.*

The damage wrought can be immense. Physical, emotional, and mental wellbeing can be severely impacted. Students may move colleges, change classes, fail courses, drop out entirely, as they struggle to cope with a significant event in their life, all while trying to manage study. Entire lives change course, hopes and dreams go up in smoke.

I use the university setting as an example in part because I see it so frequently in the criminal justice system, and because it is another institutional environment that young people occupy. But sexual violence is not limited to the university context. Many young people will have similar experiences in their first jobs, in their sports teams, on holidays, in their social lives, friendship circles, and in their family environment, regardless of whether or not they go to university. Sexual violence, harassment, and harm are not bound to, nor purely a product of, particular contexts. We must give young people the skills they need to safeguard their wellbeing wherever they may go. Whatever grounds they may walk, whatever skies they may lie under.

The question is, do we do enough when we can, while we can, to equip people for this part of life? A part of life which, for many, starts before they even leave school?

How do we get young people to that stage of their life prepared to meet it? How does *every* kid get the relationships and sexuality education they deserve? Not just condoms on bananas, but the kind designed by experts, as we discussed in Chapter 4. Do we simply hope that individual teachers, schools, parents will do a great job? Do we hope young people aren't left ill-equipped and uninformed, only to lament that they didn't have better sex-ed before they needed it? Do we leave their sexual wellbeing to chance?

Or do we deliberately spare them? Act on our duty of care and promise to give them everything they need to ensure their sexual wellbeing is protected, and they won't be subjected to sexual violence, sexual harassment, sexual harm, and unwanted sexual experiences — not on our watch?

As tempting as it may be to think of it as a matter of fate, we must face up to the confronting truth that it is a decision for us to make — to sign for those souls on board.

This is a decision Germany has made, with feeling.

Not just by individual schools, or bloody-minded advocates, or specialist providers. At the highest level, there is a commitment to safeguarding sexual wellbeing and preventing sexual violence through education. And it is no empty commitment.

I was in Cologne to meet with Christiane Erkens and Laura Brockschmidt, representatives of BZgA, the Federal Centre for Health Education. A government entity, BZgA is the custodian of sexuality education and sexualised violence prevention in Germany: it is given the legal mandate to provide the nation with information on sexuality education by the *Pregnancy and Family Assistance Act*. But, unlike the UK, whose legislative mandate has already struggled to secure RSE implementation, Germany has invested in the next step. They have put their money where their mouth is, you could say. Inside BZgA sits 'Department Four', which houses the two separate teams dedicated to sexuality education and sexualised violence prevention respectively.

Like Rutgers in the Netherlands, BZgA employs qualified professionals to conduct research and develop teaching packages, resources, materials, online platforms, and even a theatre play (*Trau Dich!*). They work with non-public sector partners, academia, the European Union, and international organisations like the World Health Organization and — critically — public sector partners like federal and state ministries, and state-based education departments and institutions.

Germany has 16 states and, as in Australia, education is governed at the state level, which means, as a federal agency, BZgA cannot directly influence what happens in schools, as each province has its own education department. However, BZgA works with those education departments to roll out national initiatives and curricula developed within Department Four, including through a biannual coordinating forum between BZgA and state representatives responsible for RSE. BZgA has developed a 'General Concept for Sexuality Education' for states to adhere to when delivering RSE, which covers tasks, goals, target groups, strategic communication approach, main topic areas, and actions. BZgA also provides all states with the relevant research and materials, ensuring the research findings trickle down to practitioners, to assist in rolling out RSE and sexualised violence prevention initiatives. All the resources are provided by BZgA free of charge. This is a useful example for those who wonder what role there is for the Australian federal government in RSE, when education here is also a state responsibility.

Some may ask whether, when it comes to teaching young people about relationships, sex, and sexuality, there ought to be a role for government at all. Not just government, but whether the community outside our own four walls should have any say in what our young people learn about this stuff. Is this a matter of civic values or personal ones?

Many people believe that bodies, families, relationships, sexuality, and sexual behaviour are subject matters only to be broached with children and young people in the home, and that the nature of that discussion should be determined by the personal values of the family unit. Comprehensive RSE, which should typically encompass all those topics, will necessarily cut across the spheres of both information and values. Some may consider that where RSE touches on values, it is not a matter for public policy. Recall the then prime minister Morrison's comments to radio shock jock Alan Jones in 2018, when he said of a Victorian respectful relationships program: 'I don't want the values of others being imposed on my children in my school, and I don't think that should be happening in a public school or a private school.'

Yet there are many social values that we consider a matter of public policy: for example, it would be uncontroversial for schools to teach pupils that bullying and antisocial behaviour of that ilk is unacceptable, or to promote anti-violence values. There are all manner of government-funded campaigns in this vein. For example, 'Bullying No Way': 'supporting school communities with evidence-informed resources and activities for a proactive approach to bullying education and prevention'.[4] 'Stop the Coward's Punch Campaign': 'Spreading awareness about the devastating effects the coward punch has on our community. We are on a mission to eliminate it from our society and save lives in the process.' In 2018, it was announced that this campaign's plans to educate young people directly in schools would receive federal government funding.[5] The 'Stop it at the Start' campaign, which began in 2016 and whose third phase was launched in 2021, is a joint federal, state, and territory government initiative under the *National Plan to Reduce Violence Against Women and their Children 2010–2022*. The campaign is designed to change attitudes and behaviours around gendered violence, and is aimed not just at parents and families of children aged 10–17, but also at 'teachers, coaches, community leaders and employers of young people'.[6] There are many values that we accept as matters of public policy, as something the community has a stake in and, therefore, the authority and responsibility to uphold and reinforce and *teach*.

But if we see the stuff of sex-ed as wholly subject to, and determined by, personal interpretation and private values, of course that feels more controversial. In other words, we might all agree that violence is unacceptable, but do we all agree on common values when it comes to sex, sexuality, and relationships? Even if we do, our own shame and discomfort about the topic may impact how we feel about whether *talking* about those values should stay in the domestic domain. As though because intimate encounters tend to be private, the values and attitudes we take to those encounters must be, too.

But isn't the point that the community *does* have a stake in the values, attitudes, knowledge, and skills about relationships, sex, and sexuality held by fellow individual citizens? Because those values, attitudes, knowledge, and skills influence the rates of sexual violence for us all? Isn't the point that we want to reset the social standard in a way that serves to protect against sexual violence and safeguard sexual wellbeing? To make sure *all* young people hold certain positive values, have the same information and skills, are on the same page, by the time they start having relationships, or acting on their sexuality? To ensure all young people have their wellbeing safeguarded? Aren't we deliberately trying to reshape the world our kids grow up in, to change what is expected of them and what we expect for them? To strengthen the social conventions about what is acceptable, respectful, healthy, and ethical in relationships and sex?

If we recognise the community has a stake, then the community gets a say. And the community will not have its say felt, if we treat this as a matter of personal convictions and beliefs, entirely the jurisdiction of individual families and homes. A significant number of us still subscribe to, or take as given, the values that drive sexual violence and unhealthy relationships: the expectations about gender roles, masculinity, and who is entitled to sexual pleasure; the assumptions about how people will behave and communicate, and the scripts they will adhere to in relationships and sexual encounters. We have seen these values, expectations, and assumptions operating on every character in this book so far, and there are many kids still learning those same things from the adults in their private lives.

There are also lots of parents and families and communities who do not feel equipped to teach the stuff of RSE in the best way, if at all. Jane Corcoran, the Australian teacher I mentioned earlier in this chapter, is also a mother. She told me: 'You think as a parent you're going to pour all your knowledge into your child's brain and their heart, but I never appreciated until I became a parent how much you rely on the institutions kids come into contact with, as a foundation of their upbringing. What are the tools schools are equipping them with?' Gesturing, she threaded her fingers together: 'You need that enmeshment [of home and school] … you need the village.'

Some families may not have the capacity in their home lives to deliver comprehensive RSE. There are those whose own experiences of sexual abuse will prevent them from being able to broach the topic with the young people in their lives. And, sadly, there are many young people for whom sexual violence and violations of their wellbeing will happen at the hands of the adults in their private lives, their family, friends, and other community members.

If comprehensive RSE has the power to safeguard sexual wellbeing and protect from harm, then everyone ought to be entitled to it. It is also a measure that only works properly when everyone has access to it. *You* may have done a marvellous job in teaching your kid very healthy, positive values around relationships and sex, but, as we have already discussed, they are bombarded with messages about these things from myriad sources. If we're talking about the impact of a world of messages on kids — not just those you are good enough to teach them — then we need to change the world outside your family home. And, at the end of the day, the relationships and sexual encounters they are going to have will be with people whose upbringing and education you had no control over. Your kid's values and skills may not be enough to protect them from someone who has very different expectations.

At a community level, this means making the call that sexual wellbeing and protection from harm is a social need that demands a collective response, not just an individual one. A collective response does not necessarily mean government, of course. I may be criticised for being idealistic, in advocating for the institutions of a colonial, patriarchal society to be deployed to combat some of the impacts of that colonialism and patriarchy. Those who experience sexual violence are, overwhelmingly, not those at the top of our power structures; how motivated, then, are those who hold the most power to curb sexual violence? Especially if doing so will diminish any of that power?

Some communities take different approaches; as Lauren French, sexologist, sexuality educator, and First Nations woman, expressed it to me:

> We are still sitting in this Western idea of education, which is very formalised. Here, we like something tangible like a curriculum, but there is more fluidity in First Nations culture and learning. It doesn't mean there are not cultural pockets, conversations happening, yarns happening. Why is it one or the other? When we really want to empower young people's voices through co-design, we have to meet them where they're at and often that's not in formal institutions.

Indeed, institutions of government and education ought not have a monopoly on RSE; rather, I ask whether, if those institutions are to continue to have a place in our society, if they are meant to serve us, can we secure a better service? While all young Australians are required to attend school, can we take that opportunity to reach every kid, to normalise the stuff of RSE in one of the key worlds they occupy? Stephanie Liow, the Victorian Year 12 student who petitioned the state government for compulsory holistic sex education, articulated it thus:

> It's quite disappointing that some schools are not 100 per cent on board because there is no legitimate reason for schools not to be trying to improve their sex-ed curriculum. It's for the health and safety of all children, and schools should be trying their best to make sure all children are safe.[7]

If we consider sexual wellbeing and safety a matter of public health, then of course we look to those we elect to use the power and resources at their disposal, to fulfil the duty of care they owe us. To ensure the wellbeing of their populace. As we have seen during the COVID-19 pandemic and with the climate crisis, individual actions alone are not the silver bullet for large-scale social problems. And, idealistically speaking, democratic governments are elected by the people, for the people. A collective, widespread response is something governments are uniquely equipped to mount at scale. After all, we entrust a government institution to respond to sexual violence, recognising it as something we, as a community, have a stake in. Why not to prevent it too?

Government input and leadership regarding RSE was something I saw in every place I visited. Whether in the form of a government department with a legal mandate, as in Germany, or funding non-government organisations like Rutgers, as in the Netherlands, or conducting a national review of RSE, as in Ireland, or providing a legislative mandate, as in the United Kingdom: the nature of the government involvement differed, but it was always there.

It seemed instrumental to the success and the scale of RSE in those jurisdictions. They recognised the need to take it up as a matter of public policy, a community endeavour. This is not to say, for example, that existing grassroots efforts have no place, or that the field ought to be cleared for government to stake a monopoly on RSE. Rather, government has a unique capacity to change the systems that will clear the way for universal access to comprehensive RSE. As Christiane Erkens expressed it when I sat across from her at the BZgA offices in Cologne: 'You always need national government to drive sexuality education and sexualised-violence prevention. If you try and use bottom-up strategies to drive it, you will never be successful.'

In Australia, it is easy to do sex-ed poorly. We need to make it easier to do well, difficult to get wrong, impossible to shirk.

If we had made the decision to ensure all young people have access to comprehensive RSE from a young age, both Dominic and Jeremy may have had a far better chance. If we had recognised their right to this information, perhaps Dominic would have been spared this experience.

We could have ensured that when he got to university, Dominic wasn't left to rely on tools like the video played at his college. A video that went no further than assuming that problematic sexual behaviour only arises from a deliberate, wilful decision by one person to violate another's autonomy with force. We would have made sure that Dominic and Jeremy had already learned about some of the pressures, expectations, and invisible forces that may come to bear in a sexual encounter, learned how to identify them and that they were entitled to resist them, that they should not wield them.

They both may have arrived at university with an understanding that the sense of obligation in a relationship can be incredibly potent. A significant proportion of sexual violence occurs in relationships and in the dating context, and this is why 'respectful relationships' education must explicitly incorporate sexuality education, explaining how respect in a relationship translates into the sexual context.

We must teach young people that being in a relationship does not mean you are safe from negative sexual experiences in that context. That even without violence or force, coercion and pressure are not acceptable: emotional, psychological pushing is as powerful as physical pushing. While you might like the fact that someone desires you, it doesn't mean you have to give in to their desires where they diverge from yours. Being pushed or worn down, when the other person won't let go of the issue and you feel it's just easier to give in, is not okay, no matter how much someone wants you.

RSE would have taught Dominic and Jeremy about healthy relationship dynamics and how they extend to the bedroom — taught them that there isn't a different set of rules once the clothes come off. That even if your boyfriend is otherwise very loving and respectful, their sexual desire doesn't override the expectation that they treat you with love and respect in bed. That wanting to make your partner happy need not come at the expense of your autonomy or comfort. That the sense of trust Dominic has with Jeremy does not mean his alarm bells are wrong, nor that he ought to be okay with having unprotected sex. Maybe nobody told Dominic that he wouldn't be letting Jeremy down, that he shouldn't fear losing Jeremy by standing up for his boundaries.

And had anybody ever told Jeremy that he shouldn't make Dominic feel like that? That as soon as he realised Dominic was hesitant or uncomfortable, he should have respected that? That he had no right to pressure and manipulate Dominic to do what he wanted. That sex is not just about what you can *get* someone to do, what you can convince them of: it is not like haggling at the markets, it's about making sure they feel comfortable and safe. That *your* sexual experience is only as good as the *other* person's worst moment.

What was it about these other jurisdictions that prompted the decision to act and ensure every young person has access to RSE?

Recall the legislation that was introduced in the United Kingdom shortly before I arrived there, mandating comprehensive RSE for all young Britons. Although many advocates were surprised it was a conservative government who took that step, the move did not come out of the blue. The Sex Education Forum, a collective of relevant stakeholders in the UK, had been advocating for improved access to RSE for thirty years already. Several reports about the state of sexual violence and abuse in the UK had paved the way, reports reminiscent of the National Survey of Australian Secondary Students and Sexual Health, telling us, every five years since 2002, the consistent numbers of young people who experience unwanted sex, with no statistically significant differences over time.[8] Or the National Community Attitudes towards Violence Against Women Survey, which usually prompts headlines about the 'shocking' and 'disturbing' attitudes about violence against women. The 2017 survey showed one in seven young Australians believe a man can force a woman to have sex if she initiated it but then changed her mind. Alice Cruttwell — who developed the Respect Yourself program introduced in Chapter 2 — told me that, in the UK, a report showing the sheer number of calls young people were making to the equivalent of Kids Helpline about their experience of sexual violence and abuse was the straw that broke the camel's back. She told me it simply could not be ignored any longer, and so the 2019 legislation was passed.

In Germany, it was the exposure of the incidence of child sexual abuse within religious institutions that acted as a trigger for politicians to truly commit to sexualised violence prevention as a matter of public policy. In Canada, increased public awareness of the need for RSE followed 'high profile legal cases involving issues of consent and a growing discussion of the importance of educating young people about consent issues', according to the Sex Information and Education Council of Canada.

Something similar happened in Ireland, predicating the national review that declared the state of sex-ed outdated and in urgent need of reform. I assumed when I was in Ireland that, given the enormous influence of the Catholic Church in their education system, the exposure of systematic sexual abuse in the Church would have been what prompted this overhaul. I kept waiting for the people I interviewed there to reference it as the reason for the review, but something else kept coming up instead. There had been a high-profile rape trial in Belfast that received significant publicity, even in the Republic of Ireland. It was an alleged gang-rape, and the media reported evidence of 'derogatory and bawdy texts' exchanged by the accused men. Those I spoke to in Ireland described a collective community outrage across the island about the attitudes to women evident in those messages. The publicity of this case and the details of the messages saw discussion about the RSE review in the Republic take on a more public quality, and calls for improved RSE intensified.

When I got back from my fellowship and published my findings, I referred to several things in the Australian landscape that I thought might represent similar catalysts for change. Things like the Royal Commission into Institutional Responses to Child Sexual Abuse, the Universities Australia 'Change the Course' report, and the powerful advocacy of Saxon Mullins after her accused rapist was acquitted.

Little did I know what would come next. The #LetHerSpeak campaign, created in 2018 by Nina Funnell and with the legal support of Marque Lawyers, had allowed seventeen survivors, including Grace Tame, to speak publicly about their experience of sexual violence. Tame was named Australian of the Year in 2021 for her bravery in fronting Funnell's campaign. Around that time, Chanel Contos asked her friends on Instagram about whether they had experienced sexual violence at school, only to be overwhelmed by thousands of responses. The petition she started afterwards, calling for better education about consent, collected tens of thousands of signatures. All of these things received significant media attention, both at home and abroad.

To be clear, none of these things represent the start of the story of advocacy about sexual violence in Australia: we stand on the shoulders of many survivors who have brought us to this point, whose experiences ought never be forgotten. Particularly those who are under-represented in our national consciousness, memory, and storytelling. Sexual assault survivors are not homogenous, even if those we learn about tend to be. Dhanya Mani, a survivor-advocate, told Junkee in early 2022 about reporting on sexual violence: 'The media's bias has meant that a lot of its reporting has been whitewashed and the intellectual property and labour of a lot of women of colour and First Nations women and other marginalised gender voices have been completely eliminated.' In the same report, Ashlee Donohue, an Aboriginal woman from the Dunghutti Nation and co-creator of the Aboriginal women's sexual assault network 'Hey Sis', spoke of how sexual violence has 'been perpetrated against Aboriginal women since colonisation', but that responses to sexual violence are viewed through a white lens.[9] To this end, Amanda Morgan, a Yorta Yorta woman and survivor-advocate, launched the Make A Seat campaign, which calls on institutions such as the media to be trauma-informed, to stop excluding the voices of under-represented survivors of gendered violence, and to ensure their experiences also inform institutional responses.

Since I returned from my fellowship in 2019, the clarion call that has been sounding for generations has been getting ever louder.

If ever there was a time to make a promise, as a community, that we will do better to prevent sexual violence, it is now. If ever there was a time for those in power to make good on that promise, it is now.

With this imprimatur, what can stop us?

6

Pounds of Flesh

Riley and Billie

Riley was to start at the local all-girls school the year after she turned ten. She was sad to leave friends from her old school behind and spent most of the summer holidays sulking about it, surliness covering her nerves. On New Year's Day, bored in the heat, she followed her mother listlessly around the backyard as she gardened. Over the fence, their neighbour was hanging out washing and Riley's mum called out to her: 'That'll dry before you've finished putting it on the line!'

It was one of those days when the air was so parched and hot you felt as though it would burst into flame if you so much as clicked, the friction at your fingertips enough to spark. The neighbour wished them a Happy New Year as she approached the fence line, basket on her hip and a hand shading her eyes from the sun.

'And how are you, Riley?' she asked kindly.

Riley's mother answered for her: 'We start at the girls' school this year, and we're a bit nervous about that.' Riley smiled feebly.

'Oh, wonderful! You'll be able to focus on school without boys around to distract you.'

Riley didn't know what to say, so she just nodded.

'Yes, she won't have to worry about trying to impress them!' Her mum patted her shoulder.

'Plenty of time for that; you're such a pretty little thing, your father will have to beat them off with a stick soon.' The neighbour laughed.

Everything was unfamiliar in this new world, with its strange corridors and stiff uniforms. Riley's class had got their pen licences the year before, knew the hardest times-tables off by heart, and obsessed over different pop stars to those who had been the favourites at her old school. Everyone had settled friendship groups, but, thankfully, there were a few girls who took Riley in and let her have lunch with them. Eventually, she found her rhythm in this place, her sadness at leaving her old life behind soon forgotten.

Later that year, Riley's teacher sat the class down and told them they would be reading a special book. It was a picture book about how babies are made, with bright illustrations explaining that when a man and woman love each other very much, the man puts his penis in the woman's vagina, and together they make a baby. That was the first time Riley and many of her friends learned what sex was.

Riley didn't think much of it at the time, but she'd remember the colourful pages a few years later when, in early high school, their biology teacher taught them about reproduction. The pictures produced this time were not cuddly characters but were instead scientific diagrams of genitalia. The teacher showed one cross-section diagram where a penis was smaller and curving downwards, and then another where it was straighter and bigger. She explained that 'When a man is aroused, his penis becomes erect.'

'What's aroused?' someone in the class called out, giggling.

'When they feel very excited and happy about having sex.' Everyone squirmed. 'Okay, last diagram.'

Riley peered at the upside-down triangle thing with a circle on each side of it, deciding it kind of looked like an alien.

'Unlike boys, the female reproductive organs are completely inside,' the teacher said, pointing out the uterus, the fallopian tubes, and the ovaries. 'When the male puts his erect penis in the woman's vagina—'

'Ewww, miss!' A chorus of embarrassed groans.

'—he puts his erect penis in the woman's vagina,' she raised her voice slightly, 'and then he ejaculates, and the sperm swim up to the uterus to find an egg, where it might get fertilised.'

'What's "ejaculates"?'

'When the male becomes very excited, and it feels very nice for him, all the sperm that live in his testicles come up through the penis and into the woman's vagina, in search of an egg to make a baby.'

'How many eggs do we have in us, miss?'

'Thousands.'

'*Thousands*?!' Everyone clutched their abdomens.

The next year, Riley took drama. When she went to the theatre room for the first class of semester, she was already nervous at the idea of taking a subject that was exclusively dedicated to potential humiliation. So when she walked in and saw a bunch of the popular girls had already gathered in the back of the room, draping themselves over the stacked boxes that doubled as set pieces, Riley's stomach dropped. These girls were so intimidating, moving around the school with an unshakeable air of confidence.

In this room, their presence seemed to lay claim to the space. The young teacher was new to the school, and seemed nervous herself. Riley sensed immediately that this teacher was not the one in charge here. In name, sure, but not really.

Somewhere in the back of her reptilian brain, Riley felt unsafe. She was hypervigilant in every drama class, hoping not to draw the girls' attention, let alone their contempt. One day she let her guard down, though, and one of them caught her looking at Emma, a petite, pretty one in their group. Riley saw them notice, and she averted her eyes immediately, but it was too late.

'Why are you staring at Emma?' the girl challenged, eyes narrowed. There was a lightness to her voice that sounded malicious, something that said she would see sport in this. They all turned to look, and Riley's heart began to beat faster; she was frozen like a deer in the headlights of their glare. They waited for an answer, not going to let this moment pass.

'I wasn't,' she faltered.

'Are you a lesbian or something?' the antagonist mocked.

And that was that: Riley became their chosen prey for the rest of the semester. They were merciless — if ever she was standing near a girl, too close as deemed by her accusers, they would brand her again. Whenever it was her turn to perform, they would whisper and giggle in the back of class, making sure their scorn was surreptitious enough that the teacher never noticed. No one came to her aid, because while Riley was the focus, everyone else was safe.

The bullying followed her out of the drama theatre, too. When they'd get changed for sport, the girls would make a show of covering themselves if Riley was near, as though she was going to perve on them. It was mortifying.

'Come on, girls, you see each other in swimwear all the time, I don't see what the issue is,' the PE teacher said, rolling her eyes.

Riley's friends told her to ignore the mean girls, but the rumours would linger for the next couple of years. It was unrelenting. If they weren't teasing her for being a lesbian, it was that she was a frigid virgin. She couldn't work out what she had done wrong. All because she had been caught looking at Emma that one time. The truth was, Riley *had* been staring, her eyes inexorably drawn to her, an airy feeling in her chest and a fluttering in her belly.

As she and her peers got older, some of Riley's friends started getting boyfriends, and 'hot guys at the brother school' became a standing item on the lunchtime agenda. Anytime there was a co-ed event, there was much preening and preparation and perseverating. For Riley, there was just pretending. She felt like she was missing something. She was completely indifferent to boys — trying to engage with them in that way was like trying to turn an engine over with a flat battery. Riley assumed she just hadn't met one she liked enough; her parents were pleased she hadn't shown interest in boys yet, and said so.

•

One year the girls got a lesson on how to use condoms, with bananas for props. 'When you get older and start having sex, this is something you have to make sure the boy wears. This is how you prevent pregnancies and STIs, girls. Take one and pass it on,' the teacher held out a basket.

The condoms made their way around the class. 'Riley, you won't need one of those,' one of the girls taunted from a few desks away. Riley tried to look nonchalant, ignoring the comment, which seemed to goad the other girl. 'Look at her pretending, like she's ever seen a dick before,' she snickered to the room at large. The whole class laughed. 'Girls,' the teacher warned.

If Riley was braver, she would have turned around and told the girl to shut up. She felt so exposed, her naiveté on display for all the world to see. After years of being pilloried, she'd had enough.

Before she knew what she was doing, she turned around and snapped, 'I have a boyfriend.'

'Bullshit,' the girl laughed.

There was a boy who caught the same bus as Riley, and they were friends. He had asked her out before and she'd said no, claiming a focus on schoolwork. But that afternoon, she marched up to him on the bus with such purpose she left a wake behind her in the aisle. She plonked herself down next to him and pulled his headphones out. 'Hey!' he exclaimed. Riley was fuelled by anger and frustration, and a pressing need to make the bullying stop.

'How about that date, then?' she asked him, by way of greeting. It took him a moment to realise what she was saying, and then she saw his eyes lighting up and a smile spreading across his face. 'Yeah, cool,' he said. 'Like, when?'

'Tomorrow night?'

They started dating, and Riley decided it wasn't so bad. He was a really good friend; they shared the same taste in music and always had heaps to talk about. Riley had convinced herself it was just a matter of time and exploration before she uncovered the desire her friends all talked about, the kind she could only imagine. It was inevitable, right?

He was keen to hook up with her, and she was even keener to prove herself. Desperate to keep up with her friends, to shed herself of the virgin and lesbian labels all at once, she suggested they have sex.

They arranged to hang out at his place one day when his folks were out.

Riley lay there, wondering when she was meant to start feeling turned on. He had his hands under her bra and his lips on her neck, and she only felt exasperated by it. If he put his tongue in her mouth again, she worried she might smack him, she was so *frustrated* by this. It had been her idea, but now that it was happening she felt like her skin was crawling.

Riley knew guys were more into sex than girls, but was it meant to feel this repulsive? Maybe it got better once you actually started. She decided they should just move to the main event, pulling out a condom and fumbling with the foil packet. They were both new to this, so it slowed things down a bit as they figured out how to get it on the right way round. As he pulled it down into place, Riley wondered fleetingly if this was really a good idea. The thought was quickly chased by the sound of the classroom's laughter ringing in her ears: *bullshit, bullshit, bullshit*. She needed to prove this to herself as much as anyone.

He began to push himself into her, and it felt like it was going to rip something inside her: 'I don't think it … I can't get it … in,' he panted. 'Push harder,' she insisted, feeling desperate. He managed to enter her and she almost yelped, the pain was so sharp and deep, and tears pricked behind her eyes. He began thrusting and there was so much friction the latex felt like sandpaper. '*Who could like this?*' she asked herself, steeling herself until it was done.

When it was over, she went to the bathroom. It burned when

she urinated. She felt hollow and strange and deeply sad, but tried to banish those feelings by reminding herself of the badge she could now claim. Hard-earned.

She told her friends the next day and hoped he would tell his, so that word would spread.

It did, and the girls at school called her a slut, and Riley cried in the school bathrooms every lunchtime, lonelier than ever.

The following year Riley joined senior debating. Like drama class years before, she worried about the public performance aspect of it, but her parents assured her it would be good practice if she wanted to be a lawyer. Riley was pretty sure she wouldn't ever want that, but signed up in the hope of making new friends. School life hadn't become any easier for her.

The teacher assigned her to a team, which would meet every Wednesday to practise. The first practice session, Riley found the room and introduced herself to the other girls. One of the girls was Billie, in the year above and super smart. She was softly spoken and funny, with wide eyes and freckles sprinkled across her nose.

Soon Wednesdays became Riley's favourite day of the week. She found herself looking forward to debating with an impatience that she couldn't articulate. She would come home from practice all bubbly and talkative. Riley thought about Billie a lot, wondering what she would think of a book she was reading, or of a band she liked. She hoped to run into Billie in the corridors at school, and on the weekends she found herself looking for her in the crowd at the local shopping centre.

Riley would take special care with her appearance on Wednesdays, spraying on fresh deodorant before she went to practice and chewing mints. During practice, if she made a bad point or stumbled over her words, she blushed for Billie witnessing it.

The two of them became close, and began hanging out after school. Billie was soon Riley's best friend. Her mum was visibly relieved that Riley seemed to have settled down after some tumultuous years. Sometimes they would have sleepovers and Riley would listen to Billie breathing in the dark, a yearning feeling in her heart.

One night Riley had a dream that she and Billie kissed, and in her sleep she felt the churning desire she had always imagined but never known. Yet, when she woke, she felt nothing but dread.

After that dream, she found herself thinking about kissing Billie all the time. Imagining what she looked like under her school uniform, what she would feel like to touch. She couldn't sweep the idea from her mind, no matter how hard she tried. It made her so anxious she looked it up online, her browser telling her it was normal to have 'girl crushes', to confuse feelings of admiration and friendship for something more.

It happened the day that nobody else turned up to practice. The teacher left the two of them alone in the classroom to work, knowing she could trust them.

Billie and Riley were looking at something on Riley's phone, their heads close together and their knees touching as they peered into the screen. Riley could hardly think, convinced Billie must have been able to hear her heart beating. She felt light-headed, not registering anything Billie was saying, and the hairs on her arms seemed to stand up. She felt Billie looking at her and was too scared to turn her face. She stared at her phone, feeling the heat rise on her neck. Then Riley decided to be brave and, her breathing shallow, she looked up.

Time seemed to slow down as Billie leaned in to kiss her, every nanosecond stretching out and expanding like a rubber band. As their lips touched, Riley started tingling like crazy down there, and she felt like she would float away, as though she was having an out-of-body experience. She realised she was gripping Billie's dress and pulling her deeper into the kiss.

They heard the footsteps at the same time, and for a split second they froze, listening to the doorhandle turning. Too late, they sprang apart as though from an electric shock. Billie wiped her mouth and Riley tried to blink her eyes back into focus, feeling the flush in her cheeks.

The teacher, for her part, knew exactly what she'd just interrupted. She smiled to herself and said nothing, playing along with the girls' pretence that they hadn't just been caught. For a while now she had suspected a blossoming romance and had toyed with saying something to make sure they knew she was a safe space on the teaching staff if they needed it. It was awkward, but she wanted to find a way to communicate that to them. The school was conservative when it came to sex-ed, nervous to go beyond the bare minimum, and the teacher knew she had to be careful. She told herself that anything in the name of health was still in line with school policy.

It was a clunky gesture, but the following Wednesday she found a discreet moment to slip Billie and Riley something in a small, thin zip-lock bag.

'What's this, miss?' Riley asked.

'It's called a dental dam. You can google it. Safe sex is not just for straight couples,' she smiled warmly.

After she left, Billie burst out laughing, 'Oh my god, that's so embarrassing, nobody uses these.'

Riley had never even heard of them, but she was burning with shame at the realisation that her teacher had seen them kissing, had seen this deepest, most secret part of her. But she also felt a kind of relief — there was something in the teacher's tone that made Riley feel safe, even though she was suggesting the same thing Riley's bullies had taunted her with all those years. There was something to it that made Riley feel seen, but not exposed.

Billie's mum found the dental dam and was really angry about it.

She phoned the school and yelled at the principal for encouraging students to have sex with each other. She threatened to go to the tabloids, to pull Billie from the school, and refused to let her see Riley anymore. Billie became withdrawn and stopped responding to Riley's texts.

They got put in separate debating teams, and a different teacher took over the practice sessions, even though the finals were coming up. The whole school found out what had happened, and the sideways glances, the whispering, and the smirks made Riley feel as if she'd just lost a game of snakes and ladders, sliding right back down to square one.

The next month, a guest speaker came to the school to talk to the girls about abstinence. Riley looked at Billie, a few rows in front of her in the cavernous hall, willing her to turn around, but she never did.

No matter the powerful advances in technology, there is something so profound about the humble tête-à-tête. Something so persuasive, one way or another, about being in the room. Such was the privilege of my Churchill Fellowship, allowing me to be immersed in my research, to spend hours, days, even weeks with people. To observe classes, to have chance meetings.

Yet, at a mere 15 minutes, the shortest interview I did in that three-month period was one of the most powerful.

And it almost didn't happen.

After much hassling on my end, I had arranged to meet with Kathleen Wynne, the former premier of Ontario in Canada, months before I started my travels. Just before I was due to leave Australia, I received an emotionless email from a staffer advising that Wynne would no longer be able to keep our appointment. She was, at that stage, the only reason I was going to Toronto, the final stop on my fellowship journey.

I managed to persuade them to find time elsewhere, anywhere, in her schedule. Eventually, they agreed to give me a brief time slot before another commitment she had, if I could come to whatever part of Toronto she would be in.

I suppose it was fitting, to meet with a politician in between her politicking. I turned up to this event at a museum, I think it was, or maybe an art gallery, early in the morning. I hovered around outside until she arrived, pouncing on someone who looked like they were in charge. Finally, I found myself sitting across from Wynne at a small table. Someone managed to find us a couple of bottles of orange juice, and the next quarter of an hour would be revelatory.

•

The Germans have a word for it, that thing we fear will happen if we talk to young people about sex: *Frühsexualisierung*. It means early sexualisation, and the idea is that talking to kids about sex will sexualise or encourage sexual behaviour simply because kids have learned what sex is, about their own bodies. As if uttering the words will cast some sort of spell on them, corrupting their innocence.

It is a fear that is invoked over and over again, like a bogeyman of sex-ed: 'You know what kids are like — if they hear about this stuff they'll go and try it,' I heard one parent say at an information session I attended, as she vowed to pull her kid out of sex-ed class.

This fear is incredibly powerful, motivating some to resist, some to oppose — and some to commit violence. I had attended that parent information session with an educator, and from the moment we walked into the room, the mood was palpably tense. Afterwards, the educator asked if I had been able to hear how dry her mouth was during the presentation. As I travelled, I would hear about rallies outside a school, protesting its programs combating homophobia; an educator who had been circled by angry fathers in a carpark after delivering a school session; others who experienced doxxing attempts; and even those who got death threats. After this particular session I attended, the parents came up to the educator one by one, pressing into her personal space, shaking heads and waving hands in concern about what their kids would be hearing in RSE.

This happens in Australia, too. People get really, really upset about the idea that we will talk to kids about relationships, sexuality, even their own bodies with any degree of detail or nuance (or at all).

But why this fear, why so potent, when the evidence shows that such information does not corrupt innocence, but rather defends it? When we know age- and stage-appropriate, comprehensive relationships and sexuality education results in *later* first sexual experiences, and a decreased likelihood of having a negative sexual experience?

Young people know this, too. In their thousands, people are connecting the dots between the deficiency in their sex-ed and their experiences of sexual violence and harassment and unwanted sex. In 2021, we saw it en masse via the Chanel Contos petition, but for years now young people have been asking for better RSE. Recall the comments Nina Funnell and I get after our university sessions: *I wish we'd learned this at school.*

At the appropriate age, Big Talk Education in the UK introduce the topic of sexual intercourse, after which they ask the class, 'When do you think people start having sex?' Most of the answers are 'When you're twenty', or 'In your thirties'; certainly nobody volunteered anything younger than 16. I saw this repeatedly, kids nominating that sex is something you do in adulthood. In one class, a little boy put up his hand to say, 'It would be good to do it before you retire.'

Sex-ed doesn't make kids want to have sex sooner. So where does this misguided belief that it does, this misunderstanding, come from? A belief so powerful that people are moved to violence over it?

Recall from Chapter 5 my visit to Cologne, where I met with the sexuality education and sexual violence prevention teams at BZgA (the Federal Centre for Health Education), who are legally endowed to provide the nation with information about sexuality education. Thanks to BZgA, Germany enjoys high-quality comprehensive RSE, and is influential internationally in this space, too. To me, Germany seemed like a sex-ed utopia. But it was there that I learned the word *Frühsexualisierung*.

I was told that it was a term used by a particular group in Germany: politicians. Conservative politicians wielded the word strategically in their resistance to improving RSE in that country, turning it into a fight against the 'agenda' of the liberal left. It became what I would call a dog whistle.

Kathleen Wynne called it a 'political hammer' when describing her experience, for this is a scenario she is all too familiar with.

Wynne's involvement in the story of RSE in Ontario did not start in 2014, when she was elected Premier. It started in 2010, when she was Education Minister. At that time, the sex-ed curriculum in Ontario (equivalent to a state-based curriculum in Australia) had not been updated since 1998: there was nothing in it about cyber safety or LGBTQIA+ sexualities and identities or diverse families or consent. In 2010, a general curriculum review was due, including of the Health and Physical Education curriculum, which was updated to improve the material about relationships and sexuality. Wynne told me that it was only after the introduction of the RSE material that some interest groups became vocal, agitated: up until that point, there had been no political angle to it.

One religious pastor managed to get people riled up about the curriculum, and the then premier Dalton McGuinty got spooked and withdrew it. They were going into an election the following year, the Catholic Church had got involved and were pushing back, and McGuinty decided he could not withstand it politically.

Wynne described herself as distraught, when McGuinty pulled the curriculum. But she campaigned for premier at the next election in 2014, making it part of her election bid that she would push for improved RSE again. She was elected and, in the following year, she introduced the updated curriculum as promised, with its new and improved RSE content. This meant that young Ontarians could expect contemporary sex-ed classes that were more holistic and inclusive than previously.

What came next was nothing short of fierce. A storm of opposition and anger followed, accusing Wynne and her government of corrupting and indoctrinating children with this new curriculum, of teaching them to masturbate or have anal sex, of failing to consult with parents. The accusers claimed that the curriculum was less sex education and more sex promotion. Hundreds of parents protested the curriculum on the lawn of Queen's Park in Toronto.

News reports of these events remind me of something Lynnette Smith said to me, when she was recounting the first year that Big Talk Education started going into one particular school that I visited with her. She told me that one parent had 'whipped up a vigilante group', telling other parents that Big Talk was showing the students pornography; this is how the opposition and protests to Wynne and the 2015 curriculum feel to me — a whipped-up frenzy.

It was a frenzy that worked: ultimately for Wynne, the backlash spelled disaster. In the following election, in 2018, her opponent Doug Ford was installed as Premier, having campaigned to withdraw the curriculum, capitalising on the fear that was being generated by interest groups and in the media. Dr Alex McKay, Executive Director of the Sex Information and Education Council of Canada (SIECCAN), recalled that the Ford government subsequently removed the proper names for genitals for the early grades from the 2015 Wynne curriculum.

Similar things happened in the United Kingdom: Smith recalled an RSE program being 'pulled from the shelves' because it referenced the clitoris, and it was only reinstated once that was removed. An LGBTQIA+-inclusive education program that promotes equality, called 'No Outsiders', was widely protested, and the program was suspended across a number of schools. I was told of similar protests occurring in the Netherlands, even with the longstanding strength and success of the Rutgers program in that country.

These frenzies, this resistance, can be influential, even politically. Programs and RSE efforts can be derailed entirely. Do those campaigning against RSE, who seem genuinely fearful and anxious for their children, know that they do so against their own interests — that is, safeguarding their kids from sexual harm, violence, harassment?

The Wynne curriculum did not teach children to masturbate or how to have anal sex, nor does Big Talk show children pornography.

That should go without saying, but it needs to be stated explicitly. McKay, whom I would meet with a couple of days after Wynne, recalled the media reporting that the curriculum was teaching masturbation in Year 5. He found himself 'all the time' asking people who had expressed concern about the curriculum whether they had actually read it, and they invariably said no. Winston Churchill is credited with saying 'A lie gets halfway round the world before the truth has time to get its pants on.' McKay recalled that the media reporting was framed in terms of the 'liberal agenda gone too far'. He described the media-fuelled backlash to the Wynne curriculum as a 'giant propaganda misinformation campaign'.

The key word there is *propaganda*: the misinformation about what RSE includes, and that it will corrupt innocence, is a lie — but it is a lie that gets airtime. I saw similar stories in every place I visited, including at the end of my fellowship when I attended the US National Sexual Health Conference 2019 in Chicago. At one session there, we were presented with a case study from North Carolina, where the media had given airtime to some parents who were actively concerned, but had misunderstood the nature of the RSE in question. The media gave those parents a platform to voice those concerns about the impact of this education on their children, which in turn significantly derailed the RSE program and its efficacy.

This is a familiar tune in Australia too: recall then prime minister Scott Morrison in 2018, agreeing on national radio that an RSE program in Victoria made his 'skin curl'. Even Safe Schools, an Australian program designed simply to make schools a safe and inclusive environment for queer kids, became the subject of a misinformation campaign that claimed the program was teaching young people about 'sexual orientation and transgender issues'. This is despite the fact that the Safe Schools program was, in the main, not a program of RSE delivery: it was designed to reduce homophobic and transphobic bullying in schools. You can read Benjamin Law's Quarterly Essay, *Moral Panic 101,* for a comprehensive look at the media's relentless propaganda efforts about the program's substance and purpose, which ultimately saw it derailed. One media report claimed Safe Schools included 'lessons on how to bind breasts and tuck in male genitalia', which was not true. Law reported in his Quarterly Essay that a conservative masthead, *The Australian*, published 200 stories about or mentioning Safe Schools.

Conservative commentator Miranda Devine called it a 'sexual indoctrination program'. Conservative politicians described it as a 'gay lifestyle promotion program' and claimed that it 'prematurely sexualised' children (there's that *Frühsexualisierung* again), arguing that the program ought to be defunded. While sexuality and gender identity are not the same thing, when it comes to sex-ed they may be grouped together and at times conflated — sometimes with dishonest and nefarious intent.

The media plays an important role here. With these examples, we see a sort of twin effort between vocal opponents to RSE and the airtime they are given in the public forum, which only serves to stoke more opposition. In turn, these seem to spook schools and politicians.

Opposition to sex-ed is often orchestrated and organised, and misinformation is a deliberate tactic. Whether that opposition merely preys on our own shame about bodies and sexuality, or whether it is a product of it, I am not sure. Has the politicisation of RSE as part of the 'liberal agenda' stoked our fear, or is it our fear that has politicised it? I suspect we are stuck in a feedback loop of doom.

Either way, what a con! People are persuaded that the very thing that protects innocence is the thing that corrupts it. That our friend is our foe, the antidote is the poison. Given what's at stake, young people ought to be able to expect that we will be led by evidence, rather than political sophistry that exploits emotion and fear. This political game, this bid for votes, makes kids' bodies and their safety an ideological battleground, and we pay for it in futures and in lives.

Back in Yorkshire, I was sitting in the front row of a group of parents, who had gathered in the assembly room of the local school their kids attended. Lynnette Smith, in her bright-purple Big Talk Education shirt, stood at the front of the room clicking through a slideshow.

Click. A drawing of a boy giving another boy a flower.

'Sometimes two boys will grow up to be men and love each other, and that's called gay.'

Next slide.

A drawing of two girls hugging. 'Sometimes two girls will grow up to be women and love each other and that's called lesbian.'

'Is that all you're gonna say about that stuff?' A woman in the audience leaned forward, arms folded.

'What stuff?' Smith said.

'Homosexual stuff.'

'Yes,' Smith nodded.

'That's all right then.' The woman sat back in her chair.

'That's like asking if you're going to tell them the sky is blue!' I exclaimed to Smith later. She nodded wearily. Obviously she was more used to this than I was. While that particular mother had been satisfied with Smith's answer, many other parents spoke to her afterwards, insisting they would withdraw their kids from the class. Smith had been taking this group of parents through the lessons their primary school kids would be getting the following week, slide by slide, word for word.

If you wonder why teaching young people a fact of life — you know, that queer sexuality exists — is so contentious, I invite you to recall our discussion in the last chapter about whether the stuff of sex-ed is a matter of information or values. Some consider that telling young people about things like the existence of the clitoris, or of homosexuality and queer identities, is a matter of values — that is, even if these are anatomical and social realities, the act of telling young people about them is value-laden. Some parents fear that simply telling their kids about LGBTQIA+ people and sexualities will somehow encourage them to join in. Maybe they think telling them about it without denouncing it will be construed as an endorsement. In the main, however, I suspect many people think of being LGBTQIA+ as only about sex, and therefore that teaching about it must necessitate discussion of sexual activity. I guess the same could be said of teaching about the clitoris — to talk about it means admitting that sexual activity may not just be for reproduction.

The idea of talking to kids squarely about sex and sexuality makes some anxious. The idea of teaching young people about queer sexuality, and/or about trans and non-binary people, even more so. This particular subject matter is a frequent source of opposition to comprehensive RSE, although not exclusively. The opposition to Safe Schools, for example, was apparently sparked by one component of the program that included a teaching resource that schools could opt in to use — a teaching resource that provided accurate, relevant, and inclusive information about queer sexualities and transgender experiences. The public, and consequently political, fear that sex-ed will teach young people about 'gay sex' or 'how to be gay' was one of the recurring issues in every place I visited overseas. Someone in charge of RSE in one municipality in the Netherlands said to me: 'The norm in Holland is that everyone should be themselves, and being gay is okay and all … but not in my backyard.'

But that isn't how sexuality works. Growing up in a world completely saturated with heterosexuality does not 'make' everybody straight, so why would it work the other way around? Nor is it how gender identity works, for those who are concerned that teaching young people about trans and non-binary people will create confusion. As a friend of mine expressed it, when I asked him what he wished he'd learned in sex-ed: 'If I had even learned the word transgender, the concept, I would have understood what I was feeling.' An asexual and gender-fluid participant in an inclusive Australian study about experiences of sex education for students with intellectual disability said: 'I feel so much better, knowing I have a name for this! It was like, yes, names help! It also makes you feel like, well, hey, if there's a name for this, I'm not the only one who's feeling it!'[1]

One of the most common things people say they wish they'd learned in sex-ed at school is about queer sexuality and identity — that is, people who are not heterosexual or cisgendered reflecting on the fact they never learned about it at school. Not talking about it did not influence the truth of their sexuality or identity, just as talking about it wouldn't have either.

Even if the act of educating young people about LGBTQIA+

sexualities and identities is seen by some as a matter of personal values, how can we justify censoring information? Some people believe in Creation, but we still have a standard of teaching young people about science and evolution. Telling young people about the reality of the world, the full spectrum of human experience, does not 'confuse them'. But failing to teach kids about it, condemning them to feeling abnormal, unseen, out of place, ashamed of who they are — that *does* cause untold harm and confusion.

We see that with Riley in this chapter, and we also saw it with Dominic and Jeremy (Chapter 5). The comments from Dominic's head of college did nothing to assist Dominic or anybody else in the room, by failing to contemplate that any of the men there would be anything other than potential perpetrators against women. No wonder Dominic tuned out. Those comments never considered what skills, tools, information he may have needed for his own sexual wellbeing and those he would be with.

So too for Riley: the information she was given at school about what sex was, and what it would look like, completely left her out. The 'official' information was that sex = penis + vagina. Consequently, how relevant, and therefore helpful, were those school lessons about 'sex' to any other kinds of intimate activity that looked different to penis-in-vagina? Riley was taught that safe sex meant stopping pregnancy through condoms, with no mention of the benefits of condom use for men who have sex with men, or dental dams for women having sex with women. Did Dominic know about PrEP, an antiviral drug that assists in HIV/AIDS prevention? Do we want him learning about it after he's already had that experience with Jeremy? Are we happy to just wear that risk — even though he would be the one to wear the consequences?

And it is not just the physical health warnings: what about other lessons, about things like relationships and consent? If young people grow up learning, from 'official' and authoritative sources like teachers at school, about relationships that don't sound like the relationships they want to have, how can that education be relevant and inclusive to all kids? When *we* divide sex-ed classes into boys and girls, when *we* assume relationships will be heterosexual, and when *we* suggest the gender of the participants determines how they will act, we create limited expectations – for *all* young people, not just queer kids. For example, if we say that boys want sex more than girls, so much so that they will sometimes pressure girls for sex, does that mean boys don't pressure boys? That girls don't pressure girls? What if you are trans or gender-diverse? Is it even 'rape', if it doesn't fit the heteronormative stereotype we're sold? What does that mean for people who don't fit that mould when they want to seek help, when they're at school or later in life, if they feel concerned about something in their relationships or if they experience sexual violence? Who do they go to in a world that ignores or is openly hostile to their existence? What can help to mitigate and challenge that hostility?

It is not that young people cannot find that information elsewhere, but when we leave it out of RSE, when young people have to go looking for it because we have erased it elsewhere, we are communicating that heterosexual relationships and heterosexual sex are the only kind that's 'real', the only ones worth talking about, the only ones that are 'sanctioned'. And so we are condemning anyone who feels different, whose world looks different.

The erasure of queer sexuality throughout Riley's life, the assumption that she would be straight, which we saw from her mother, her teachers, and even from the neighbour, dovetailed with the homophobic bullying she was subjected to by the kids at school. This compounding pressure had a material impact, making her feel like she had to prove that she fitted in by having a sexual experience she did not want.

But this isn't just about *potential* harm: when we erase people's identity, we treat them as less than, as inferior, as different. Can we not all agree that we ought to be guided by a vision that all kids grow up happy and healthy? Withholding information about LGBTQIA+ sexualities, identities, and experiences did not make Riley straight. It only left her unhappy, hurt, and isolated, and feeling shame about her desires. When she finally found joy, it was quickly snuffed out.

This censorship claims lives: the rates of depression, anxiety, self-harm, suicide attempts and suicidal ideation in the LGBTQIA+ community are a tragedy. A 2020 report from the Australian Research Centre in Sex, Health and Society at La Trobe University confirmed that:

> There is a substantial body of research revealing that LGBT communities experience higher rates of depression and anxiety than the general population, which has been associated with stigma, prejudice and discrimination that create a hostile and stressful social environment. Previous research has revealed that LGBTQ people have comparatively higher levels of suicidal ideation and suicide attempts than in general populations.[2]

A fidelity to cis- and heteronormativity and sex-for-reproduction collects pound after pound of flesh.

'There was no political gain for me in implementing a contentious curriculum. It was about the safety of kids,' Wynne said to me.

Sex-ed is politicised even before politicians and governments get enthusiastic about it. We saw that with the response from Billie's mum, and I saw it in many of the protests I learned about overseas — opposition often comes in response to actions by individual teachers, or schools, or external sex-ed providers. It is inevitable that RSE will be politicised, one way or another, and it leaves politicians and governments nervous to make the decisions we need them to make.

The fear of backlash, the perceived political risk that it represents, is one of the greatest barriers to RSE. It is enough to make politicians do a 180 so fast it'll give you whiplash — as we saw with McGuinty, and with the Australian government when it withdrew its funding for the Safe Schools program once the flames of controversy were raging. It's enough to see politicians ignore the evidence, to make excuses, to deflect responsibility. A bureaucrat involved in the national review of RSE in Ireland reported that, at the time of the review, the Department of Education asked why they should be responsible for sex-ed instead of parents. 'Bags-not-me' seems to be the motto.

However, government leadership is the very thing that can mitigate backlash. Look at how quickly the school capitulated when Billie's mum complained. The leadership shown by a single teacher was not enough to resist a single parent's complaint — let alone if there had been a protest outside the school. I use this example because in my research I found that it was common for schools to succumb to community (usually parent, but not always) pressure and dial back RSE efforts in the face of opposition. Perhaps if, in this scenario, Riley and Billie's teacher had the support of the school's powers-that-be, it might have gone differently, but the school was wary of the threat to their reputation, the unrest it might cause in the parent community, the tabloids picking it up. If the school had the support of their sector, of the Education Department, of the Minister, they would have been far better able to respond to the concerns raised by Billie's mum, without sacrificing the sex-ed of every other student. This reminds me of what I learned from Breanna Coyle, whom I met with in Dublin. Coyle is a clinical sexologist, and a former facilitator and training co-ordinator with the Irish Family Planning Association (IFPA), who has extensive experience in the delivery of, and training for, RSE, including for young people with disabilities. During her time with the IFPA, she delivered a program in Ireland called Speakeasy, funded by a government agency and designed to equip parents with the information and skills they need to have conversations about sex and relationships at home. Coyle described some of the challenges she faced while co-ordinating the program and other training. Teachers were fearful that certain board members would actively shut down attempts to deliver RSE to students. Coyle's role required the skills to negotiate resistance to the content of RSE workshops, which was often followed by requests for information to be dropped. Even when teachers expressed the strong desire to provide their students with the information and knowledge they knew the students needed, there were times when, for example, fear of a bishop on a board, who represented a school's biggest funder, created obstacles that restricted access to essential education. Schools should not be left in this position: this is why strong government commitments, formal policies, and even legislative mandates are vital for schools and teachers in insulating RSE programs from opposition.

Time and again, those I spoke with overseas cited these things as instrumental to their ability to do the work of RSE. In the Netherlands and the UK, legislative mandates to provide RSE include the requirement that they teach young people about diversity in relationships, about LGBTQIA+ people, in the name of equality and anti-discrimination.

After the session when the mother asked about the 'homosexual stuff', many parents told Smith they'd withdraw their kids from the Big Talk classes. I asked her later how she felt about parents being able to do that, to prevent their kids from accessing RSE despite the legislative mandate.

I was surprised to find that Smith supported the parents' right to withdraw, but I soon learned that so did most RSE advocates I spoke to. Even though all of them were fiercely committed to young people accessing comprehensive RSE, they recognised that parents ought to have the option to withdraw their kids. Smith described it as 'catching more flies with honey than vinegar', assuaging concerned parents by providing them with this choice. In turn, this may prevent vocal minorities and individual parents from derailing RSE initiatives entirely, acting as a kind of safety valve.

It can be very disempowering for parents to be told by institutions what to do when it comes to their child's education: most importantly, allowing parents the option to withdraw their kids from RSE helps to empower parents and caregivers to better appreciate the importance of it, and to reinforce lessons at home. I heard of many parents and caregivers who initially exercised the right to withdraw their kids from sex-ed at school, only to change their minds once they realised theirs was the only child missing out, and once they understood the nature of and need for RSE.

Building receptivity in communities, ensuring that parents

are not made to feel as though they are failing, is imperative. SIECCAN's Executive Director Dr McKay warned against getting into a 'pitch battle of one ideological world view against another, because you won't win'. He said to me: 'The population as a whole need to have their hearts and minds changed: they need to be educated themselves on what comprehensive sexuality education is, and what it is kids get taught developmentally when they're better informed. If you explain to people what you want to teach, a pretty strong plurality would be supportive.' Even with a legislative mandate, arguably the strongest step a government can take, there are still mechanisms to respond to the concerns that will flow.

The trick is that we all — including government — need to stand our ground. To be brave. The director of a college at a Group of Eight university in Victoria told me he gets angry phone calls from parents about his efforts to ensure residents have access to comprehensive RSE, even though their kids are no longer living at home. I got a bit choked up when he told me, 'I would rather have a hundred conversations with angry parents than one conversation with someone who has perpetrated or experienced sexual violence.'

Backlash, opposition, and public hand-wringing about what we are teaching kids in sex-ed are the things we need to face, not run away from.

Wynne described it as very hard for her when McGuinty backed down on the improved RSE curriculum in Ontario in 2010. 'If a straight Catholic man had just stuck to his guns, we wouldn't have then had the situation where a lesbian Protestant woman had to push it,' she told me. Her courage to go around again, to stand on the evidence in defence of young people's wellbeing, is an example to us all — even though she was 'obliterated' for her stance on sex-ed, to use the words of another Ontarian I spoke with, and ousted at the next election.

We were starting to get the wind-up signal from her aides, and I knew there was one more question I wanted to ask before our time was up.

'What would you have done differently?'

Unhurried by her staffers, Wynne stayed seated. She told me she would have been specific and explicit about the consultation the government had already conducted with parents, the data they had showing *most* parents were supportive of better RSE for their kids. Let me divert for a moment to note that this is similar in Australia: we have data that shows a significant majority of parents and caregivers are supportive of school-based RSE for their youngsters[3], including data showing 82 per cent of Australian parents support the teaching of sexuality and diversity in schools.[4] Topics for inclusion in school-based RSE such as 'information about masturbation', 'gender identity', and 'sexual pleasure' are extremely well supported by parents overall.[5] The Ontario example shows us how we need to use that data effectively, to remind ourselves that the loudest voices raised in opposition do not represent a majority.

Wynne also told me she would have provided schools and parents with information about the dangers of *not* providing comprehensive RSE. A better and pre-emptive public information campaign, one that was explicit about what was to be included in the curriculum, things like consent and personal boundaries. She would have given clear media briefings, framing the discussion so that the danger in opposing the curriculum, in exposing kids to harm by failing to give them improved RSE, was laid bare.

Her answer was one of the final puzzle pieces that fell into place for me. I realised that those other places I'd visited where they do RSE well, where their governments walk the talk, are not inherently different from us (except perhaps in political courage). They are not magically exempt from anxiety, backlash, and outcry about sex-ed. You could have everything you need to succeed: bloody-minded advocates, the best experts, great educators, engagement with parents, even political will. But if you aren't prepared for the winds of ignorance, apathy and — most of all — opposition, it will all come tumbling down. Wynne had the courage of her convictions, but her plan, her strategy to meet the inevitable resistance, was lacking.

•

So, what happened when Ford was elected in 2018, rolling back Wynne's sex-ed curriculum in favour of reverting to the version two decades old?

Hundreds of teachers marched on Queen's Park in Toronto in protest. On a September afternoon, tens of thousands of students walked out of class from over a hundred schools. Shoulder to shoulder, in the fight for lives and futures.

This battle lost, perhaps, but the journey far from over.

7

Fear and Self-Loathing

Olivia (and Felix)

Olivia's first memory of feeling something nice *down there* was when she was still a little girl.

Her grandmother had an old rocking horse in the back bedroom where Olivia would sleep when she stayed over. Its leather saddle was cracked, and it was missing an eye from where the paint had worn away over the years. It creaked a little when it was ridden, a faint protest as though it was weary.

Olivia was playing in the back bedroom one day, her grandmother baking in the kitchen. Tired of her toy dinosaurs, Olivia clambered onto the rocking horse, hoisting herself into the saddle, her legs not quite reaching the stirrups. Back and forth — creak — creak — creak; it gave her a funny feeling in her undies. It was a nice feeling, though, and she kept going.

'Olivia.' Her grandmother had entered the room, her tone sharp and an expression on her face Olivia did not recognise. 'That's enough. Come and watch television.'

In early primary school, Olivia and her best friend would play doctors in her cubby house and examine each other's private parts. There seemed to be an unspoken agreement that this was a secret game — if ever they heard a parent calling them, they would hastily pull up their pants.

As they drew closer to high school, she and her friends got really into a book series that one of them had discovered in the young-adult section of the library. A sex scene in book three became a hot topic of conversation, the well-thumbed pages of that chapter practically memorised between them. They would talk about what they imagined it would be like to kiss someone, wondering out loud what sex was like. One day a teacher overheard them: '*Girls*,' she said with a warning in her voice. After that the librarian wouldn't let them borrow those books anymore, frowning over her glasses as she said that they were too young to be reading them.

One time Olivia made a joke about sex in front of her parents, and her dad said her name in the same tone the librarian had used. The same tone in her grandmother's voice when she had been on the rocking horse all those years before. It was a reprimand, but mixed with something else. It made Olivia feel embarrassed and uncomfortable, self-conscious somehow.

In her first year of high school, her biology teacher talked about the cells that exist in all living orgasms, sending the class into peals of laughter. The teacher blushed as she corrected herself: 'All right, don't be silly, obviously I meant organism.' Olivia didn't know what was so funny, writing a note to her friend: *I don't get it.* 'It's something that happens in sex,' her friend whispered back.

Olivia had never heard of it. *Or-gaz-em* — she rolled the word around in her mind, curious. Later, she searched for it on the internet: ***did you mean orgasm?*** the computer prompted. *Oh, that's how it's spelled*, she thought to herself. All these results about sex came up and, although she wanted to know more, she was on the family computer and didn't want her parents to find her looking at this stuff. She closed the browser, still wondering what it was.

The next year, Olivia was sleeping over at a friend's house. They were talking about celebrities they thought were cute, giggling about what base they would go to if they had the chance. After a pause, Olivia's friend asked if she had ever seen porn.

'No,' Olivia answered, trying to sound nonchalant.

'Do you want to watch some on my phone?' her friend asked, a note of challenge in the question.

Olivia sometimes got butterflies, and a strange tingly feeling in her lower belly, when she thought about kissing someone. Sometimes she couldn't stop thinking about her crushes. She liked admiring them, and she imagined being admired by them. She imagined being their girlfriend, making out with them like the cool girls at school talked about. She'd heard them talk about things like fingering and blow jobs, but she didn't really know how those things were meant to work. She knew what sex *was*, and that it was supposed to feel good. But she couldn't really imagine it — she had only just worked out where her vagina was with the advent of her period and learning to use tampons.

Now, lying side by side on the bed on their tummies with the light of the phone illuminating their faces in the dark, Olivia and her friend watched two naked people having sex. Olivia had never seen people having real sex before and she laughed — half in embarrassment, half in thrill at their daring in watching something so grown up. The video made her feel kind of icky, but also curious. The woman in the video was making weird noises but was smiling and saying *yes* a lot: 'Why was she doing that?' Olivia asked when the short clip was over.

'She's turned on,' her friend answered, letting a few moments pass before asking, 'Have you ever masturbated?'

Olivia had first heard the word in sex-ed in primary school, and it was a word that made her feel embarrassed. She knew it was something boys did, but she wasn't sure how she knew that. She had a memory of a family holiday to the beach once, with her brother taking really long showers and being teased about it. She remembered that everyone knew he was masturbating, and it was this kind of joke, her uncle laughing that he was *becoming a man now*.

'No,' Olivia answered, not wanting to admit that she wouldn't know how.

Besides noticing that it felt nice if the seam of her jeans rubbed against her down there in a certain way — the same feeling she remembered from the rocking horse — Olivia had never touched herself deliberately to get that feeling. The idea of doing it made her feel kind of gross — she didn't think she would like putting her finger in her vagina. She decided she was happy to go on daydreaming about kissing guys she thought were cute.

As high school went on, those urges got progressively stronger. By 17, Olivia had had her first kiss but hadn't done anything more. She thought about sex constantly, and occasionally it would make her feel really turned on. It was an insistent sensation that sometimes demanded her attention with an urgency she couldn't understand.

When she felt like this, Olivia remembered her friend asking her if she'd masturbated. One night, after everyone had gone to bed, she decided to try it. Alone in the dark, she felt embarrassed; shy in her own company. The very act of touching herself there seemed meaningful in a way that touching no other part of her body did: it carried a feeling of scrutiny even when she knew nobody was watching.

Under the watchful eye of that intangible audience of her mind, she carried on. She didn't really like the feeling of putting her finger in her vagina, it felt kind of weird. But she noticed that there was this bit just above it, kind of near her pubic bone, that felt really good when she touched it. So she did, over and over.

That night, alone in the darkness of her room, Olivia finally learned what an orgasm was.

She started masturbating once or twice a week, and worried she was obsessed. It was like an itch she just had to keep scratching.

Even though it made her feel really good during, afterwards she always felt kind of dirty and gross. She almost felt embarrassed that she had done it, that she had wanted to do it, even though she was totally alone. Nobody knew, of course. She worried that if her parents found out, they might be disappointed in her. It would be totally mortifying, and they would be ashamed of her for doing something disgusting, she thought. She felt ashamed of herself. So it was her secret.

She didn't tell any of her friends at school either — since that sleepover years ago, she'd never heard any of them talk about masturbating. Olivia didn't know why she couldn't stop thinking about sex, why she always felt so horny. She became convinced that she was weird and abnormal; nobody else seemed to be plagued by these feelings. She wished they would leave her alone.

It was around this time that Olivia met Felix, when she auditioned to be in a play that a couple of schools were collaborating on. They had a few scenes together, and he was really good. She thought he was hot and got the sense her feelings were reciprocated; when they waited in the wings in silence, the air seemed to crackle with chemistry.

He made her feel nervous; he was funny, and she liked him. At some point they found each other on social media and, on the nights they weren't rehearsing, began messaging with increasing frequency.

Olivia started to feel emboldened: she put out flirtatious feelers and Felix responded in kind. It seemed easier to talk to each other online. Olivia found herself drafting salacious messages — things that she would never have been able to say out loud, with his eyes on her. This way she could type it and then dare herself to hit send, the risk invariably paying off when he would say something just as exciting in return.

She enjoyed being able to put words around the physical feelings she had. Describing the things she wanted to do was fun, and felt more comfortable than actually doing them. She wasn't sure she was ready for that. But reading the things Felix wanted to do with her would send a shot of adrenaline down into her belly, a delicious thrill that made her feel all hot and tingly.

Olivia loved that Felix was excited by the things she would send him. He never made her feel weird or embarrassed for her feelings or desires. Sometimes their conversations would turn her on so much that she would masturbate afterwards; on one occasion she even tried to do it during their exchange, but it was too hard to do while typing — her dominant hand unable to be in two places at once.

Felix was really into Olivia. They had fun together, and he felt comfortable talking to her. He was stoked to discover her risqué side when they started sexting. She was bold with it, and creative. He hoped they would graduate from this to real-life action, but for now it was hot and exciting, a secret pastime they shared.

As great as the words were (so good he had to be careful where he read them), he was more a visual person. He wanted to see more of her. One night, he asked Olivia to send him a photo.

She obliged with a selfie, and he told her she was pretty. But he wanted more and he asked for it, followed by the blushing emoji. She told him she was shy, and he reiterated that she was beautiful.

It's only fair, if you're gonna get a guy this excited 😉, he sent.

Olivia was nervous. She was worried about seeming easy, but maybe she had been leading him on a bit. Besides, she *wanted* to send him a photo of herself — she loved how attractive he made her feel, it excited her.

You'll keep it to yourself? Olivia asked.

Of course! he replied.

Several minutes went by, and he was just starting to think that she might have decided against it, when his phone buzzed. The notification that popped up made his heart beat faster; the anticipation was fleeting, though, because he hit that button so quick he could have strained his thumb.

She was standing in front of the mirror topless, and she looked so good. He could hardly believe she'd actually done it. He took a screenshot of the photo before it disappeared, replying with a bunch of love hearts.

Your turn, she said.

He pulled off his shirt and stood in front of the mirror, ruffling his hair to get it just so, before taking a few photos until he got one he was happy with.

Sexy, she replied.

His ego purred.

A few days later he was sitting on the oval with his mates at lunchtime, when one of them asked him how it was going with the girl in the play.

'Olivia,' he reminded them. 'Yeah, she's cool.'

'You hooked up yet or what?'

'Nah, just like messaging and stuff.' Felix was still feeling so pleased with himself that she had sent him that picture, he couldn't help but gloat about it to his mates. 'She sent me a photo of her tits the other day, though.'

'She did not,' his friend exclaimed sceptically.

Felix didn't hesitate to pull out his phone to produce the evidence, not giving Olivia a moment's thought in his quest to prove himself. He wasn't thinking of the photo as hers, now it had become his — a feather in his cap, the photo said something about *him*.

School was Felix's world, and here girls and sex were treated as a kind of game — but, somehow, a really important game. One in which you seemed to score points for the things you said and the things you did. In Year 7, Felix went to the school social, and the boys did this challenge where they ran around the dancefloor pinching the girls' bums. The teachers told them to stop running inside. As he got older, the lads would rate the girls with numbers, talking openly about who had the biggest boobs and which ones they'd like to screw. His best friend Mark once hit on a girl at a party, and she'd kissed him but then declined to sleep with him; the next day at school they all nodded when Mark declared her a bitch and a dyke, agreeing he'd been robbed. The teachers never said much, although one boy did get in trouble for taking a photo up a girl's skirt — he got suspended or something.

'Holy shit!' The boys passed around Felix's phone. 'Send it to the group chat,' someone laughed.

'Nah, I'm not going to do that.' Felix remembered he had promised Olivia he'd keep the photo to himself and he intended to keep that promise.

'Mate, she's obviously not shy!'

Word spread that the girl from the play had sent Felix a topless photo. It took on a life of its own and, by the time Felix realised that everyone knew, he couldn't put that toothpaste back in the tube. He could only hope Olivia wouldn't find out.

That night, Olivia's phone pinged with a DM from a name she didn't recognise. She opened it:

Nice rack

Straight away the penny dropped and so did her stomach. She blocked the sender. But then she got more messages like that, all of which she blocked and deleted. She felt mortified — everyone knew. Total strangers knew. And she couldn't get away from it because they kept finding her on social media.

In some of the messages they called her a slut, and someone even sent her a dick pic. A bunch of the messages came from people at her school. How could she possibly face those corridors the next day? She burned with humiliation and complete disbelief that Felix would do this to her.

She couldn't tell her parents, so she had to catch the bus like normal the next day. She felt sick, and her hands were shaking. All day it felt like everyone was looking at her and whispering about her.

In the afternoon, she was pulled into the principal's office. Horrifyingly, she had found out somehow. Olivia was embarrassed, but also relieved that the principal might be able to help, might know how to put a stop to it.

Olivia sat down, on the verge of tears and expecting sympathy. Instead what she got was a lecture about why she should not have sent a boy such a photo — 'You know what boys are like!' — and that she ought to be concentrating on schoolwork and not boys, that she had damaged her reputation and the school's. The principal wasn't yelling but Olivia could tell that she was angry, as well as disappointed.

'What on earth compelled you to do that?' the principal asked, her voice carrying notes of that same tone Olivia had heard so many times before.

Olivia stared down at her hands in her lap and felt naked, covered only in shame.

In mid-2021, I participated in the World Association for Sexual Health Congress, co-presenting a symposium about whether 'consent education' is the solution to addressing sexual violence in Australia. One of my fellow presenters was Dr Melissa Kang, whose career has specialised in youth health, adolescent sexuality, and sexual health. During her segment, Kang showed us a photo of a handwritten letter. On the left-hand side of the page, familiar characters decorated the margin: Winnie the Pooh, Piglet, Tigger, and Eeyore. In cursive that stayed carefully between the lines, young handwriting:

> Dear Dolly Doctor
>
> I have a problem. I masturbate all the time!
>
> Can you tell me if there is something wrong with me, and how can I stop?

Dolly Doctor is a now-historical figure since the death of print magazines, but until it closed in 2016, the Australian girls' magazine *Dolly* had a section specifically dedicated to readers' questions about health and sexual wellbeing, which the doctor would answer. Kang, a personal hero of mine, was the doctor behind Dolly Doctor from 1993 to 2016.

After 23 years receiving letters from teen girls, Kang is well placed to tell us just how common it is for young women to ask whether they are 'normal'. She wrote in *The Conversation* in June 2021:

> Many questions from girls suggested they needed information about desire and experiences of sexual pleasure. Those discovering sexual arousal and masturbation often seemed ecstatic (pun intended), although, even from a young age, these desires were often seen as problems and silenced.
>
> Somewhere between the delights of sexual self-discovery during early puberty and becoming sexually involved with a partner later in adolescence, I had a sense young women fell into a chasm of sexual repression, objectification and instruments for male pleasure.

I cannot help but feel emotional as I imagine the lass writing out that letter so carefully on her Winnie the Pooh notepaper. Putting it in an envelope and searching for a stamp, walking to the nearest letterbox and pushing it through the slot. I wonder if she listened for the sound of it landing, straining to hear that softest of thuds. Waiting for the next issue to hit the magazine stands, hoping for an answer to tell her how to stop feeling this way. How to put a stop to herself.

Of course, there was nothing wrong with that girl who wrote to Dr Kang all those years ago — the tragedy is that we made her feel like there was. How did we manage that? And how did Olivia end up feeling so unhappy and distressed about her sexual exploration and expression — at first alone, then later with Felix? Lauren French, sexologist, sexuality educator, and First Nations woman, tells me that to this day, in all the Victorian schools she visits as an external sex-ed provider with Body Safety Australia, the most common question she gets in the anonymous question session is 'Am I normal?' All year levels, all genders, young people are asking about

> things that touch on that idea of shame, around genitals, how they look — because it's not discussed, they get a narrow view of what is normal. It becomes a concern about what they are going to do for their life, and relationships — they are wondering 'can I ever have sex with anyone?', 'is it normal to be interested in sex?', 'is it normal to have crushes on people of the same gender?'

What are we doing, or not doing, to make young people feel this way, and why does this matter to the story of sexual violence prevention?

To answer these questions, let's take a closer look at a term I've been using throughout this book that you may have wondered about. I talk about the power of RSE to safeguard *sexual wellbeing*, but the term can attract some consternation. People often think sexual wellbeing is synonymous with sexual pleasure, or 'orgasms for all', as someone once scolded me. Although I firmly believe everyone should feel entitled to (consensually) experience sexual pleasure, that isn't what sexual wellbeing means.

To me, sexual wellbeing is something more holistic than that. Sexual wellbeing is a necessary component of sexual and reproductive health — and therefore overall health and wellbeing — as well as sexual safety. The World Health Organization defines sexual health as not merely the absence of diseases or negative experiences, but as including the 'possibility of having pleasurable and safe sexual experiences'.[1] Thus, sexual wellbeing includes freedom from sexual violence and harassment, or unwanted sexual experiences. It is freedom from shame, guilt, and distress about your own sexuality, your own body. It is a feeling of confidence, safety, and autonomy with respect to your body and your choices and your lifestyle.

It is also freedom from anxiety caused by standards of beauty that make you feel you need surgery to 'fix' your labia, or make you feel embarrassed about your penis size. Freedom from embarrassment and anxiety about menstruating, from asking friends to check the back of your skirt to make sure you're not leaking, or hiding tampons in your hand as you walk to the bathroom. It is freedom to seek help about the impact of gender incongruence/dysphoria or endometriosis or vaginismus, and how they affect your sex life. It would be confidence in knowing that those things will be treated just as seriously as erectile dysfunction is.

Sexual wellbeing may be having no interest in sex, and celebrating your asexuality. It may include feelings of desire and eroticism, the pursuit of sexual pleasure if that's what you want, feeling just as entitled to sexual pleasure as your partner/s. It may be choosing to practise celibacy. Or to masturbate without feeling disgusted at yourself, free from guilt. Freedom from the fear that healthy sexual feelings and behaviours are somehow unhealthy. Freedom from kink-shaming. Freedom from the idea that virginity is something that you 'lose' or have 'taken away', or that its 'loss' changes your fundamental character. Freedom from judgement and stigma about being 'frigid' or a 'slut', freedom from the fear of being derided for your personal choices when they have no impact on anyone else at all. Sexual wellbeing may be curious sexual exploration, joyful sexual expression, free from shame. Sexual wellbeing is freedom from feeling that your sexuality is — that *you* are — a problem in need of a solution.

This is what sexual wellbeing is, and it is about so much more than consent and sexual violence prevention. This is what sexual wellbeing is and, unless we name it and set our sights on it, we will never be able to reach it. And reach it we must, for so much damage can be inflicted without a single moment of violence by one person against another. It is damaging for young people to feel abnormal or deviant for having intense feelings of desire or wanting to masturbate as they move through puberty, or for feeling attracted to someone of the same gender, or for not feeling interested in sexual activity at all. It is damaging for them to feel their sexuality is worthy of shame, or that expressing their sexuality deserves judgement. To think of sexual feelings and activity as a minefield of risk and indignity. The feelings of abnormality and fear that prompted all those letters to Dolly Doctor make me despair. By failing to tell them these things are normal, by failing to talk about sexual wellbeing at all, we are teaching young people to feel confused, even disgusted with themselves. Even to hate themselves. And doesn't *that* destroy innocence? That gift of fear and self-loathing? How carelessly, how devastatingly we wield our weapons of silence and shame.

And what does any of this have to do with sexual violence prevention, you ask? Well, how do you avoid hurt and harm and shame and risk in a sexual experience when you don't know any better? How do you advocate for what you do *not* want if you have no concept of what you do want, or are entitled to want? How do you find your way to greener pastures if you don't know what they look like or where they are? A world where sexual violence thrives and unwanted sex is commonplace is not necessarily a world that celebrates those things and endorses them; it might just be a world that refuses to celebrate and endorse the alternative.

It was during that symposium that Kang explained the history of sex-ed in settler-colonial Australia, as I outlined in Chapter 1. Recall that she described it as telling a story of 'deficit and reactionaryism', with sex education focused on disease and pregnancy prevention, and then, more recently, harm prevention via a consent-based discourse.

When I went overseas on my fellowship in 2019, I too had that focus: I was determined to find out how RSE can prevent the sexual violence I saw in my professional life on a daily basis. How sex-ed could be used to stop rape. That angle must have been obvious in my questions, because at some point in my meeting with Christiane Erkens and Laura Brockschmidt from BZgA in Cologne, one of them stopped me: 'You must stop conflating sexualised violence prevention and sexuality education. They are different. Related, but different.'

Erkens and Brockschmidt insisted that young people must not learn about relationships, sex and sexuality only by reference to 'avoiding sexual violence', nor should they learn that sexual violence is simply sexuality gone wrong. They see a danger in framing discussions about relationships and sex *only* in terms of harm prevention.

Working in the criminal justice system for years, I suppose I had become blinkered. *How do we stop this hurt and ruin?* was the only question that mattered to me, and so it defined my perspective of the purpose of sex-ed. The funny paradox of RSE, I discovered, is that the more it focuses on avoiding something — pregnancy, disease, violence — the less effective it can be in equipping people to avoid those things. It's like when you're driving towards a pothole in the road: the more you focus on it, the harder it is to miss.

Let me try to demonstrate how that works when it comes to sex-ed, as someone who started with her eyes fixed on the pothole. In Germany, I learned that their approach to sexuality education seeks to frame relationships and sexual wellbeing in positive terms, and their sexualised-violence prevention work supplements that baseline. They recognise the harm that comes from teaching young people about sex and sexuality through a negative lens only. The harm that comes from failing to set a standard of holistic sexual wellbeing, from failing to paint a picture of what that looks like and what young people should expect: a picture of joy and excitement and fun and fulfilment and connection. After they pointed this out to me, I couldn't unsee it in every other place I had already been or would go on to visit. Everyone I spoke with overseas on my fellowship shared this approach, as did the RSE experts at home.

I can understand that some will feel uncomfortable about the idea of taking a sex-positive, sexual wellbeing approach to sex-ed. Perhaps you feel more comfortable with sex-ed that speaks to the clinical, the reproductive, and the prevention of actual violence and abuse. Perhaps you consider that feelings of shame or fears of abnormality are not quite as important, and are simply a part of growing up. If that's the case, I understand why you would believe RSE should have a singular goal of preventing violence, avoiding risk. However, if that is your view, focusing sex-ed content narrowly on sexual violence prevention is not only a problem for the sex-positivity, sexual-wellbeing proponents among us — it's a problem for you, too. It is the pothole effect.

What I have learned over the past decade in the criminal justice system is that you can draw a direct line between our refusal to talk about people's right to sexual wellbeing and every sexual offence matter that comes across my desk. Sexual violence is not a necrotic limb we can simply cut off, a cancerous tumour we can excise. It is not extraordinary, somehow separate from 'good sex', the sanctioned kind, the ordinary way we think of bodies, sex, relationships, sexuality: it is born of those things.

My years in the criminal law have shown me that the opposite of sexual violence is not merely its absence. In each chapter we have looked at the danger of playing too close to the margin of consent, of only avoiding 'no', of operating inside a narrow idea of sexual violence. It makes the line a blurry one, and it is harder to recognise when we're close to it, even when we've crossed it.

We need to get as far from the line as possible, aiming for expectations of sexual experiences that are not just free from violence but are *far* from violent. We need to shoot for the other end of the spectrum, not just this side of legal.

But if we are going to do that, we need to know what we're shooting for. In previous chapters I have described consent-focused RSE as a deficit model, and asked whether there is anything else we teach solely by reference to what *not* to do. I have said that we don't teach kids how to drive or how to swim with the words 'don't crash' or 'don't drown'.

Kerrin Bradfield, accredited sexuality educator and current national chair of the Society of Australian Sexologists, regularly delivers relationships and sexuality education to young people. She says that when we focus on the legalities of consent, rather than on rights and positive ideas of what consensual and ethical behaviour looks like, we don't help young people navigate complicated moments. I was once asked whether the nomenclature of 'consent education' was shorthand for all of this, shorthand for comprehensive RSE that takes a positive approach to sexual wellbeing. It may be for some, but in a subject so contentious and fraught, many will believe or feel relieved that consent and the avoidance of sexual violence are all that should be on the lesson plan. This is why, as I argued in Chapter 2, the introduction of 'consent education' into the national curriculum was not so politically contentious at all.

When we teach young people that sex is risky and dangerous — don't get pregnant, don't get an STI, don't get raped, don't get a reputation for being easy — then risk and danger are the characteristics we associate with the activity. If sex is something fraught, something to be anxious about, can it ever look like something else? And if so, what? How can we aim for that if we don't know where we're going? So often we tell young people 'just wait until you're ready before you start having sex'. Do we ever tell them what 'ready' may feel like? If nobody ever tells you what healthy, positive, enjoyable sexual experiences look like, or what it means to feel confident and safe and respected, then how can you find your way there? How do you know that you deserve and ought to expect *those* experiences?

We have seen the consequences of this in every chapter so far: Elliot did not recognise that Amy was freezing in fear, because he had never been taught that positive sexual experiences mean mutuality and communication, nor how to engage in that communication. Max didn't recognise Bec's brake lights because he had only been taught to respect the word 'no', and he felt he could get away with not being fully honest with her; meanwhile, Bec felt like she owed him something, not recognising that she should expect to feel happy and safe in every sexual activity, or what that would look like for her. Leon was sure that as long as he didn't cross the line into rape (his narrow idea of rape), all was fair in his pursuit of Nadia. Ashley didn't even contemplate that Xavier might not be interested in sleeping with her, and Xavier couldn't comprehend a world where he didn't have to. Jeremy was comfortable exploiting the sense of obligation Dominic felt to him and their relationship in order to get his way, and neither of them recognised that a good relationship shouldn't feel like that. Riley had a painful and unwanted sexual experience with the boy from the bus because she didn't feel anything else was possible, nor had she been shown what that possibility could look like. And when Olivia explored her sexuality, by herself at first and then with someone she liked, she was punished for it.

All of these people were left to rely on trial and error. I imagine them standing in a long corridor lined by closed doors, told only to avoid doors one (disease), two (early pregnancy) and sometimes three (rape). But they are never shown which is the door that leads to the healthy, safe, respectful, joyful experiences they deserve — left to try every other door no matter what may be on the other side, hoping for the best.

The key to choosing the right door is empowerment: feeling knowledgeable, confident, and capable in your own body, sexuality, and the choices available to you. Feeling able to communicate about those things, and safe in the expectation that you will be respected. Feeling interested and able to find out what the other person/s wants, where their comfort zone is. This is why it is so important to foster healthy and positive attitudes to sexuality, to talk about sexual wellbeing in a way that empowers while also building knowledge around risks. This is why it is imperative that we pursue holistic, comprehensive RSE, the kind I outlined at the beginning of this book.[2] If we all believe that everyone is entitled to this high standard of sexual wellbeing, then the further away from it we find ourselves, the more likely we will notice and act.

If we resort to silence, we cannot empower young people. And they will never feel entitled to that empowerment whilst ever we actively corrode it with shame. If empowerment is freedom, then shame is a cage.

Some may consider that the answer is to tell young people not to open any of the doors in that corridor at all: an abstinence model of sex-ed. But what does that mean for them when they get to the age and/or circumstances when we think it's appropriate for them to start engaging in sex and relationships? They still won't know which door to open, and, as we've considered in previous chapters, by then it is too late to teach them.

Teaching abstinence-only is a blunt instrument, and it's

counterproductive; sexuality isn't a part of us that just flicks on when we hit the age of consent or adulthood. Sexual development happens gradually, in a process that 'consists of an interaction between physical, cognitive, mental, social, relational, ethical, religious, and cultural factors'.[3] Dr Kang recalls people as young as 11 writing to her with questions about sexuality and sexual arousal. It is completely normal for young people to have feelings of desire, whether in the form of imagining being with someone romantically, or how it feels just to kiss someone, or wondering what it is like to have sex. It does not mean they will immediately want to go off and act on those feelings with someone else, as we saw with Olivia in her younger years.

Those feelings are powerful and naturally occurring, so we cannot simply eliminate them. Anne Philpott, a public-health professional who set up the international education and advocacy organisation The Pleasure Project, which promotes sexual health and agency through a focus on 'good sex', has said: 'Pleasure is arguably the most powerful motivating factor for having sex and yet has been absent from sex education or sexual health interventions.'[4] Trying to teach young people to ignore and suppress feelings of desire and curiosity about sexual pleasure is completely ineffective, even in achieving the measurable outcomes we have traditionally been concerned with in sex-ed: the abstinence-only approach leads to earlier first sexual intercourse, higher rates of teen births, and higher rates of pregnancy terminations, compared to comprehensive and positive RSE. For example, the Netherlands — with its longstanding, more comprehensive approach to sex-ed — has very low teenage pregnancy rates.[5] Negative sex-ed messaging is also worse for safe-sex practices to prevent disease (recall the Oxford study about the influence of pleasure-based messaging on condom use).[6] Even in pursuit of risk-reduction, it turns out it's still better to teach young people to engage positively with their feelings and navigate them safely, healthily, and ethically.

Young people are not going to learn to engage with those feelings if they are too uncomfortable to even dwell on them, because they feel wrong and dirty somehow. Lauren French tells me that young people feel weird to be interested in sex, when sex-ed is so clinical. This is why abstinence-only messaging is not empowering: we use shame to teach young people to suppress those feelings. Instilling in children a sense of fear or guilt around their sexuality is not going to keep them safe — even if it stops them from having sex before they're ready (or before we're ready), it will damage their future sexual encounters, leaving them ill-equipped to navigate those encounters with the nuance that is required. Comprehensive RSE does not remove abstinence as an option available to young people, nor does it ridicule those who choose it. It is simply that imposing abstinence on young people as their *only* option is dangerous to their safety and wellbeing, in both the short and long term. We must not sacrifice the safety and wellbeing of our kids at the altar of puritanism and fear.

I think the reason we so readily resort to abstinence-only messaging is our own shame: we live in the cage ourselves. We still carry entrenched notions that being sexual, physical, is somehow lesser and sinful. Or at the very least, frivolous and unimportant. Not only that, but the idea of talking to kids about sex feels especially wrong and inappropriate, particularly to speak of sex in positive terms. But there is a way to do it that is age-and stage-appropriate, empowering them so that their sexual wellbeing is *protected* not *corrupted.*

I remember Lynnette Smith of Big Talk Education saying that when we worry about talking to kids about sex, we are thinking of sex with our adult brains — imbuing it with all the meaning that we, as adults, ascribe to it. But children don't do that. How many songs do kids sing along to with abandon, never understanding the innuendo in the lyrics until they're much older? How many double entendres do they slip into kids' films, just for the parents, because they know they'll go straight over little heads? Smith said to me: children won't stop wanting to fly kites and build sandcastles just because they've learned about their bodies and sexuality in an age-appropriate way.

Conversely, as I see in my job, it is when they don't learn those things that they are at greater risk of abuse and harm.

So, what about sexual pleasure, then? I have said that sexual wellbeing is not synonymous with it, but how does it factor in? I said in Chapter 1 that refusing to be open about the fact that people often have sex because it feels good may be the most dangerous thing we do. To understand the full impact of shame about our bodies and sexuality, and how that contributes to not only poor sexual wellbeing, but also sexual violence and unwanted sex, we must consider our expectations of sexual pleasure and who is entitled to it.

The belief held by Leon (Chapter 3) and Xavier (Chapter 4) that they were 'red-blooded men', that they were expected to always want sex, does not exist in a vacuum. It is held in a patriarchal, cisnormative, and heteronormative binary that says men want sex all the time and women don't. And that, when women do want and enjoy sex, they do so in a way that happens to align with and cater to a man's desires — and/or they're a slut, deviant somehow. This construct promotes sex as more for men than for anyone else.

Recall how Bec in Chapter 2 was more concerned with Max's experience of her and with her, and how she struggled to identify what she desired. Or, in Chapter 6, Riley's bewilderment that anybody could enjoy sex. Riley didn't know what to expect of her own experience of sex at all, let alone that she was meant to enjoy it. She didn't even realise that the experience — one of pain and frustration — was the very opposite of how it should be. That her lack of desire for that boy, or any boy, perhaps revealed that this was not the kind of sex for her, rather than being something to panic about. She understood something of the arousal system for anyone with a penis, what it meant for them to be turned on: erections and ejaculation are staples in any sex-ed class that explains reproduction and how to avoid pregnancy. But Riley had no idea what desire would feel like for her, and even when she began to identify her desire for Billie, her internet searches led her to think that wasn't what it was at all. She had no idea what being turned on would feel like for her, that she would feel tingles and butterflies and that her genitals would become engorged and lubricated — the wonderful feelings she discovered when she kissed Billie.

We erase sexual pleasure for more than half of the population, including but not limited to our censorship of an entire body part in the clitoris. We do not learn that these folks should also expect to enjoy sex on their own terms, and we learn to shame them for it when they do.

For Olivia, the delights of self-discovery felt deviant, abnormal, and a source of guilt. Even when she was alone, she did not feel like it was 'my body, my rules' — she felt scrutinised by others' expectations of her behaviour with her own body. That fear was vindicated, sadly, when she expressed her sexuality with Felix, and was shamed for it by others. For Olivia, exploring sexual pleasure became fraught, her agency less relevant than others' judgement.

And what of the representation of 'female pleasure' that Olivia saw when she watched pornography with her friend? She saw a woman performing sexual pleasure without any concept of what that might actually *feel* like — physiologically or emotionally. Without any concept that not everyone experiences pleasure in that way or in those circumstances. Without any notion that authentic pleasure, on her own terms, matters more than performing pleasure for another.

What does that mean for Olivia and her sexual experiences with other people? It is just a hop, skip, and a jump from 'your (authentic) pleasure is irrelevant' to 'your autonomy is irrelevant'. If Olivia feels she is not entitled to pleasure, because she has felt ashamed of her sexuality all along, then how is she to advocate for her right to it in a sexual encounter with someone else? She can barely advocate for it to herself. How is she to recognise when she is in an unwanted encounter, when we have taught her she isn't supposed to want sex anyway? Or that she is only supposed to want it on another person's terms? When the moment she engages in any sexual expression and agency she gets called a slut?

Words like 'slut' and 'whore' and 'tart' and 'floozy' remind us that only straight, cis men are entitled to sexual pleasure, and that anyone else who pursues sex and pleasure is trouble: a straight cis man's sex drive is put down to biology, everybody else's says something of their character. The impact of harmful stereotypes like these is compounded for people of colour, trans folk, disabled people, and the queer community.

By centring one type of sexual pleasure, we actively make it difficult for anyone else to explore or openly express their sexuality, their wants and desires — especially if those wants and desires diverge from the heteronormative, penetrative standard. Many young people with vaginas and vulvas grow up expecting their first experience of penetrative intercourse to hurt, for example. We sell the lie that sex without authentic pleasure is normal, to be expected, for a significant group of people. As though sexual pleasure is not for them and they do not deserve it. Or that the only pleasure they can expect is the kind that is performative and serves others' desires. But then we also use words like 'frigid' to shame people who want to wait to have sex, or those who do not want to have sex at all, their asexuality treated as abnormal. Talk about being caught between a rock and a hard place.

No, 'normal' sexuality belongs chiefly to men — especially white, straight, able-bodied, cisgendered men.

So long as we teach young people that sex is defined by the sexual pleasure of only one type of person, we set up these lopsided expectations. Expectations that are repeated in all those innocuous places: films, shows, podcasts, social media, our stereotypes, our jokes, our language. Repeat something long enough and it takes on an air of incontrovertible truth. But, to quote Ericka Hart, a US-based sexuality, racial and social justice educator, in Episode 1 of Netflix's *The Principles of Pleasure*: 'Accessing pleasure just in our bodies ... is political because of the systemic structures that impact our bodies that say that we are not supposed to experience pleasure. It makes a difference that you actually name them as structures and not the truth.'

I remember as a young person being shown a picture book in sex-ed that only mentioned masturbating in terms of 'something boys do'. I remember a friend of mine telling me at school that 'Boys have to do it or it's painful, they get blue balls.' From such a young age, we learned that masturbating was something inherently masculine and that it was healthy, even necessary, for boys. The propaganda that sexual pleasure is more for cis men than for anyone else, that it is something *they* need for their health and wellbeing, starts early.

Big Talk Education in the UK uses a series of illustrations in its primary school sessions, one of which is an illustration of a young person scratching inside their underpants during class. Big Talk staff tell the students that if you want to touch your genitals, you should do it in private. Then they show an illustration of a girl who has her hands in her underpants and is smiling: 'This girl has her hands in her underwear, and it's okay because she's doing it in private — see how she's by herself in her bedroom and the blinds are closed?' This illustration simply emphasises young people's bodily autonomy, teaching that curiosity and self-discovery is normal and healthy.

This does not promote masturbation, encouraging young people to run home and take part; it simply speaks to the fact that young people are already curious about their own genitals and aware that touching them sometimes feels nice. It's not as if kids simply ignore that part of their own body until they reach puberty, but we seem to be more okay with it if the genitals in question are a penis: 'You know what boys are like, obsessed with their willy from day one!' We normalise it for some kids, but not for others.

Imagine if Olivia had grown up in a world that celebrated and endorsed sexual wellbeing. Imagine if she'd received RSE lessons that taught her that self-discovery was not only normal, but important for her to work out what her desires were, and where her comfort zone lay. What if she had never been shamed for her sexual expression? So too for Riley in Chapter 6. Learning to expect and prioritise their own sexual wellbeing may have saved both Olivia and Riley significant distress. They may not have seen themselves as shameful, so at odds with the world around them. They may not have had negative sexual experiences if they had known that this was not what they deserved. They would have known to expect something so much more than their mere consent.

•

Lessons alone would not have been enough to spare them, though. For both Olivia and Riley, the experience was significantly influenced by things that happened outside of the classroom too. As I said in Chapter 4, the opportunities to delve into the stuff of RSE will arise in all manner of ways — and we must be ready to meet those opportunities, even and especially when they crop up outside the class timetable.

Olivia was influenced by her grandmother, her parents, her uncle, her friend, her teachers, even the school librarian — they all contributed to shaping what she understood about her own sexuality. Then, when she was older, she was shamed by her peers for her sexual agency and expression with Felix, with the principal bringing up the rear. Riley was influenced by the adults in her home life and the girls at her school, as well as by the internet and her teachers — influenced both by what they did and did not say.

Sex-ed classes and the information they offer are, on their own, not always going to be enough to influence individual behaviour and values. Our worlds are shaped by the behaviour of those around us, not just by what we rationally know or are told. If you're in a stadium and everyone around you starts running for the exits, you're probably going to follow them even if you don't know what they're running from.

Culture, community, society: the behaviour and values of those around us are incredibly influential. We can give kids the very best RSE lessons, designed by the experts, packed full of useful information, and delivered by a charismatic, well-trained teacher. But the moment they leave that classroom and hear one of their peers calling another boy 'gay' as an insult or calling a girl a 'slut', then that brilliant lesson is immediately diluted, if not washed away altogether.

The way Riley was bullied for being a lesbian weighed heavily on her, making her feel she needed to prove that she was straight. The teachers who observed that bullying tacitly endorsed it by responding with no more than an eye-roll and a '*Girls*', instead of recognising it as homophobic. When the internet suggested Riley just had a 'girl crush', an opportunity to validate Riley's curiosity about her sexuality was missed.

When Olivia was bombarded on social media after sharing that photo with Felix, when she was called a slut and was sent unsolicited dick pics, that public ridicule reinforced that she ought to be ashamed. Being chastised by the principal for sending the picture at all communicated to Olivia that the fault lay with her, for having the desire to do it in the first place. The desire to sexually connect with a boy she liked, to explore her own sexuality, to feel admired — those things were treated as the problem, rather than the way *he* had acted. The principal should not have shamed Olivia for her sexual expression, but should have explained instead how Felix was in the wrong for sharing the photo.

Teaching that focuses on sexual behaviour as problematic, even pathological, 'eliminates the opportunity for young people to explore and experience normal, healthy, safe and pleasurable activity', and the literature suggests that 'there is a need for, but little evidence of, teaching that views teen sex as normative'.[7] Olivia used sexting to explore her sexuality with a boy she liked, in a way that, to her, felt comfortable and seemed safe. Telling kids 'Just don't do it!' doesn't allow them the respect and agency they deserve, and they will rightly feel resentful of that. The principal could still have explained the repercussions of sharing nude photos, especially as someone under 18, without making Olivia feel wrong for having the desire to do it, and without destroying her confidence to explore intimacy in the future, out of fear she was likely to get screwed over.

The principal may never deliver a sex-ed class, but Olivia's encounter with her sent a very strong message about sexuality, one personally addressed to her. This is why it is so important to complement those brilliant RSE lessons in the other corners of the world our kids occupy. As Jan Hargrave, the local council RSE expert in Lincolnshire in the UK said to me, 'Everyone needs to be on board: teachers, janitors, school governors, dinner ladies' —

whole-school policies are critical to the success of RSE. And why stop there? What about coaches, music teachers, paediatricians, babysitters, driving instructors?

We'll take a closer look at how parents and community can be engaged in RSE in the next chapter, but school remains a major part of most young people's worlds. It can be one of their core communities. What they see and hear and do at school really matters: a whole-school approach cultivates an environment that extends far beyond the classroom and out into the corridors.

A different school environment might have ensured that Olivia didn't leave that meeting feeling humiliated; a different environment at Felix's school might also have influenced him. It is not enough to only tell the Olivias of the world to be cautious about whom they sext and send photos to. I wonder how many sons get the same sexting talk that daughters do. I doubt Olivia would have been surprised to learn that Felix suffered no such reprimand, no such scolding as she did — young people know they get treated differently based on our gendered expectations, and by maintaining those expectations we communicate that this is just 'the way it is'. When we say things like 'that's just what guys are like', when we make jokes about fathers having to lock up their daughters, we create an air of inevitability about behaviour that we ought to challenge. We must teach the Felixes — and all of Felix's friends — to care just as much about the person who sent them that photo, no matter who they are, as what their friends think of them. To respect her sexuality, her right to sexual expression, and her sexual wellbeing just as much as their own.

Felix saw the way his peers behaved, the way that behaviour was waved away by the adults in his life, when he looked around for examples of how to be a young man. It is both a cop-out and a hall pass when we say 'boys will be boys' and will always want to show off their conquests. Of course they will, if they see that they'll be celebrated for those conquests. If they occupy a world where pinching girls' bums at a school event is treated as some kind of game, and the adults around them shrug it off.

The expectation that boys are entitled to sexual gratification, and to girls' bodies, was thriving at Felix's school. When he suggested Olivia owed him a photo if she was 'gonna get a guy excited', Felix was invoking the idea that she'd somehow led him on. When he showed his friends the photo she'd sent, it was because he could think of it as a trophy he'd earned. While that sense of entitlement may have only been a kernel in Felix and his friends, it has the potential to bloom into something much darker.

It is this same entitlement to sexual gratification, and to other people's bodies, that drives some to carry on in the face of *no*. Sometimes *no* may even provoke it, offending that sense of a birthright to access another's body. I remember a young man who was sentenced for forcibly sexually assaulting a junior staff member at his casual job, the judge remarking sympathetically that he had 'only wanted a girlfriend'.

It is said that justice must not only be done but be seen to be done. That is, what is justice if the community that has a stake in it cannot observe it, or detects any hypocrisy in it? This idea that boys are entitled to sexual gratification, girls and their bodies be damned, is fostered in places both ordinary and extraordinary. It is an entitlement that survives at the expense of others' sexual wellbeing, an entitlement built upon the denial that *everybody* shares the right to sexual wellbeing.

We must ensure that every corner of our community, of the environments that young people occupy, celebrates a right to sexual wellbeing for all. It is not enough for us to simply say that we do, young people must know it and feel it — that we have the same expectations of everyone and for everyone.

When it comes to our expectations that everyone has the right to sexual wellbeing, those expectations must not only be held but be seen to be held.

8

Through the Looking-Glass

Lina and Charlie and Erica

They were on their second date and swapping travel stories, when South America came up. 'Have you been there?' Charlie asked.

'Yeah, I went there with my ex,' Lina said.

'When did you go there with him?'

Here we go, Lina thought as she chased an errant piece of gnocchi with her fork. *It's time to do the reveal.* Her heart began to beat a little faster and she cleared her throat.

'My ex wasn't a guy.' Lina made sure she looked at him as she said it.

'Oh, right — sorry, shouldn't have assumed. You like girls too?'

'Yeah, all genders. It's fluid for me.'

'Cool,' Charlie nodded, only a little too casually.

Lina was relieved to have that out of the way. She liked Charlie a lot, and wanted to keep seeing him. Revealing her sexuality was always a moment of trepidation; people often thought she was confused or experimenting — and if they didn't, Lina worried they did. She felt her shoulders relax as the conversation moved on.

He was easy to talk to, and they had much in common. Charlie was younger than she was, and she could tell he was trying to impress her, but he was fun and smart and handsome. As the wine flowed, so did their wit. Lina decided to go home with him tonight, if he asked.

•

He did.

His small apartment was minimalist — more by young bachelorhood than by design — but clean. She loved when a man kept his place clean. He had a decent booze collection and, nightcap in hand, she was admiring the collection on his bookshelf when he came over to her. The two of them locked eyes, and Lina touched his arm as they leaned into each other and kissed.

They moved to his bedroom and began to undress. Lina was glad to discover the spark was very much accounted for.

Charlie seemed quite confident, if a little hasty — there was already a lot of tongue involved and he had dispensed with her bra expeditiously. *No worries*, Lina thought, *first time is usually a little nervy*.

He went down on her early in proceedings — she hadn't quite warmed up yet, but she appreciated his intention. She enjoyed cunnilingus, so chances were this would get her going.

But he didn't stay there for very long. His tongue was doing an awful lot — too much — and just as she was working out how she would ask him to be more gentle, he stopped and moved up her body. Maybe she should take the reins here for a bit.

She started to give him head. She fancied herself quite good at it, and she could tell he was enjoying himself, so she was rudely surprised to feel his hand on the back of her head, pushing it down further. *Oop, don't like that,* she thought warily. Lina pushed back and assertively moved his hand away. She kept going for a bit, trying to set the pace of their foreplay, before coming up for air.

Next thing she knew he had pulled out a condom — *Okay, at least we don't have to have that discussion,* she thought — and she put it on for him, again trying to slow things down a little. She kissed him, embracing him in the hope they might simply do that for a bit, when she felt his erection nudging her impatiently. *So much for setting the pace.*

She guided him into her — and then it was on, and he seemed

to want to do it all: standing, sitting, against the wall, from behind, on top, underneath.

It was fun, but a bit frenetic. They'd just be getting into a rhythm, and he'd flip her around somewhere new. Lina felt like she was at a HIIT circuit, running between exercises and barely getting the hang of one station before the instructor was yelling at everyone to rotate.

'I'm coming,' he gasped eventually, and then she saw him looking at her expectantly and realised it was an announcement, a cue, so they could coordinate and come together. In a split second, she had to decide whether or not to fake it. It was a catch-22: if she didn't, he might be disheartened or think there was something wrong with *her*; but if she did, would he do anything different next time?

'Did you come?' he asked, panting into her collarbone.

'Absolutely,' she replied, legs akimbo.

She had gone for option B.

Their next rendezvous might be better; maybe this was first-time nerves.

The next time, it was more of the same. He wasn't always confident on the location of her clitoris and, when he happened to stumble across it, he didn't seem to know what to do with it. Lina decided to offer more guidance, and he took it well when she gave directions. This definitely had potential and, on account of her growing feelings for him outside of the bedroom, she kept seeing him.

Still he favoured penetrative sex, and always asked if she came. While his stamina was impressive, he seemed to think that simply thrusting in and out of her was enough to send her into the throes of ecstasy. Foreplay was always the same: kissing, he'd go down on her briefly (albeit improving in technique), followed by her giving him head. His idea of variety was to attempt every imaginable position, and, credit where it's due, he was creative on that front.

She decided to try to improve the situation, suggesting to him that they mix things up a bit. She hoped a change of formula might enhance the synergy between them, so one evening when they were having sex in a position that worked for Lina, she asked him to keep going like that.

Charlie was only too happy to oblige — her saying what she wanted was hot, and he really was trying to impress her. But in the front of his mind was her comment that she wanted to mix things up. He knew women like being choked as much as he loved doing it, and he hadn't done that with Lina yet, so he reached down and put his hands around her neck. Lina didn't mind a hand lightly resting at the base of her neck, but this was different: Charlie started squeezing.

'What the *fuck*!' Lina sat up and shoved him off her.

'You have to *ask* first, don't you fucking know that?'

'I thought you wanted to mix things up!' He looked at her imploringly.

'I meant do things a bit differently, I didn't mean frighten me,' she snapped.

'I'm so sorry.' Charlie was horrified and forlorn, clutching the sides of his face. 'I'm so, so sorry, other girls I've been with have liked it, I swear it won't happen again.'

Lina softened a fraction and shook her head. 'Maybe we need to do more talking in the bedroom. About what we like, what we don't like.'

'Yes, please,' he said, with an earnestness that tugged at her heart.

And so they did. Naked and relaxed, they lay on his bed and spoke.

Lina's heart rate was finally starting to slow, and her breath evened out again after the shot of fear she'd felt when he had grabbed her throat. She was just thinking that this conversation had turned surprisingly sexy, when Charlie remembered something he'd been wanting to ask: 'How did you do it with your ex?'

'What do you mean?' Lina asked, wary.

'Well, like, what sort of stuff did you do?' He was sheepish now, and the question had killed the mood a little.

Gently, Lina explained that she didn't tend to reach orgasm from penetration alone. He asked her a lot of questions about what she'd done with previous girlfriends, very eager for detailed descriptions. Lina had been right to be wary: this wasn't uncommon, for guys to be titillated to think of her with women, once they discovered she wasn't straight.

Still sheepish, but not so much as to arouse his better judgement, Charlie volunteered that he would like to watch her with a woman. Lina rolled her eyes: 'Yeah, sure, maybe for your birthday,' she said, her voice sarcastic. She almost gave him a lecture about how her sexuality wasn't a performance for his viewing pleasure, but she remembered how vulnerable he had allowed himself to be in this conversation already, and decided to save it for another time.

Charlie didn't pick up on the sarcasm, or he chose to ignore it, already building ménage à trois fantasies. A quick look at his porn search history would reveal his penchant for threesomes, and now he was entertaining the idea that this could happen for him in real life. He was starting to think he'd scored the jackpot.

Over the next while, he and Lina continued to see each other, and he got better at listening to what she wanted in bed, letting her teach him what she liked and trying not to be offended that his penis was not the answer to her orgasmic prayers. Lina was impressed, ready to award him 'Most Improved' and relieved she wouldn't have to break up with him.

Charlie remained excited by the thought of Lina having 'lesbian sex', as he called it in his head, often imagining it while they were being intimate. When they were on dates at bars, pubs, restaurants, at the beach, he would point out hot women, asking if she found them attractive.

Lina wasn't sure why she kept letting him do it — it made her uncomfortable and gave her a bit of the ick. She was going to have to say something.

Charlie ended up saving her the trouble, though — he started to detect that she didn't love talking about it as much as he did, so he stopped doing it. Anyway, he reckoned by now he had got a sense of the kind of women she liked (he hadn't).

•

The waitress brought over dessert, and Charlie's had a candle in it that was starting to slide, thanks to a lack of structural integrity in the sticky date. 'Make a wish, handsome.' Lina winked at him as he blew out the flame. He grinned gleefully.

Later they caught up with a group of his friends at a bar for his birthday drinks. Lina was nervous to meet them for the first time — she felt a little old, but they were as charming as Charlie and very welcoming. A woman named Erica was kindly making a concerted effort to ensure Lina felt included, speaking to her if ever she was left alone, offering to refresh her drink whenever it ran dry. They hit it off, enjoying a lively and interesting conversation over the course of the evening, and Lina found herself having a good time.

As the evening wore on and the crowd thinned out, Lina, Charlie, and Erica were left in a dim booth at the back of the bar. A live jazz band started playing, and they had to lean in to each other to be heard. Several times, Erica spoke so close to Lina she could feel her breath tickling the downy hairs behind her ear. Gradually, she would put her hand on Lina's knee when she leaned forward to speak to her.

Wedged between the two of them, Lina suddenly noticed they were all sitting very close together — acres of leather upholstery around them, and yet she could feel the length of Erica's thigh against hers.

Is something going on here? The thought rushed into Lina's mind, and she rubbed her eyes, trying to bring some clarity to her tipsy head. She noticed that Charlie's eyes were darting between her and Erica, following their every interaction. She thought she caught a look between them, fleeting eye contact across her body as she sat there trying to work out what was happening.

Suddenly she felt Erica's fingers stroking the soft skin of her inner thigh, and she looked down in surprise, to see them disappearing under the hem of her skirt. Then Erica's lips were on her neck, and Lina could hear the band playing 'Cheek to Cheek'. She turned to see what Charlie was doing and, before she could say a word, he kissed her mouth. It felt surreal, as though everything had turned back-to-front.

She was acutely aware that she had two different tongues on her in a public place. The panic and embarrassment that flowed seemed to sober her up, and she pushed them away.

'Sorry, I'm not really up for this,' she managed, before extracting herself ungracefully from the booth and making for the exit. Outside, she steadied herself on a lamppost and the music dulled as the door closed behind her. It blared again when Charlie emerged on her heel.

Lina rounded on him: 'I told you to ask before you just do things! I didn't want that; you never asked if I wanted that.' Her anger rose.

'It just happened! You said we could do this for my birthday, and Erica happened to be into it!' he said defensively.

'I was being sarcastic when I said that! And don't lie to me, you clearly worded her up.'

'I didn't — I just told her you also liked girls!'

'Yeah, I like them for me, not for us. Or at least not without talking to me first. I'm not just some fantasy you can play out. You planned this! I thought you learned from that other time that you can't do stuff without asking first.' Her voice was raised now.

'But this isn't like that! I totally get why you freaked out that time, and I shouldn't have done it without asking, but this isn't like that! It's different, it's not like she was going to hurt you or anything!' he pleaded, clasping her hands in his.

Lina swore at him to leave her alone and wrenched her hands free before hurrying out to the street and hailing a cab that was passing, desperate to get away from him.

'We don't let him have a phone, and we monitor his use of the computer at home.'

This is how I heard one parent explain their tactics to stop their son from seeing pornography, in response to hearing statistics about how early young people are exposed to it (early double digits on average, if not sooner for some).

The role of pornography in shaping young people's attitudes to and understanding of sex is a common concern. We may worry that young people will borrow the standard script of a heterosexual porn clip for their own sexual encounters: cunnilingus, fellatio, intercourse in a predictable sequence of positions, and, finally, the money shot. We may worry that these videos will teach young men to objectify and degrade women, and their real-life sexual proclivities will be defined by those features; that young people will grow up thinking sex includes choking and anal sex and ejaculating on someone's face as a matter of course. We may fear the impact of genres like incest, rape, and deflowering pornography in normalising sexually violent material. We may be concerned about the way porn perpetuates racist stereotypes by fetishizing the bodies of people of colour.

Some people report that they feel negatively influenced by pornography — for example, those who say it has made them feel they need to act a certain way or look a certain way during sex. We should believe people when they say watching pornography caused them harm, as pop singer Billie Eilish did in late 2021, speaking publicly about how seeing porn at the age of 11 affected her.[1]

But the limitations of my expertise mean I cannot make claims about the way pornography influences attitudes and sexual behaviour at a societal level, the science of what it may do to the human brain, or the extent to which it contributes to its consumers perpetrating sexual violence.

For that reason, this chapter is restricted to what I *do* feel able to comment on: the importance of comprehensive RSE in a world where pornography and other sexually explicit media is ubiquitous, and the danger in our readiness to blame pornography as a unique source of sexually violent behaviour and attitudes.

We love a scapegoat and, *hoo boy,* this is a good one. Graphic, abundant, and external, porn is easy to point the finger at. But we should be cautious before we assume that young people engage with pornography completely uncritically, that they take no literacy to it whatsoever. Some data suggest that young people are not all simply confusing pornography with 'real sex', that they have a 'more sophisticated and nuanced understanding of how pornography works', with some even expressing a preference for 'amateur porn' because it seems more 'authentic', varied and 'real'.[2] Let us not forget that, in respect of digital media, 'young people's literacies are recognised as often surpassing that of adult educators and researchers', and — as ever, when it comes to RSE — we ought to eschew the 'long history of adults discussing young people's "needs" without inviting young people into such discussions'.[3]

Sexuality educators I spoke with overseas told me that they get questions from young people about pornography, asking about things they've seen, such as someone ejaculating on another's face. This suggests that young people are not all simply mimicking what they see in porn uncritically, but it also suggests that — at the very least — porn leaves them with questions. I've said in previous chapters that comprehensive RSE is a chance to set the record straight, to help young people make sense of all the messages they are bombarded with from the world around them. Do they get some of those messages from porn? Of course.

'Sexually explicit media does a great job of providing information,' my friend Kerrin Bradfield says. She is an accredited sexuality educator and current national chair of the Society of Australian Sexologists, the peak body for qualified sexuality educators and therapists.

> But what is that information? Much [heterosexual porn] may be about conservative gender norms, that cis women's role is one of submission. It may be information that fetishises the bodies of women of colour. It may provide information about communication in sex, but largely that you should use derogatory language, if you are talking at all.

Bradfield emphasises that people may very well enjoy some of these things and consent to them. Equally, some research suggests that porn can be a 'useful resource when sexualities education is inadequate'[4] — for example, it may help people explore or even discover their sexuality.

But, as Breanna Coyle, the clinical sexologist and former facilitator and training co-ordinator with the IFPA, put it when I met with her in Dublin, 'while pornography might offer some an opportunity to explore the erotic mind, there are times it is experienced as compulsive, not pleasurable, which is not about the pornography itself. There could be underlying sexual shame, insecure relationship dynavmics, a need for self-soothing, digisexuality, or psychosexual issues'. There is significant danger when sexually explicit media is the *only* source of information for young people. Bradfield says it's not the fault of sexually explicit media that it has become the default educator, nor is it young people's fault for going to it for information — they usually go to it out of curiosity at first. According to the last Australian Survey of Secondary Students and Sexual Health, 79 per cent of young people accessed information about sexual health online — a figure that has almost doubled since 2013. That statistic doesn't mean 79 per cent of young people are solely going to porn for information about sexual health, but it does show that a great number of them are seeking out information online.

One of the greatest perils of porn is not so much the noise it contributes, but the silence that it occupies.

Attempting to prevent young people from accessing pornography, while completely understandable, is by itself an unrealistic guardrail against its impact. Protecting against early exposure is something RSE can address in primary school lessons, by teaching young people to recognise a situation as risky, if someone else attempts to show them pornography, for example. We may be able to delay how early a young person is exposed to it, but as a long-term strategy, it is far from watertight.

Young people are curious and clever. And they have friends. Siblings, cousins, teammates, other kids on the bus. Unfortunately, we simply cannot eliminate every opportunity they will be exposed to pornography now that it is in everybody's pocket. Before that, kids were finding the magazines and the Mills & Boons and sharing them around, too.

Even if we can delay kids from accessing it, by contributing to the vacuum that pornography helps to fill, we leave them ill-equipped when they eventually do see it. Pornography is a powerful industry driven by profit and the patriarchal, colonial gaze, but the messages it sends are not separate or external from our everyday life. This is why Bradfield uses the term sexually explicit media: it's not just porn.

We worry about porn, but remember all those messages young people get from other innocuous places? Bradfield explains that sexually explicit media can include things on social media, like videos and memes and gifs, as well as television shows and films. This is media that is mainstream, free, and not always designed to arouse — it may be comedic or shocking or simply trending.

Bradfield had previously told me that in 2019 she'd attended a school-leavers event in her capacity as a sexuality educator. She was astounded by the number of young women walking around with bruising on their necks, 'as common as hickeys were only a few years ago', she said to me. My first assumption was that it was probably because choking in heterosexual pornography has become so commonplace. Now that may be so, but in reflecting on her comments about sexually explicit media, I realised I was seeing it somewhere else too — somewhere far more pervasive. I'm not *that* online and I'm also not that young, but even I had noticed this shift, that memes about choking and rougher sex had become ubiquitous online.

I'm not saying breath control play and rough sex are new, it's the ubiquity of it that feels new. When this sort of content is everywhere, and if it fills up a silence that we have created, it becomes the only information on offer. And its ubiquity may lead to a sense of expectation. Is it any wonder that young people may be under the impression that choking is standard and that they are abnormal if they don't want to participate in it? Young people do speak of feeling pressured to be more kinky, worried that they are boring if they are too vanilla. Women report being choked during one-night stands without ever being asked, assumed to be up for it. A 2021 survey of undergraduate students at a United States university found that half of the college students who had been choked reported they had never or only sometimes been asked for consent prior to being choked.[5] In a 2022 qualitative interview study (also in the US) of young women's experiences with choking during sex, participants discussed accepting being choked for their partners' pleasure, even when they didn't personally find it arousing. Most participants in the study shared that choking was something they did not ask for or initiate and that, even if they enjoyed it, for most it had occurred either without consent or with assumed consent. Sometimes consent was sought during the act itself.[6]

I use this as an example to highlight the danger in pointing the finger only at porn for any *non-consensual* sexual behaviour of individuals. Perhaps these messages arrive in places like social media after crossing over from pornography, but if we are talking about *where* young people are finding their information, cutting off their access to porn won't account for the more innocuous places.

By bringing up social media, I'm not substituting one scapegoat for another. As Bradfield says, online and offline are not separate realities for young people anymore. Social media platforms can be places where young people express their agency, places to critique and lampoon things like toxic masculinity and binary gender roles. There is plenty of content on these platforms that celebrates affirmative consent and healthy relationship models. But those things compete with media that normalises toxic relationship behaviours like possessiveness and jealousy, often represented and interpreted as a sign of love. Similarly, the idea that guys are always up for sex, and women less so, is a common meme across platforms. In the face of this information competition, it is not as simple as the platforms themselves being the issue — it's that people interacting with them are often bereft of the knowledge and skills to make sense of the messages they find there.

It is too easy to blame pornography and social media as external forces that emerged out of thin air to corrupt our kids' brains and their way of interacting with the world. We are quick to let ourselves off the hook when we say porn is the problem, chiefly responsible for problematic attitudes around sex or for setting 'unrealistic' standards. Yes, cis women in heterosexual porn seem to orgasm from penetration alone, despite the fact most don't climax that way. But how many movies and shows are there where the same thing happens? We might think of films and shows as art that imitates life, and yet there these kinds of sex scenes are the norm.

Is anybody telling young people that it doesn't really happen like that? Do we tell young people about the clitoris in biology, as we teach them about the uterus and the penis? Do we tell them that it is shaped like a wishbone and extends down into the vagina? That plenty of folk orgasm from clitoral stimulation alone, and it might take a bit longer to get there than what you see in the movies? Much pornography and many sex scenes in films reinforce heteronormative, penetrative sex as the standard, no different to sex-ed classes that do the same.

What about the way that actors in lots of porn don't talk much, moving from position to position in a sort of seamless dance, with nothing but some over-egged ecstasy to fill the silence? Where have we seen this before? In Chapter 1, Elliot saw that, on the silver screen, people seem to rely on telepathy to communicate their mutual lust before they lock lips and strip off. Similarly, possessiveness and jealousy as symbols of romance has long been a favourite trope of Hollywood, and literature before it. Meanwhile, heteronormativity remains dominantly represented in popular culture.

And what of the degradation and objectification of women that we see in a lot of pornography — is that so novel? In late 2019, a group of schoolboys from St Kevin's, a prestigious school in Melbourne, were filmed shouting a chant on a tram. With one voice and with gusto they bellowed: 'I wish that all the ladies, were holes in the road, and if I was a dump truck, I'd fill them with my load.' I wonder how long this chant has been around, if it's anything like those at university colleges around the country that similarly paint women as instruments of male degradation — chants that many of us would be familiar with from a time well before porn was only a click away.

A former student of that Melbourne school recalled, from years before, a teacher getting some of the boys to chew up pieces of a cookie and spit it into a glass, by way of demonstrating what it was like to sleep with a woman who had already been with other people.[7] It's not hard to imagine how a culture like that would embolden its boys to gleefully perform a degrading chant on public transport. This isn't something they see only in the privacy of their bedrooms at night, through the looking glass of their screens, an illuminating portal to a dark world far away from the rest of us. This is the stuff of broad daylight, even among strangers.

Is porn a place where these messages are exaggerated and saturating? Yes. But it is a place that is not so different from the others we occupy without remark. It reflects and reinforces the expectations we have already created, taking inspiration from the world around it. Still, we find it easier to point a finger than to look in our own backyards.

It is in our backyards and lounge rooms and around our dinner tables that we must fill the silence that sexually explicit media occupies. I can understand why many parents would endeavour to block a young person's access to pornography with a view to mitigating its impact. But unless we are going to lock kids away, we can't prevent them from encountering or being confronted by moments that call on them to make decisions. Isn't it better to equip them with the information and skills they need to make decisions that are right for them?

Self-evidently, the fact that young people are asking about things they have seen in porn means that it is leaving them with questions. Our job is to answer those questions.

Bradfield, in her practice as an educator, sees that young people recognise what consent and rape are technically, but they do not recognise as easily things like compliance or pressure or coercion — and we've seen that with characters like Elliot in Chapter 1 and

Jeremy in Chapter 5. I imagine if Charlie had seen porn clips where a man has sex with a 'sleeping' woman, hopefully he would have still known that in real life that would be rape. He may have seen women in porn whose character has been forced to have sex with the male protagonist and known that the subsequent pleasure she apparently experiences is unrealistic. But knowing those things did not mean Charlie knew how to communicate with Lina, to discuss what they each liked. Knowing what *not* to do did not mean he knew what to do instead: he thought he just had to put in a solid performance and figure it out as he went along.

The problem isn't simply that young people look at porn and think it is realistic, something they must mimic. It's that they look at porn and see no alternative models. They may know porn is not realistic but still not know what *is*. They may know that they ought not behave like *that*, but not how to behave instead. Lynnette Smith of Big Talk Education in the UK said to me, 'We need to challenge some of the things young people see in porn with RSE, otherwise it will become the only reality.' Pornography leaves young people wondering about things like how to start a relationship, how to talk about what you like, how to find out what you want in a way that is safe and helpful. This is why it is so important that we talk about the things we see in sexually explicit media, why we should explain it rather than hoping young people won't ever see it.

Understandably, many parents feel a bit at sea when it comes to this stuff. They often don't know how to answer the questions they may get, how to bring up these kinds of conversations with their kids in a way that isn't impossibly awkward, how to talk about sexual wellbeing and relationships and consent and pornography. England's Children's Commissioner produced a guide called 'The Things I Wish My Parents Had Known: a guide from teens and young adults on dealing with sexual harassment online', to help parents 'negotiate tricky conversations about children's online behaviour, using advice from teenagers and young adults based on what they wish their parents had known'. The Commissioner said:

> The overriding message from our focus group is talk early, talk often. You might be surprised how early our young people felt parents need to start the conversation. My advice to parents and carers is to create the culture before the crisis. Children have told us they want their mums and dads to create a safe, judgment free space for them to talk about these issues. It's better to do that before you hit a problem rather than trying to create that mood while you're dealing with one.[8]

In every place I visited on my fellowship overseas, the task of engaging with parents, caregivers, and community was a key plank of RSE. Every person I spoke with emphasised the need to explain to parents what their young people will get in RSE classes at school, but also to provide parents with information and resources to continue the conversation at home. Recall Siobhan O'Higgins at the University of Galway, whom I introduced in Chapter 1, who prioritises information sessions for parents in advance of any RSE delivered to students. So too, Big Talk Education in the UK runs an information session for parents before delivering RSE in a school — every time. Many RSE providers in Australia undertake similar engagement work when they deliver at schools.

Research has shown that 'parents who received training [about RSE] had better communication with their adolescents about sexuality compared with those who did not',[9] But it is critical to the success of RSE that we meet people where they are, that we are sensitive to their needs and understanding of their concerns. Some of those concerns may arise out of faith and culture, for example. Breanna Coyle said of her experience at the Irish Family Planning Association, delivering Speakeasy, the program aimed at parents: '[Those] who grew up in a very Catholic Ireland, where are they supposed to get the confidence to talk about things that they were told were dirty, use words they were told were dirty?' These sorts of programs may be organised by community too: in Canberra, I attended an evening session called 'Awkward Conversations', organised for parents and by parents. At a local watering hole, a number of experts volunteered their time to talk RSE-relevant issues that parents had questions about.

Should it be left to private providers, community sector organisations, and individual parents? Or is there a role for government here, too? Municipal health departments in the Netherlands conduct parent engagement, through activities like information sessions, when they implement Rutgers' RSE resources and programs. Rutgers also produces books and pamphlets for parents, which provide useful guidance on how to navigate this topic at home. BZgA in Germany creates and distributes similar material. In March 2022, the Australian federal government released the fourth stage of the 'Stop it at the Start' campaign that we considered in Chapter 5: an advertising campaign encouraging parents to speak to young people about respect, aimed at changing attitudes about violence against women. While this campaign aims to encourage parents (and others) to engage in these conversations and emphasises the importance of their role, the ads themselves do not provide any detail about how to navigate those conversations (although the campaign website has a conversation guide). At the time of writing, the campaign is also focused on that higher level and sometimes amorphous concept of 'respect', which is an important plank of RSE but does not engage with specific detail of sexual health, wellbeing, and consent.[10] This is because the advertising campaign has a broader, more general goal of preventing violence against women. Of course, an advertising campaign is necessarily limited in purpose and scope: this is why greater investment in engaging parents in RSE is necessary. As with the implementation of RSE in schools, government resources can go a long way to engaging and educating parents, caregivers, and community at scale — provided they do so in consultation with RSE experts, of course. A 2022 ad campaign launched by NSW government targets young people directly with depictions of how to communicate consent in sexual settings. The campaign was designed in consultation with a wide range of stakeholders, including young people. More of this would be wonderful.

In terms of how to navigate sexually explicit media, one important thing we can do is explain that pornography is a type of entertainment, not a how-to manual, and one that does not depict consent or communication. If we are going to use the word 'unrealistic' to describe porn, we ought to explain what we mean by that, because 'real' sex is not only for married heterosexual couples in the missionary position. We might explain that there are many different ways to experience pleasure in sex, and that it is not only cis men whose desires matter. That women have sexual agency and like sex, too, but not necessarily in the way shown in most porn. And, on that note, we ought to explain that not all women look the way most are depicted in porn. That even though the actors don't seem to be using protection, it may be because they've all been tested for STIs. Most of all, we should explain that in real life people do not just start having sex without communicating about it, and that communication in sex need not be degrading. This is why consent to one thing does not mean consent to another — everyone has different ways of enjoying sex, and the only way to find out is to ask.

The conversation should extend beyond pornography, to those other kinds of sexually explicit media and innocuous places. What about the relationship dynamics in the programs and sitcoms we watch over dinner? What about the possessiveness and jealousy that participants display in reality TV shows about 'finding love', like *Married at First Sight*, *Love Island*, and *Too Hot to Handle*? Possessiveness and jealousy are not signs of love at all, nor are things like love-bombing and negging: red flags, all of them. Are we also watching programs like Netflix's *Sex Education*, which celebrate queer relationships, not just heterosexual ones? Charlie enjoyed pornography that depicts threesomes (between two women and a man) and 'lesbian' sex, and in a world that privileges heterosexuality as the norm, and an absence of comprehensive education about LGBTQIA+ sexualities and identities, he was left alone with the repeated messages that two women having sex was for his titillation. He treated Lina as an avenue to that.

Of course, these conversations can feel incredibly stilted,

unnatural, and uncomfortable, and I appreciate that young people aren't always receptive. But, as Australian psychosexual therapist Lisa Torney says, the more you practise talking about sex, the less difficult it becomes — and it's our job to show that the everyday adults in their lives will help to normalise this topic for them. We need to work out how to talk to our kids about sex in a way that feels most comfortable. It is important that young people have trusted adults they can talk to, people they feel safe to ask questions of. This isn't just parents and caregivers — it could be a trusted aunt, uncle, grandparent, older sibling, cousin, or family friend. Ericka Hart, the US-based sexuality, racial, and social justice educator featured in Netflix's *The Principles of Pleasure* said in Episode 3: 'My advice for parents or guardians when you're talking to your kids about sex is to not shame them. Whatever they ask, try your hardest not to be like, "Ew!".'

If talking is simply too uncomfortable — and even if it's not — what about books on bodies (ones that don't censor out the clitoris!) and consent that young people can read in their own time? Providing evidence-based sources of information is key to young people making sense of the messages they see. Young people need to know where to get accurate information: we can give them options, but they need to know what those options are.

Comprehensive RSE in schools is, ideally, an evidence-based source of information for young people. Parents and communities should feel empowered to advocate for their kids' right to information both at home and at school. I know of many parents who, as key stakeholders of their kids' school, have encouraged the school to implement better sex-ed. EducateUS (an RSE advocacy group in the United States) has produced a guide for parents and other community members who want to advocate for improved RSE in schools, called 'So You Want to Speak Up For Sex Education'.

Schools already teach young people to 'read' media critically, and can incorporate an RSE perspective in that. If we're going to keep teaching Shakespeare, are we talking about the gendered and relationship dynamics in his work? The expectations of how the protagonists in the syllabus texts will behave romantically? In history class, are we teaching about the way masculine and feminine ideals developed — and whether they've changed? Do young people (including boys) learn about why the contraceptive pill was so instrumental to women's liberation, for example? As Alice Cruttwell, the Respect Yourself RSE program designer I met with in Shropshire, suggested: 'Does the science lab have pictures of influential women scientists on the wall as well as men?' This is part of a whole-school approach that we looked at in the last chapter as well, ensuring RSE lessons are supported across the curriculum. Incorporating sex-ed into existing subjects and across the curriculum is the practice in the Netherlands, and a review of three decades of sex-ed literature offered strong support for comprehensive sex education that is embedded across subject areas as having the potential to improve sexual, social, and emotional health (as well as academic outcomes!).[11]

Both at home and at school we can give young people the information they need to make sense of the messages they get from porn and other sexually explicit media. As Bradfield says, 'If we don't talk about sexuality, about pleasure, about consent as something we value and embody, then we are not giving young people the information they need to prioritise that for themselves. We can't just tell them they need consent, we need to tell them why it matters.'

I want to return to the example I gave earlier, of people who have experienced choking during sex without being asked beforehand. What does that say about the comfort level and capacity to communicate about sex — before, during, and after?

We saw how, after he put his hands around her neck without asking, Lina and Charlie were able to have a conversation about what they enjoyed sexually, even though Lina felt frightened and Charlie felt mortified. Not everyone would be able to do that, in those circumstances especially, but perhaps even at all. Lina has had some prior positive sexual experiences, is a little older than Charlie, and was willing and able to have that discussion with him. But what if it was her first sexual experience? Or if she felt unable or unsafe to say anything to Charlie? What if she froze? What if Charlie got defensive and sulky, or insisted that she would like it? That these two were able to have a conversation, that Lina was able to show Charlie what sexual pleasure looked like for her, and that he cared enough to listen and respond, is not a universal experience.

Good for Lina and for Charlie, but it should not have been left to her to educate him that consent to one act isn't consent to another. Or that consent to one person isn't consent to another. What if he had gone into the relationship with better knowledge, if he had developed those skills earlier, more comprehensively? Even after that conversation, at best, Charlie still did not really know how to talk to Lina. At worst he didn't care enough, clumsily orchestrating a sexual experience that he wanted to have, without talking to her about it first. He may well have had absolutely no idea how to approach the idea with Lina, but he was also deliberately underhanded.

According to Torney, teaching young people that they have a right to happy, healthy, pleasurable sex lives is key to supporting people to have open conversations with each other about sex. We need to reshape our expectations and learn 'how to have sexual conversations and to be curious without shame, stigma, and embarrassment,' she says. And again, the more you practise talking about sex, the less difficult it becomes. *What are you into?* can be incredibly powerful, along with *Is there something you'd like to do instead?*

But many of us believe that communicating during sex will kill the mood, or we simply don't know how to do it without ruining the vibe. It comes back to what we looked at in Chapter 3, the expectations we've cultivated that nobody talks about sex or during sex. That it's embarrassing or awkward or clinical.

Much porn doesn't show you how to say I've changed my mind, how to ask for something. How often does it show people asking, 'Can I pull your hair?' or 'Can I put my hand on your throat?' and how often do they just do those things? Does it show people answering no to those questions, or responding 'Can you spank me instead?' Does it depict any kind of communication that is required for mutual navigation, or just people apparently getting pleasure out of exactly the same thing without ever establishing what that might be? Miraculous!

I'm going to break my rule of no food analogies for sex and consent, in aid of this point: if you have guests over for dinner, you probably ask if there is anything they don't like or are allergic to. Better yet, you probably ask if they like what you propose to serve. You might even ask if there is something in particular they want you to make for them. But in sex, too many of us prefer to leave it to guesswork. Or to use the sexual act *as the question*, as I said in Chapter 3. But in sexual activity the stakes are just too high, and once you have your hands around someone's neck, for example, it is too late to ask if that's okay or set any ground rules.

The idea that talking kills the mood is an idea we have created; it's made up. We make all sorts of things sexy — different clothes, hairstyles, body types. Hirsute men were sexy in the seventies and eighties, but by the nineties, denuded men were all the rage. The fashion of body shapes fluctuates every decade. We somehow made it attractive and a sign of romance for a man to act jealous and possessive about a woman he loves — I think we can work out how to make it sexy when someone gives a damn about what someone else wants in bed. Because you know what actually does kill the mood? Someone having a bad time, a negative experience.

Torney says we need to not just teach young people *how* to communicate, but work at normalising that type of communication. Normalising that it's ok to be vulnerable, to expect to have your choices respected. She says this will lead to more satisfying sexual experiences for everyone — including not having them if you don't want to.

In some of our workshops with university students, Nina Funnell and I do a particular activity that is always a favourite for the participants. It is popular because it gives them a concrete, practical example of how to communicate *during* sex. It also happens to be an exercise in reading sexually explicit media — something that we obviously can't do by showing pornography in a classroom!

There was an HBO program called *Tell Me You Love Me*, and in it, a character goes out to a bar and picks up a handsome young lad and they go home together. They begin to hook up — they're kissing, they get undressed, they're both enthusiastic. She suggests they have sex and goes to get a condom, before they continue with the kissing and the touching. But then, all of a sudden, her mood shifts. In the context of the show, the inference is that she realises she doesn't really want this anymore. The camera focuses in on her face, a tight frame. Then the guy stops and asks, 'Are you not into this?' She doesn't respond. In fact, she hasn't said anything at all for the whole scene, since she went to get the condom. The guy says 'That's all right. It's okay,' and rolls off her to sit on the floor next to the couch where she is still lying.

We pause the scene there and ask the students whether that was a 'successful' sexual encounter. Some say yes, some say no. But those who say yes, cite the fact that he picked up on her mood shift and respected it, that he didn't try to press on. We discuss the things he might have noticed, given she didn't say anything at all — her change in body language, that she went still, that she wasn't making eye contact anymore and was covering her face with her hand. As I argued in Chapter 3, these things alone don't automatically mean she was not consenting — but that's just the thing: he asked. We discuss with the students not just what her conduct and body language communicated, but what he did in response. The way he asked and made it safe for her, hitting the brakes at the slightest inkling that her enthusiasm had dissipated.

I do wish there was more sexually explicit media like this in the world, but until there is — the least we can do is talk about it. It sounds almost too simple, but the reality is that when we break it down with the young folk in these sessions, you can almost see the cartoon lightbulbs going off above their heads.

It sounds almost too simple, but sometimes the answer is right in front of us.

9

Lessons Earned

Ethan and Oscar

Oscar sat across from the school counsellor, having been summoned to her office. The small room had only one tiny window, high on the wall, under stairs that led up to the music classrooms, which meant you often had to talk about your feelings to the strains of badly played instruments.

He looked at the counsellor expectantly. He didn't know what he was here for; he hadn't been told. He didn't think he was in trouble for anything, though, because surely that would mean the principal's office.

'Oscar, I know you're relatively new to the school. We haven't had a chance to meet yet.'

He wasn't sure if he was meant to say anything to that.

'How are you finding things?'

'Good.'

'You're making friends okay?'

'Yep,' Oscar nodded awkwardly.

'That's good, that's great.' She shifted in her seat as she seemed to search for what to say next. 'Look, we've just noticed that you've been spending a lot of time with Ethan.'

'Yep.' He was aware he was giving monosyllabic answers, but had no idea what she was getting at.

'I just wanted to talk to you about that. You shouldn't feel obliged to spend all your time with Ethan if you don't want to.'

'He's my friend, though?' Oscar was confused.

'Well, that's very nice. That's honestly lovely to hear, because he can struggle sometimes, socially. But we just want to make sure you're comfortable and don't feel any pressure. He can be quite rigid.' The counsellor paused, and Oscar felt like she was expecting him to nod along or murmur in agreement.

The counsellor dropped her voice slightly. 'Ethan is on the autism spectrum.'

Upstairs someone fumbled in the middle of piano practice, the jarring sound of discordant keys punctuating the tension.

'Yeah, I know...?' Oscar said, cocking his head to the side.

Of course he knew Ethan was autistic — even though Oscar was new to the school, it wasn't like it was a secret. He was just Ethan, and it was part of who he was. Since coming here, Oscar hadn't noticed anyone treating it as a big deal, so he was taken aback by this oddly serious briefing from the counsellor.

But Oscar hadn't been at the school long enough to know of the *Incidents*, so-called, in documents buried deep inside filing cabinets in the administration office.

When Ethan was 13, there was a school camp. They'd travelled by bus to a semi-rural area near the coast, where there were cabins and bunk beds and a mess hall. They did a bunch of activities like abseiling and archery and team games. There seemed to be two kinds of kids on that trip: those who loved the camp activities, and those who hated them. Ethan was firmly in the latter category.

They did get to go swimming, though — there was a shallow part of the creek that was safe to swim in, and Ethan's parents had dutifully packed his bathers as per the preparation list that had been sent home. His camp group had been allocated swimming time one afternoon, and their instructor was focused on helping some of the kids, the sun high in the sky.

They were all swimming together. Ethan watched the girls splashing around in their togs. He'd grown up with most of them, but this year something was different. They looked different; their bodies had changed, and he felt different about it. For whatever reason he was fascinated by them, and didn't want to take his eyes off them. It made him feel funny inside, an almost-uncomfortable kind of stirring in his tummy.

He was floating around alongside them when he rolled over onto his back in the water. One of the girls squealed and pointed at him. 'ETHAN!' She covered her mouth with her hand, her eyes laughing. 'Do you have a boner?!' He looked down and saw that he had an erection.

All the girls started giggling and some even covered their eyes. He wasn't sure why it had to be *such* a big deal — he remembered when it first started happening to his older brother a few years before, and he'd explained to Ethan how it was just part of growing up. But Ethan didn't like being made fun of, so he rolled over to tread water, covering his crotch with his hands, willing it to go away.

'Poor little Ethan,' one of the girls cooed. Sometimes the girls liked to baby him, because he was autistic. It was annoying.

'Ethan, have you touched boobs before?' the same girl said in a singsong voice, the kind his mum used to speak to the family labrador. The rest of the girls laughed.

'Of course he hasn't!' Stephanie giggled. 'Do you want to touch mine, Ethan?'

Ethan wasn't sure if they were still making fun of him.

'Go on, try it.' She paddled towards him.

At that moment, the instructor called to the kids to come out of the water.

Only a few months later, they had the school swimming carnival. Ethan sat in the bleachers, his feet uncomfortably damp in his thongs and his legs poking out from his shorts with a greasy white sheen on them, from sunscreen that refused to be fully rubbed in. The smell of chlorine filled the humid air. He sat alone, listening to the older boys behind him talking about how the girls looked in their swimmers, sometimes even wolf-whistling. A teacher scolded them for being show-offs.

Stephanie had just won the hundred-metre freestyle in the year group and was making her way back to their house area in the bleachers. She sat down near Ethan, not right next to him but close enough that she heard him say, 'Congratulations, Stephanie.' She turned to see who had spoken, 'Oh, thanks, Ethan.' She smiled, pulling off her swimming cap.

She was wearing the same bathers as she had at camp. Ethan stared at her chest as he remembered her offer in the creek that day. One of the boys behind them whooped, 'Look at this kid, checking out her rack! Don't make it weird, my man, you need to be more subtle.' Egged on by his mates' laughter, he carried on. 'Here, wear my sunnies.' The guy made a show of mockingly holding out his sunglasses. Everyone was looking now.

'Oh my god, Ethan!' Stephanie muttered, mortified, covering her face with her hands, before pulling her towel around her and disappearing to the toilet block.

The teacher saw the incident unfold, and called Ethan aside to tell him off. There was something different in their tone, compared to the one they'd used to scold the other boys earlier — there was a note of panic in it. Later, Ethan was sent to the counsellor's office, and she spoke to him in a saccharine voice about inappropriate behaviour and how he had made Stephanie feel embarrassed. Ethan felt frustrated: being mocked had made him embarrassed, too. He wondered if any of the other boys were spoken to.

A couple of years later, there was an afternoon when his year group and the one above were filing down to the gym for PE. As they were heading there, Ethan was pulled aside by his homegroup teacher: 'Ethan, would you like to go to the library and work on your science project instead of going to PE?'

This happened once or twice a year; Ethan hated PE and he liked the library, so it suited him. At some point he had figured out that this occurred when the other kids were getting a special sort of health class to do with puberty and sex and stuff, but he was used to this arrangement, and to being singled out sometimes on account of being autistic.

This time, Ethan was leaving the library at the end of the hour at the same time as some of the boys from the year above were returning from PE. They saw him and realised he hadn't been in the session with them.

'Didn't you want to learn about *sexting*, Ethan?' one of them called out.

He turned around. 'What's sexting?'

The boys looked at each other, grinning. 'It's something you do when you like a girl, mate. You send her a photo of your … you know,' he whistled and gestured at Ethan's crotch.

Ethan looked at them, unsure.

'Nah, for real. We all do it.' He gestured to the group around him.

It was true that in the last year or so some of the guys had started swapping nudes with girls they liked or were dating. Of course, it was almost always in circumstances where the other person was receptive, or at the very least where the sender knew they wouldn't get in trouble for it.

'When you're chatting to a girl who you like, you just—' he whistled again, making a masturbatory gesture with his hand, 'get it up and then send her a photo of it. They love it.' Ethan didn't notice that the guy's smile was more Cheshire Cat grin. The other boys nodded.

Ethan liked it when the guys included him, instead of mocking him. They usually oscillated between the two, sometimes being quite protective of Ethan and other times giving him a hard time. He liked it when he didn't feel on the outer.

That night he thought about what they'd said, and he felt good about the idea of being able to tell them the next day he'd done it, of feeling part of their group.

Everyone found out Ethan had sent a dick pic to one of the girls in their grade, because he got in trouble for it. This incident had earned him another trip to the counsellor's office and another discussion about inappropriate behaviour, and she used that voice again.

There were a few other incidents over the years, and it always went the same way. The school kept careful notes each time, in tones of increasing concern. And each time, Ethan was left increasingly confused.

Oscar started halfway through Year 11, and he and Ethan became friends quite soon after. The more time they spent together, the more natural it felt to Oscar that he and Ethan were drawn to each other. Finding each other outside the library most mornings as they waited for it to open, they were at the start of a beautiful friendship — although one that would experience scrutiny.

Ethan found himself thinking about Oscar a lot. He craved his company and something about being with him felt like home. He'd never had a boyfriend or a girlfriend, but Oscar gave him those fluttery, airy sensations he had experienced the other couple of times he'd had a crush on someone. Oscar was interesting to talk to, and made him laugh. He was also handsome, with lips that looked really soft. Ethan wondered what it would be like to kiss him. He hoped he wasn't imagining that Oscar also seemed interested — he would read the books Ethan talked about, and would suggest shows or music that he thought Ethan would enjoy.

Oscar realised he was developing a thing for Ethan when he found himself buying extra red frogs at the canteen every lunchtime because he knew Ethan liked them, handing them over in that little white paper bag like a love letter. He noticed himself waking up most mornings excited to go to school, to get to the library and spend time with Ethan before classes started. Some days he felt like he had to sit on his hands to stop from reaching out and taking hold of Ethan's.

As they spent an increasing amount of time together, Oscar asked his friend Cass about him.

'Do you think Ethan likes me like that?'

Cass was quick to shake her head. 'I don't know if he would see anyone like that. He probably just wants to be your friend.'

Oscar's heart dropped a little, but he wasn't sure he agreed.

He decided to take the next opportunity to say something. It arrived when they were walking from the bike rack to the library one morning. Rather than meeting him there, Oscar had intercepted Ethan where he knew he locked up his bike. He figured it would give him enough time to say something without being interrupted by the librarian unlocking the doors. He was also impatient; now that he had decided to profess his feelings, he couldn't wait a moment longer.

As they made their way across the oval, Oscar was glad to be walking side by side so he could look at the ground in front of him as he spoke, nervous and shy suddenly. He finished saying his piece as they passed behind the equipment sheds on the side of the oval.

'I guess what I'm saying is, I'd like to go out. Like on a date. If that's something you would like,' he concluded awkwardly, his heart beating in his ears as he waited for what felt like an eternity before Ethan replied.

'I would like that too,' Ethan said with a little nod, happiness bubbling up inside him. Something about that nod, so small but so sure, made Oscar's heart sing, and he stopped walking to reach for Ethan's hand.

'Can I kiss you?' Oscar ventured softly, desire starting to hum across his skin.

The idea of it made Ethan feel a rush of excitement, he'd thought about it so many times already. Now that the moment had arrived, his stomach knotted up with a thrill, but the nerves weren't only for Oscar. Ethan felt anxious: anytime he had done or said or been anything remotely 'sexual' at school, he'd been reprimanded for it. He was worried about getting in trouble, about being regulated.

He was right to be: some teachers had been watching the developing friendship between Ethan and Oscar and were 'keeping an eye on it', worried that Oscar might be feeling a bit wedged in by Ethan's 'rigidity' and a fear of being rude. Oscar hadn't even told Ethan about his own trip to the counsellor's office.

But the urge to kiss Oscar was stronger than his anxiety, and so Ethan nodded. Oscar's back was to the shed, and he pulled Ethan into him as their lips met.

Just then, one of the PE teachers was walking down to the oval to set up for the first period. They saw Oscar's back against the shed and Ethan's hands either side of him, palms against the wall as he kissed him.

Oscar heard the teacher bark Ethan's full name and jumped in shock, taken aback by the sternness in it. 'I think we're in trouble,' Oscar whispered, as the teacher approached them.

The spell of his first kiss broken, Ethan knew he was. He waited for the reprimand but it didn't come at first. He saw the teacher's hand outstretched towards him, in the way the crossing guards would hold up their hand to stop traffic outside the school gates to let the kids cross the road. But the teacher wasn't looking at him, they were looking at Oscar.

'Oscar, are you all right?' the teacher asked.

'Our students all have complex needs; they'll never have a relationship.'

When a school for students with learning disabilities in the UK refused to send school staff to RSE workshops, run by a team at the Lincolnshire County Council, this was the reason they offered.

Lincolnshire is an area in England not far from Doncaster, and I had travelled to the town of Lincoln after my time with Lynnette Smith and the Big Talk team. It's a quaint place, which is home to an original 1215 Magna Carta and boasts the fourth-steepest hill in England — helpfully named, in case I had missed the burning in my calves, Steep Hill. I was there to meet with Jan Hargrave and Elita Cozens, the Lincolnshire Council team's specialists in RSE, with an emphasis on students with disabilities. The pair were extensively involved in RSE delivery and implementation in Lincolnshire Council (recall that, in the UK, county councils are responsible for education and social care for their area). Hargrave and Cozens supported schools and training providers to develop and implement RSE to meet the diverse needs of all students.

Just as in this school in England, which had decided on behalf of its students that they had no need of RSE, kids with disabilities all around Australia and the rest of the world are getting pulled out of sex-ed classes.[1] And that's if they are at a school where it is even offered. 'Young people with disabilities may never access relationships and sexuality education, even if they're in a mainstream school,' Breanna Coyle, clinical sexologist, had told me back in Dublin. And if young people with disabilities do access RSE, 'many do not receive sexuality education that is oriented to their needs and development, promotes a positive image of sexuality, or aims to empower them'.[2]

As we have explored throughout this book, we already punt RSE to the too-hard basket — for disabled and neurodivergent kids, it's even worse. Here is where our fear and shame around sexuality, and our apathy about RSE as less important or too contentious, intersect with our systemic failings for people with disabilities. The inclination to deny agency, to exclude and segregate, to think of accessibility as too much trouble. When it comes to RSE for disabled and neurodivergent kids, these things collide in spectacular fashion.

A scoping review of obstacles to sexuality education for young people with disabilities in the WHO European region identified seven barriers:

> (1) social misperceptions of people with disabilities as asexual and (2) in need of protection, combined with (3) limited support for educators, resulting in (4) non-comprehensive and normative sexuality education. Additionally, educators seem (5) to redirect responsibility for the provision of sexuality education to one another. Furthermore, (6) diversity among children and young people with disabilities, even within one specific type of disability, is large, making a general approach difficult. This diversity in types

> and severity of disabilities is combined with diversity in religious and cultural backgrounds. Finally, (7) competing priorities related to the health of children and young people with disabilities may position sexuality education low down on the list of issues to be addressed.[3]

The limits of my expertise and lived experience mean I am not able to speak to the whole story of RSE for young people with disabilities, and I don't wish to speak 'for' a group of people that I do not and cannot represent. I can, however, speak to what I've learned about the way schools and other institutions respond to this need, and demonstrate how all the other factors needed to successfully implement RSE — young people's agency, government support, specialism in design and delivery, qualified teachers and equipped schools, engaged parents — are even more important when it comes to disabled and neurodivergent kids.

Ethan was treated as though he was a potential perpetrator of sexual harassment by his school, whose primary concern seemed to be that his autism was a liability to the other kids in this way. The things Ethan did or said that the school freaked out about were things you could well imagine any of his neurotypical peers doing too — indeed they often were doing those things, and more — but the school reacted as though being autistic made Ethan a ticking time bomb, and he was treated as a challenge the school had to deal with.

When I was in Holland, I spoke to Robert van der Gaag, an RSE professional in a municipal health department in Leiden, who talked about how our fear of the unknown drives us. 'Parents and teachers are fearful about sexual behaviour displayed by a young person; they may not know whether it is normal or if it signals something worse, like they've experienced child abuse,' he said. He told me of entire primary schools in Holland 'falling apart', because of this fear of the unknown, when *incidents* happen.

It is a fear that is accentuated when it comes to neurodivergent and disabled children. 'Schools are fearful about neurodivergent kids displaying sexualised behaviour, so much so that anything with a sexual connotation is seen as sexualised behaviour even if it is not,' Hargrave said to me. She told me a story about a young neurodivergent boy at a school they worked with, who lifted up a teacher's skirt one day. The school was very concerned about this incident, fretting about what it meant and what they ought to do about it, but it transpired that his last teacher had left on maternity leave, and this kid was checking whether his new teacher was pregnant.

Van der Gaag optimistically identified this fear of the unknown as an opportunity to improve RSE in schools, to equip teachers to feel more confident about it, and to assist parents to learn as well. Recall that he was the one who told me of a sex-ed triangle: education of children, education of parents, and education of teachers. However, as we've examined in previous chapters, we might be fearful of sexual behaviours and the unknown, but we're also afraid that sex-ed will promote those things.

We worry that RSE will encourage young people to do things they aren't ready for, or to cross boundaries and behave inappropriately. But, as Hargrave said to me, 'If kids don't know what's appropriate how will they know what's inappropriate?' RSE equips young people with the information they need to understand boundaries, what kind of behaviour is okay and what isn't.

The Lincolnshire Council team expressed it thus: 'Young people with disabilities have the same risks as others, just amplified.' We know that disabled people face a much higher likelihood of experiencing sexual violence and abuse: Australian Bureau of Statistics data showed that 16 per cent of adults with disability have experienced sexual violence after the age of 15, compared with 9.6 per cent without disability.[4] The Australian Law Reform Commission has noted that while there is a lack of research that documents the extent of sexual violence against people with disabilities, one 2004 study found that 90 per cent of women with intellectual disabilities had been sexually abused; and 68 per cent of women with an intellectual disability will be subjected to sexual abuse before they reach 18 years of age. This prevalence is consistent with overseas studies.[5] Different dependency needs may mean disabled and neurodivergent people are at increased risk of abuse in their own homes and in institutionalised settings, for example.

RSE alone will not eliminate this risk; there are many other instruments and systemic changes we must invest in as well, to ensure the safety and wellbeing of people with disabilities. As highlighted by the 2021 Rapid Evidence Review of the Royal Commission into Violence, Abuse, Neglect and Exploitation of People with Disability: 'Few to no studies examined the role of perpetrators and the systemic factors that enable the perpetrators to target people with disabilities, often repeatedly. Rather than identifying the ways in which the people who are closest to the person with disability, care workers, communities and society fail, the research generally focuses on the ways in which people with disability struggle within existing systems.'[6] In respect of RSE, as Christiane Erkens, the sexualised violence prevention professional at BZgA in Cologne, expressed it to me: 'We want to build resilience in kids, without putting responsibility entirely on them to protect themselves from sexualised violence.' That said, RSE that equips disabled and neurodivergent people with information and skills to recognise healthy relationships, to assert their own and to respect others' boundaries, and to navigate consent, remains a significant protective factor.

As we have seen in previous chapters, however, the purpose of RSE must not be limited to protecting against sexual abuse and negative sexual experiences: 'In practice, this means … providing people with the means to experience sexuality positively (i.e. through sex education programmes) and to include topics such as sexual diversity and how to have pleasurable sex.'[7] Indeed, 'incomplete and inadequate sexuality education has been identified as a main factor impeding the development and execution of the sexuality of people with disabilities'.[8] We will return to this a little later in this chapter.

The call for universal access to RSE means just that: universal.

Schools must ensure all kids have access to RSE and that it's delivered in a way that is accessible and inclusive for all students, rather than waiting for an 'incident' to happen in the school community and then panic-reacting. This is a frequent response, when we let fear drive us. 'Incidents' seem to be a common trigger for schools recognising the utility of RSE, whether for the whole school community or for neurodivergent and disabled kids specifically. Schools will rush to do some RSE, often bringing in expert external providers or figures like police officers, as a 'sticking plaster' on the issue, as Lynnette Smith of Big Talk Education described it.

But, as we have seen in earlier chapters, it is imperative that RSE is lifelong, starting from a young age and embedded across the curriculum, delivered consistently and frequently. We have already seen how inconsistent, and often rare, this can be. With Ethan's story, we see how the factors needed to implement sex-ed effectively are especially important for people with disabilities.

Often, disabled and neurodivergent kids are pulled out of sex-ed because there is uncertainty about whether the content is going to be too confusing. Teachers may not know how to teach it in a way that accommodates that child's learning needs. As we saw in Chapter 4, teachers are hardly trained in RSE, if at all — let alone with the additional specialism required to make relevant accommodations for kids with differentiated learning needs. Imagine if we had the kind of public commitment to relationships and sexuality education that I saw in places like the Netherlands and Germany, the commitment to RSE as a specialist area that deserves investment of resources and experts. People whose whole job is dedicated to making sure sex-ed is designed with the needs of all kids in mind. People who have the capacity, resources, and lived experience to modify RSE curricula to accommodate different learning needs and to ensure those who deliver it are equipped and feel confident to meet those needs in a way that is relevantly accessible. The resources and capacity to ensure disability-specific sexuality education is delivered, such as lessons that include appropriate tactile experiences for vision-impaired students, or providing materials that are also available in Braille, and building sex-ed websites that have speech-to-text functionality, as I saw in Germany, or dedicated material for young people with autism, as I saw in Ireland.

Some Australian high school girls with intellectual disabilities participated in an inclusive study about their sex education experience, and suggested that their sex education could have been improved by things like simplified language, visual aids, explanations of vocabulary, and the use of a question box for students to pose their questions about sexuality anonymously.

Visual resources like books and videos, as well as modelling and role-playing of skills, have been found to be useful aids in delivering RSE to students with intellectual disability. Individualising RSE delivery for these students is also important to its efficacy.[9]

There are certainly examples of such approaches and materials in Australia and other countries too, but this book is concerned with the structural: as ever, it is not good enough to pin our hopes on individuals and schools and grassroots efforts. *All* schools must be supported to deliver RSE, with confidence, to *all* their students, so that kids like Ethan don't get sent off to the library because it's too hard, or because it seems like a convenient time for kids with disabilities to catch up on other lessons. School is where many kids develop extrafamilial relationships — especially for disabled and neurodivergent kids — but so many schools don't know where to start. Hargrave and Cozens' team in the Lincolnshire Council help conduct RSE audits at schools to get the lay of the land and to identify what needs work. They then help those schools to develop targeted action plans that are inclusive of disabled and neurodivergent kids, as well as things like peer support groups for teachers who are learning to deliver RSE.

The lives young people have outside of schools must be brought into the equation too. As we saw in Chapter 8, it's vital that parents and caregivers are engaged in the RSE effort. This is particularly important for parents of neurodivergent and disabled kids, in part because of potential dependency needs, some of which may be long-term. As Coyle said to me: 'What supports are there for someone parenting a child with disability — is the infrastructure there?' Furthermore, 'lives outside school' does not just mean parents: relationships education for people with disabilities will be relevant to things like supported apprenticeships and supported living. It is important to equip all professionals and caregivers of people with disabilities, for those professionals and caregivers may 'react negatively, express disapproval, and perpetuate negative emotions (e.g. guilt, remorse, shame, etc.) when encountering sexual expression and/or normal sexual behaviours in people with … disabilities'.[10]

A 34-year-old woman who 'lives with cerebral palsy, a mild to moderate intellectual disability, epilepsy, paralysis on the left side, and is partially sighted and hard of hearing', told Australia's Disability Royal Commission that at the first group home she lived in, she 'shared her desire to date men and experience intimate or sexual relationships, but found staff dismissive'. She had a set of rules imposed upon her that were not imposed on other residents, which forced her 'to have dates away from the house. She was not allowed to receive visitors after 6pm and was told to leave the door open when she had visitors during the day. Even when she was engaged to be married, in 2014–15, she was not allowed to have her fiance visit her room with the door closed or stay the night.' On one date that she had away from the group home, she was sexually assaulted. Ultimately, one staff member organised sex education for the woman, which she 'described as "minimal". She wanted face-to-face teaching from a female support worker and DVDs about sex and relationships but instead got "childish" picture books about how sperm fertilise eggs.'[11]

RSE is a protective factor for all young people, including for neurodivergent and disabled kids who are at increased risk of abuse and exploitation. In Ethan's case, perhaps if his school hadn't excluded him from sex-ed and had done more to instil values of respect and inclusivity in his peers, they may not have so readily exploited him, finding fun in encouraging Ethan to send an unsolicited dick pic to someone. Wanting to fit in with peers, feeling pressure to behave a certain way sexually, is something all kids experience — perhaps especially those who are already treated as different.

This is the price of throwing up our hands because it's all too hard. Of the particular risks faced by disabled and neurodivergent kids, Coyle said: 'If you know this protects somebody, why are you not jumping to act now? What happens if you knew you could protect and safeguard through education, and you didn't do it?'

When I heard about the school that said *Our students will never have a relationship*, I wondered: was that an assumption? Or was it a threat?

Hargrave and Cozens showed me a report into the needs of young Britons with disabilities who are at risk of sexual exploitation.[12] It reported an oft-held view on the part of institutions and social workers that the young people in their care will 'never be allowed to have any relationship and will never be allowed to have sex'. This approach to kids with disabilities or who are neurodivergent is common, and while it may be driven by a desire to protect them from exploitation, to me it sounds like a paternalistic threat.

Even as I advocate for the protective power that RSE offers, we must not pursue protection at the expense of agency. Yes, RSE may mitigate against the greater risk disabled people face of sexual violence, exploitation, and harassment, but as I have argued in the last two chapters, there is very real danger in framing RSE as a tool only for harm-prevention. As we have seen, the key is empowerment, not paternalism.

When it comes to RSE, there is danger in pursuing the idea that we can prevent young people from being exposed to all the things we believe are a risk to sexual wellbeing, rather than equipping them to navigate the myriad situations and moments they will meet in life. For example, participants in the Australian study of the sex education experience of students with intellectual disabilities had a common experience of teachers 'warning them of the internet and its dangers, rather than preparing them for safe use of the internet or [providing them] with the skills needed to navigate the online world'.[13] For disabled and neurodivergent people, this approach is often driven by a fear that *any* relationship or sexual activity will risk their sexual wellbeing, as though they do not have the capacity to consent to sexual activity, or that they are childlike forever. Magenta, a young person with cerebral palsy, wrote for the ABC's Triple J in 2021: 'It wasn't just the minimal sex-ed, either. Teachers actively discouraged us from romantic and sexual relationships. All they were doing was further perpetuating the stereotype that people with disabilities are essentially non-sexual creatures, which couldn't be further from my truth.'[14] As we saw in Chapter 7, sexual wellbeing is more than the absence of harm. It should go without saying that disabled people have fulfilling relationships and active sex lives, and that the right to sexual wellbeing belongs to everybody — it is not a privilege of the able-bodied and the neurotypical.

If 'our students will never have a relationship' was not a threat, it was an assumption. The same report Hargrave and Cozens showed me also included comments from institutions that 'our pupils don't have sex or don't think about it'. The assumption that people with disabilities are asexual is common, and we saw it in Cass's attitude when she said she did not think Ethan 'sees anybody like that'. If not asexual, it may be assumed that disabled and neurodivergent people are unlikely to find romance, that they won't have sexual experiences. We saw this in the attitude of the young girls in the creek when they patronised Ethan, when one of them offered for him to touch her in an apparently charitable gesture. And, whether they assumed he was asexual or that his feelings were not reciprocated, the school's default was to think of Ethan's behaviour as problematic and unwanted by Oscar. They did not contemplate the possibility that a mutual friendship was afoot, let alone that a romance was blossoming. These attitudes are magnified for disabled people of colour, who may be infantilised or pathologised to an even greater extent.

This is why it matters that RSE is inclusive, not just in ensuring everyone has access to it, but also in the way it teaches about sexuality and sexual wellbeing. RSE materials and lessons for all students must depict and represent people with disabilities: RSE must teach about the full spectrum of human experience, and that includes the fact that disabled and neurodivergent people enjoy fulfilling relationships and sex lives. Sex-ed has a role to play in dispelling, for all kids, the assumption that they don't. Perhaps such RSE could have dissuaded Ethan's peers from seeing his sexuality as something of amusement for themselves. Again, the expectation that *everyone* has the right to sexual wellbeing must be held, and be seen to be held.

Whether assumption or threat, 'our students will never have a relationship' attempts to strip disabled and neurodivergent people of agency and self-determination, and denies their right to sexual wellbeing. Cozens said to me, 'Every young person has the right to a relationship if they want it, but they deserve to understand what they need to do to keep themselves and each other safe.'

Hargrave told me of a neurodivergent boy she worked with who said, 'I'll be sixteen soon, and I'm worried because it means I'll have to have sex'. He had learned that 16 was the age of consent, and thought it meant he had to have sex at that age — he was very relieved to learn that he didn't. Equally, I read of a 19-year-old man with a disability, who asked whether he was allowed to say the word 'sex', because he had a girlfriend he wanted to have sex with but nobody would talk to him about it. Coyle said of her work, 'Young people are afraid of getting in trouble. We explain that it's not about punishing them for their sexuality, but giving them the support, information, and skills they have a right to.' We saw this fear of getting in trouble for one's sexuality in Ethan's story, as we did in Olivia's. For Ethan, it added a layer of anxiety to his first kiss with Oscar. This fear of being punished (whether by shame, embarrassment, or something else) can negatively impact self-esteem, willingness to explore intimacy and, ultimately, self-determination.[15]

Fear begot fear begot fear.

Paternalism often ignores the voices of those we purport to protect. A critical part of RSE for people with disabilities is 'consumer ownership'

— that is, 'the people for whom the program is intended … should be involved in all levels of the program development, including planning, implementation, evaluation and advisory boards'.[16] As I have emphasised throughout this book: including young people in the design and delivery of RSE is essential, and is a recognised core principle of quality RSE. It is critical that people with disabilities are involved in the design of RSE that meets their needs and promotes empowerment and sexual agency. The Sexual Lives and Respectful Relationships program in Australia, for example, was 'co-developed with individuals with intellectual disabilities. Importantly, the programme centres the lived experience of people labelled as intellectually disabled and makes use of peer education. In doing so, it challenges conventional ideas about "who the expert is in relation to sexuality in the lives of people with an intellectual disability" as well as "who the holder/s of knowledge are".'[17]

In Lincolnshire, Hargrave and Cozens told me of young people with disabilities who were undertaking training to be mentors for other young kids with disabilities: 'Children and young people with disabilities, their voices are not heard in terms of making changes. We need to encourage their advocacy, not just hide behind "I don't want to have this uncomfortable conversation",' Hargrave said to me. 'But,' she smiled wryly, lifting her hands to make air quotes with her fingers, '"adults know best".'

What if we took a different approach and recognised young people's rights to have those conversations that might make us uncomfortable? Article 23 of the United Nations Convention on the Rights of Persons with Disabilities provides for the right to:

- Free choice of marrying and starting a family
- Free choice concerning the number of desired children
- Access to age-appropriate information, reproductive and family planning education.

Article 25 of the same Convention provides for persons with disabilities' right to be provided 'the same range, quality and standard of free or affordable health care and programmes as provided to other persons, including in the area of sexual and reproductive health and population-based public health programmes'. Notably, Article 4 states: 'In the development and implementation of legislation and policies to implement the present Convention, and in other decision-making processes concerning issues relating to persons with disabilities, States Parties shall closely consult with and actively involve persons with disabilities, including children with disabilities ...'

There is recognition in the international community that the 'sexual and relationship needs of young people with ... disabilities are the same as for other young people, even though they may sometimes be expressed differently'.[18] Germany, for example, has ratified this particular UN Convention, and its Government's Action Plan for its implementation expressly supports the rights of persons with disabilities to marriage, partnership, and sexuality. To put that lofty support into practice, BZgA has a guidance document that expressly acknowledges that the 'goal of sexuality education is to support [people with disabilities] in accordance with their specific needs. It should enable them to have a sophisticated, self-determined ... relationship to their own sexuality'.[19] While Australia also ratified this Convention, in 2008, Australia's Disability Strategy 2021–2031 makes no positive commitment to RSE.[20]

This recognition that people with disabilities have a right to sexuality ought not be a radical concept, although perhaps it seems that way if we allow ourselves to be led by fear. Do we recognise a right to sexuality, to sexual wellbeing, at all? And what of the right to access education and information about those things?

On my last day in Lincoln, I visited the castle there. It has a vault the public can visit, where an original 1215 Magna Carta sits on display. The Charter represents the first time in British history that subjects of the Crown — individuals — were afforded legal rights and is widely considered a foundational document in the evolution of modern human rights.

As I rushed back up the hill to make my train, I wondered: can we ever truly promise empowerment, if we are ourselves governed by fear? Do we not have the courage of our convictions? Do we not take courage from the evidence, about the power of relationships and sexuality education? Do we not have faith in the next generation?

Perhaps we might if we listen to their voices, their advocacy. I have argued that to change course, to promise future generations their sexual wellbeing and freedom from sexual violence, we must talk and we must teach. But we must also listen.

In the Quietest of Places

We started this journey in Galway, the first stop on my fellowship. Remember my friends Sarah and Shaggy, who took me to the Cliffs of Moher? After bidding them goodbye, I hopped back on a train to Dublin. Apart from those I was interviewing for my research, there was one place I really wanted to visit in Ireland's capital.

I lined up for quite a while in the grey drizzle to get into the Long Room of the library at Trinity College — another very old and prestigious Irish university. Despite the wait and the weather, I was determined to see it, and to get my parents a souvenir from the gift shop. In my family, libraries are almost holy places.

The Trinity College Library is what's called a legal deposit, which means a copy of every book published in Ireland must be provided to the library free of charge. The purpose of a legal deposit is to preserve every book, and the knowledge it holds, for future generations, to make sure nothing is lost to history. Like a perennial gift, one that literally keeps on giving.

In Australia, the state libraries and the National Library are our legal deposits. The National Library sits on Lake Burley Griffin at the centre of Australia's capital city, among other imposing institutions that are meant to represent democratic freedoms, like the Australian Parliament House and the High Court of Australia. My parents worked at the National Library the year they had me. They are both librarians by profession: disciples of the transformative power that is access to information, and custodians of the precious right to do so. My parents taught me that education is a gift, knowledge is power, and the right to access information is sacrosanct.

I stood at the end of the Long Room and wished they could see it too, the rows and rows of books under those lofty ceilings, tourists marvelling in hushed tones at this beautiful building and the wisdom in its walls. I wonder at these places we create, these institutions we build up to represent us and serve us. And through them, the promises we make to ourselves and to each other.

'Access to information that can be used to make autonomous decisions is a right,' Dr Alex McKay said to me as I sat across from him in a Toronto café. He was the last person I interviewed for my fellowship before I made my way home, and with that simple statement I found myself having an epiphany over my flat white.

McKay, the Executive Director of the Sex Information and Education Council of Canada, said something that I realised I had been hearing expressed, in various ways, for months. While they all had different language for it, every person I spoke to about young people's access to RSE understood this information to be something young people are fundamentally entitled to.

And if we recognise that all of us have a right to sexual wellbeing, or at the very least the right to live free from sexual violence and harassment, then how do we ensure that right is protected and realised? The criminal justice system only recognises this right once it has been infringed (and even then, only sometimes). Looking back, we declare the violation of it wrong, unlawful, deserving of punishment. As though the right only matters, maybe even that it only exists, once it has been broken. And it depends entirely on the individual whose rights were traversed to speak up. What of those who are unable to secure, or even to seek, justice in the legal system? What of those who are never able to speak up, or who do not wish to travel that road? What of those whose right to sexual wellbeing and to live free from sexual violence has not been violated — yet?

Are there other rights that we only worry about once they've been violated? Or do we pour our efforts into protecting them in the first place? We build up institutions that are supposed to make good on the promise that we are all 'born free and equal in dignity and rights', purporting to ensure the right to freedom of thought, to a fair trial, to the highest attainable standard of health and education.

It would be dystopian if we refused to build hospitals and schools, only to later declare an individual's rights to health or education violated when they found themselves ill and unable to access necessary medical treatment, or unable to secure employment without adequate schooling. It is our duty to take positive steps to fulfil the inherent and inalienable rights that belong to us all, otherwise they have no meaning. So how can we justify only acting on the right to sexual safety and wellbeing once it has been abrogated? We shake our fists in outrage and wag our fingers in rebuke, with hands that must be numb, we've been sitting on them for so long.

We teach young people next to nothing of sex, sexuality, bodies, relationships, and the nuances of consent. We give them almost no guidance in a world that still perpetuates the drivers of sexual violence and, when the damage is done, we may reach for the biggest cane available to us in answer. Treating sexual violence as so grave that it warrants criminal punishment is one way of recognising that the right to sexual safety matters, and that a violation of it will be taken seriously. Working in her halls, I have seen how limited a role Lady Justice plays in the greater scheme of society when it comes to sexual violence. Sometimes the courts feel like castles in the sky: in reality, our justice system is clunky, blunt, imperfect, and necessarily concerned with its own functions.

As I said at the start of this book, the criminal justice system reminds me of a pawn on a chessboard: it is one piece of many, and can only advance in a limited way. When pawns are used strategically, they can be very influential — but no chess master would reach only for them. I do not say that the criminal justice system has no role to play, just as I do not say that relationships and sexuality education is a silver bullet. But when the stakes are so high, how do we justify doing anything less than everything, to protect the right to sexual safety and wellbeing?

While the right to sexual safety and wellbeing, or 'sexual rights', is not expressly recognised in fundamental human rights documents, it arguably flows from other rights. The WHO claims 'the application of existing human rights to sexuality and sexual health constitutes sexual rights'.[1] For example, the right to the highest attainable standard of physical and mental health ought to capture sexual safety and wellbeing (Article 12 of the International Covenant on Economic Social and Cultural Rights), as does the right to privacy (Article 17 of the International Covenant on Civil and Political Rights), which speaks to the 'physical and moral integrity of a person, including his or her sexual life' (*X and Y v the Netherlands* 1985). Furthermore, nobody could dispute that sexual violence seriously impacts quality of life, liberty, and security. The World Association of Sexual Health endorsed a revised Declaration of Sexual Rights in 2014, which was originally proclaimed in 1997.[2]

Formally recognised rights aside, we can all agree that everyone should expect to live free from sexual violence and harassment, and free from fear of those things. I hope we all agree that everyone should be free to pursue and safeguard their sexual wellbeing — whatever that means for them. As I argued in Chapter 7, sexual wellbeing is not just about sexual behaviour and pleasure: it is more holistic than that, and it is intrinsically linked to autonomy. The parts of us that crave intimacy, meaningful relationships, the joy of connection and sexual experiences are not an optional extra, not hedonism or vulgarity, not sinful: they are essential to the human condition, as important to us as eating, drinking, exercising. The violation of sexual safety and wellbeing can ruin lives, those who experience it irreversibly changed and futures cruelled. That alone should demonstrate how fundamental sexual safety and wellbeing are to our health and happiness. To our humanness.

One of our most basic human instincts is to seek out connection, friendship, love, and intimacy — and another is for autonomy. At the core of the human condition is a need to exercise autonomy over our bodies, and to engage in intimacy and sexuality on our own terms. We must recognise this as inherent and inalienable, the most fundamental of freedoms.

We may speak of human rights as lofty things, the concern of government machinery and international bodies and public institutions. But surely our cardinal human rights, those that speak to our inherent dignity and equality and freedom, are just as important in the moments we are most intimate, most human with each other. Perhaps they are *most* important then: if we do not cherish those rights in the quietest of places, what does that mean for us in the loudest? How can we hold ourselves up as bastions of human rights in the glare of the public eye, if we don't care about those rights when nobody is watching?

If we recognise that sexual safety and wellbeing is a fundamental right that warrants protection, then without *access* to that protection, it is a right in name only. As we have seen in each chapter of this book, the right to sexual safety and wellbeing, to pursue fulfilling relationships and connection, cannot be realised without access to information and education about those things. In fact, we have seen how the absence of that education not only leaves safety and wellbeing to chance, it may actively promote harm — at both an individual and a collective level. We have seen how comprehensive RSE can articulate positive values, can challenge harmful power structures and accepted norms that drive sexual violence and unwanted sexual experiences.

This is not radical, for we know the transformative power of education: people have crossed oceans, have risked everything in pursuit of it, as my grandparents did. Others have died in its name. One of the first mechanisms of oppression is to censor information and restrict access to education. We have long understood that education is key to securing justice, equality, opportunity, and freedom, and for that reason we recognise that the right to it belongs to us all.

This is what McKay meant when he said, 'Access to information that can be used to make autonomous decisions is a right.' Choices are not free — they are hardly even choices — if we do not know what it is we are choosing. If we do not know the choices available to us, nor how to give expression to them. If our choices will not be respected by others, who may not know, or care, to respect them. If our choices are governed by unspoken assumptions and social pressures that — without information and education — go unchallenged.

McKay's comment, which speaks to the relationship between information and autonomy, reminds me of my parents, the librarians. Because of them, I do not take the right to access information for granted. Because of them, I understand the purpose and symbolism of institutions like legal deposit libraries: access to information and ideas must be guaranteed for every generation. It is not that the preservation of books is the only way to do that (cultures with strong oral history traditions tell us that), but contemporary Australia gives life to this idea in the form of institutions such as the National Library of Australia. It is no accident that the National Library of Australia was built alongside places that represent democracy and the rule of law, places that are supposed to guarantee our freedoms and serve us all equally. At the highest levels and in the most formal places, we recognise the relationship between information, education, freedom, and autonomy. We promise young people their right to access information, their right to education, and with these things their freedom, their futures, their full potential.

And yet too many young Australians are denied access to information and education about *their* bodies. *Their* sexuality. *Their* wellbeing, their experiences and the choices they will face. We teach them about planets far away from here and people who died long ago, but too many will be refused information and education that matters to them here and now. Things critical to their daily, corporeal existence. Things that will materially impact their lives and futures, far more profoundly than the rings of Saturn ever will. We recognise that education is the answer to all manner of social issues, and yet all too often we consider sexual violence, unwanted sex, unhealthy relationships, poor sexual health and wellbeing the exceptions to that.

If we fear that young people accessing this information and education will be emboldened to behave sexually before they are 'ready', we are missing the truth that denying them that information before they need it, while we still have the chance to shape their expectations, denies them the autonomy and freedom they need to defend their own, and each other's, sexual wellbeing and safety as they get older.

Failing to give young people this education does not simply mean they might encounter a few tricky moments in life. That they may need to learn to stand on their own two feet and deal with conflict. That they just need to 'have self-respect'. It is not good enough to throw up our hands and say sexual violence and unwanted sex are just a part of life, that it's just how it is. Our failure to educate, to give young people accurate and relevant information about relationships, sex, and sexuality, actively causes harm to their lives and futures. And we let ourselves off the hook.

In my notes from a meeting I had in Dublin, all the way back at the beginning of my journey, and two days before I visited the Long Room of the library at Trinity College, I scrawled something at the bottom of a page. I can't remember if it's something my interview subject said, or my own musing: 'What if an individual takes legal action about their rights being abrogated because they didn't get RSE?' Two and a half months later, at the other end of my fellowship, McKay would tell me how, after Doug Ford was elected premier of Ontario and replaced Kathleen Wynne's updated RSE curriculum with the 20-year-old one, the Ontario Teachers Federation filed a court action against his government on the basis that it was a harm to the students. Transgender youth also filed a human rights action against the government on the same basis. In both the ensuing court and human rights tribunal proceedings, McKay appeared as an expert witness, carefully outlining the material harm that flows from a failure to provide comprehensive and accurate information about bodies, identity, gender, sex, sexuality, and relationships.

I understand that, in both the court and the tribunal proceedings, the matters were decided on a jurisdictional basis rather than on the substantive issue. Internationally, whether the state owes a positive obligation to provide relationships and sexuality education remains contested, although there are those who argue it flows from other human rights[3], such as the rights of children, the right to education, the right to health (which includes mental health), or from the right, insofar as it exists, to sexual safety, health, and wellbeing. The United Nations has promoted comprehensive sexuality education that allows 'young people to learn about their bodies, understand relationships and make informed decisions about their sexuality, and stand up against sexual harassment, exploitation and abuse'.[4] In a 2010 report, the UN Special Rapporteur on the Right to Education stated that 'sexual education should be considered a right in itself and should be clearly linked with other rights in accordance with the principle of the interdependence and indivisibility of human rights'.[5] In any event, I would not be surprised if this kind of legal action continues to be brought, as we have seen with the rise in climate litigation brought by young people staking a claim on their future. If the institutions expressly responsible won't act, young people may go to other institutions to defend their welfare. Whether *those* institutions will, in fact, respond is another issue, but by taking action in this way, young people are exposing the fault lines in those institutions as well as our hypocrisy.

We operate as though 'adults know best', but from where I sit in the criminal justice system, we are getting something very, very wrong. And young people know it. We must listen to them when they say they need us to step up, that they need the institutions responsible for their education to step up. Dani Villafana, a Sydney Year 12 student in 2021, founded Youth Against Sexual Violence Australia that year, with 'the peak of sexual assault and harassment circling the news cycle', saying that 'as a survivor myself and still in high school and being disenfranchised by the system it was really frustrating to see that the people who could do something about it weren't'.[6]

Villafana went on to say: 'We are often overlooked in these conversations but we're impacted by this so so much.' As I have reiterated throughout this book, the youth voice is crucial to the development of relevant, comprehensive RSE, in both content and delivery. Young people routinely report what they want from their sex-ed: not just condoms on bananas and puberty, but also consent, sex positivity, and pleasure. Queer sexuality, trans rights, bodily autonomy. How to navigate intimate relationships and decisions they will face. There are consistent themes in young people's call for better education in this space. Education and information they know will not corrupt them or confuse them. Throughout this book we've seen that it is not the information that unleashes damage, it is *our* silence, *our* shame, and *our* fear.

The kids, on the other hand, are all right. Young people know this is something they not only need but are owed. We owe it to them to act not as gatekeepers of this information, but as guides. When Wynne told me what she might have done differently in the fight for better RSE in 2015 Ontario, she said she should have engaged young people as allies. Young people like those schoolkids who staged a walkout after Ford pulled the updated RSE curriculum and who were, like their counterparts around the world, fighting for the right to access this information.

But young people are not our allies — we are theirs. They are crying out for access to this information with an urgency that won't be ignored, and those of us with the power to answer that call must do so. By staging walkouts and protests, by initiating legal actions claiming harm in consequence of our failure to adequately educate them, by launching a petition for better sex-ed that collects tens of thousands of signatures, young people are revealing that they understand something we seem to be slow to grasp. They understand that this kind of education is critical to their welfare, to their lives and their futures, and that by failing to give it to them we put that in jeopardy. They understand that their village is forsaking them.

To call on institutions that have the power to protect the right to sexual wellbeing and safety *before* it is traversed is to better understand the nature of sexual violence and unwanted sex. To better understand its root cause, and therefore its cure.

Young people recognise that we promise them a life free from sexual violence, we promise them their sexual safety and wellbeing, we promise them freedom and autonomy. We have given them a legitimate expectation for the lives they will lead, and they are doing no more than asking us to keep that promise.

Within Reach

In my job, we respond to sexual violence one case, one file, one name at a time. In the criminal justice system, the story of sexual violence is one of an individual accused, and, once found guilty, an individual culprit. And it is those individuals that we have put on trial, those who find themselves in the dock awaiting sentence, in the sombre hush of a courtroom. In that place, for me at least, an unspoken lament seems to hang in the air: *why didn't we stop this?* Am I alone in thinking of it as something we, the village, could have done more to prevent?

Beyond the accused, the prosecutor, the defence counsel, the judge, the jury, the victim, there is an unnamed presence in the courtroom. What that person and those around them believed, what they knew, what they cared about, what they expected and what was expected of them in the moment they chose to visit sexual violence upon another — those things seem to be there in the room with us, echoing around the cavernous space. Beliefs, knowledge, values, expectations, and choices that did not come from nowhere.

What you have read in these chapters are features of every single sexual-offence matter the courts deal with. Power, sexism, racism, ableism, shame, cis- and heteronormativity, the erasure of sexual agency and pleasure for some, entitlement to others' bodies, ignorance, apathy, inability or a lack of care to communicate, masculinity and other gender norms, ideas of obligation in relationships, dangerous expectations of how we will or ought to behave in moments of intimacy — these are the building blocks of sexual violence. They are its lifeblood.

These are things that, as a community, a collective, a culture, we are all responsible for. And until we are ready to put those things on trial too, a world free from sexual violence, sexual harm and unwanted sexual experiences will never be within reach.

Comprehensive RSE does put those things on trial. It challenges and mitigates those things. It can look to the future and ensure young people have the information, knowledge, and skills they need. It can set new, brighter expectations. This book has looked to the solution of comprehensive RSE, and has focused on its systemic, interconnected nature, for this is not an individual responsibility, it is a collective one. We have seen how a good curriculum, a legislative mandate, a brilliant teacher will never be enough in isolation. Parents, teachers, families, friends, peers, community members, politicians, and advocates — we all have a part to play, and to wash our hands of responsibility is to be culpable.

It will take all of us investing in this solution. Investing in the power of sex-ed and social change to defend and to secure autonomy, safety and wellbeing for all of us. To ensure relationships and sexuality education can reach its full potential, so future generations can reach theirs. To set expectations of sexual experiences that are not just free from violence, but are far from violent.

Acknowledgements

I will start by thanking the network of sexuality educators and advocates, both at home and abroad, who welcomed me with open arms — you are such collaborative, generous and determined people. Young people's education, and their futures, are in excellent hands with all of you on the job. May I continue to have the honour of putting my shoulder to the wheel alongside yours.

Special mention to Jacqui Hendriks, Kerrin Bradfield, Tim Bavinton, Melissa Kang and Deanne Carson, who have become personal mentors and friends, and are always willing to answer my calls.

To those I met with overseas on my Churchill Fellowship, and every single person I have quoted in these pages: thank you for your time, your labour, and your voices. Thank you to Catía and Mikey for your help and generosity in reading some extracts and sharing some of your personal experiences with me.

Thank you to those at the Winston Churchill Memorial Trust Australia, who gave me the opportunity to undertake my research overseas, and for everything since. I hope I can do it justice, in my efforts to pay it forward.

Special thanks to everyone at Rape and Sexual Assault Research and Advocacy, and the Relationships and Sexuality Education Alliance ACT. You are all so marvellous and working with you is a constant delight.

Shane Drumgold SC, ACT Director of Public Prosecutions, you ensured I was able to write this book in more ways than one. As one of my referees for the Churchill Fellowship, you believed in this advocacy long before a book was ever on the cards.

My darling Nina Funnell, whose inimitable passion and power make a difference in the lives of survivors and young people every day. I will look up to you forever, dear friend. I would not be who I am — personally and professionally — without you.

Alex Lloyd, whose idea this was in the first place, thank you for reaching out to me, setting this train in motion, and for your contribution to the nascent words. This book would not exist if not for you.

To Bri Lee: you had faith in this book from the moment I told you about it and as much as you will wave away any credit, you were instrumental to its coming to fruition. Your advocacy continues to echo across this country, and I am proud to know you.

Grace Heifetz, my beautiful agent! You've grabbed this project with both hands since the moment you read those early pages. I am still tickled pink that you chose to represent me, and hearing how much you wanted this book to come to life has kept me going. Thank you to everyone else at Left Bank Literary who has been so welcoming and supportive.

Marika Webb-Pullman: my editor, my coach! It feels like we've been arm in arm, charting a course in these pages, and you helped me to believe in it again every time I lost sight of where we were going. You brought clarity, compassion, and guidance to this endeavour — it is better by an order of magnitude, thanks to your vision.

Thank you to everyone else at Scribe who made this book a reality.

To my loved ones, who have been so patient and encouraging — including my extended family: aunts, uncles, cousins, and in-laws. My friends who celebrated with me: Erin, Sara, Emilija, Bec SC, Hannah, Verity, Elle, Skye, Kieran, James, Lydia, Amanda, David, Bwalya, Jess, Kylie, and everybody else I've no doubt forgotten to name. Special thanks to Soraya, Kelly, Katie, Angus, and Kirsten, who not only offered constant support but also read many of these pages and gave me vital feedback.

To my PhD supervisor, Dr Rachael Burgin, with love, for putting up with me going MIA on the thesis for a while, and for cheering me on in this project in the meantime.

Saxon Mullins — you are a force of nature and no other words do you justice. I am privileged to exist in your orbit.

To my Oma, you are a beautiful, admirable woman and have influenced me in ways you will never fully know. Your unwavering support acts as a pillar for me.

To my beloved Djedo: resolute, in the winter of your life, you continue to capture my imagination and inspire me with your forbearance. Your legacy will never, never be lost.

To my mother and father: I owe everything to you. I love you so much, and am not sure what I did to deserve the greatest parents in the world. You made my life beautiful, and our family is woven into the very cells of my heart.

Dearest Ariel, my best mate: you have been the wind at my back, patiently keeping the home fires burning while this project occupied my time and my attention. You celebrated every word, challenged every doubt, and advocated for me, to me, more times than I can count. I respect and admire you in new ways every single day. Life with you is a joy.

To every survivor of sexual violence — those I have met in my work and those whose names I will never know — I am in awe of your courage.

To young people everywhere: may we all add our voices to yours, in the call for better sex education, and may you get the education you deserve. You inspire me, and this is for you.

Endnotes

It Takes a Village

1 Australian Bureau of Statistics 2021. *Sexual violence — Victimisation: statistics about sexual assault and childhood sexual abuse, including characteristics of victim-survivors, victimisation rates, and police reporting*. 24 August 2021 <abs.gov.au/articles/sexual-violence-victimisation>

2 Nkyala Afshariyan, 'Trans and gender diverse people "four times more likely to experience sexual violence".' 23 September 2019, triple j *Hack*; Callander D, Wiggins J, Rosenberg S, Cornelisse VJ, Duck-Chong E, Holt M, Pony M, Vlahakis E, MacGibbon J, and Cook T (2019). *The 2018 Australian Trans and Gender Diverse Sexual Health Survey: Report of Findings*. Sydney, NSW: The Kirby Institute, UNSW, Sydney.

3 Australian Institute of Health and Welfare 2020. *Sexual assault in Australia*. Cat. no. FDV 5. Canberra: AIHW.

4 Australian Human Rights Commission 2017. *Change the Course: National Report on Sexual Assault and Sexual Harassment at Australian Universities*. August 2017.

5 Australian Institute of Health and Welfare 2018. *Family, domestic and sexual violence in Australia 2018*. Cat. no. FDV 2. Canberra: AIHW.

6 Ibid.

7 Australian Bureau of Statistics 2021. *Sexual violence — Victimisation: statistics about sexual assault and childhood sexual abuse, including characteristics of victim-survivors, victimisation rates, and police reporting*. 24 August 2021 <abs.gov.au/articles/sexual-violence-victimisation>

8 Anna Prytz, 'Teens take lead in anti-harassment fight.' 25 July 2021, *The Sydney Morning Herald*.

Every Moment Counts

1 Sexuality information and Education Council of the United States, Position Statement 2018.

2 Botha M, Hanlon J, and Williams GL (2021). 'Does language matter? Identity-first versus person-first language use in autism research: A response to Vivanti.' *Journal*

of Autism and Developmental Disorders, 1–9. Advance online publication. https://doi.org/10.1007/s10803-020-04858-w

3 Layla-Roxanne Hill, 'How colonialism has shaped the way we view sex and our sexual identities.' 9 June 2019, *The National*; *The Sex Agenda Podcast*, 'Episode 2: Decolonising Sex Education.' 22 July 2020.

4 Braun B (2015). 'An interpretation and analysis of the prevention of sexualised violence.' BZgA Sexuality Education and Family Planning FORUM 2/2015 at 16.

5 Ramírez-Villalobos D, et al. (2021). 'Delaying sexual onset: outcome of a comprehensive sexuality education initiative for adolescents in public schools.' *BMC Public Health* at 2.

6 Ibid.

7 Goldfarb E and Lieberman L (2021). 'Three decades of research: The case for comprehensive sex education.' *Journal of Adolescent Health* 68:13–27.

8 Ketting E and Ivanova O (2017). 'Sexuality education: Lessons learned and future developments in the WHO European region.' Conference Report, Berlin, 15–16 May 2017 at 32.

9 Amanda Sibosado and Michelle Webb, 'Consent education needs Blak voices for the safety and well-being of young First Nations people.' 22 March 2022, *The Conversation.*

All the Time in the World

1 Breuner C and Mattson G (2015). 'Sexuality education for children and adolescents.' *PEDIATRICS* 138 (2) August 2015.

2 Jacqueline Hendriks, 'Relationships and sex education is now mandatory in English schools — Australia should do the same.' 9 September 2020, *The Conversation*; Ezer P, Power J, Jones T, and Fisher C (2020). 2nd National Survey of Australian Teachers of Sexuality Education 2018. La Trobe University.

3 Johnson B, Harrison L, Ollis D, Flentje J, Arnold P, & Bartholomaeus C (2016). '"It is not all about sex": Young people's views about sexuality and relationships education.' Report of Stage 1 of the Engaging Young People in Sexuality Education Research Project. University of South Australia, Adelaide; Jacqueline Hendriks, 'Relationships and sex education is now mandatory in English schools — Australia should do the same.' 9 September 2020, *The Conversation*; Sophie Meixner, 'Does Australia's sex education curriculum need to include more on sex positivity, LGBTQI+ relationships and intimacy?' 27 January 2021, ABC News.

4 Ramírez-Villalobos D, et al. (2021). 'Delaying sexual onset: outcome of a comprehensive sexuality education initiative for adolescents in public schools.' *BMC Public Health* at 2.

5 MacNeela P, et al. (n.d.) 'Development, implementation, and evaluation of the SMART consent workshop on sexual consent for third level students: Report summary.' School of Psychology, NUI, Galway.

6 See, for example: UNESCO. (2018). International technical guidance on sexuality education: An evidence-informed approach (Revised Edition); Lundgren R and Amin A (2015). 'Addressing intimate partner violence and sexual violence among adolescents: Emerging evidence of effectiveness.' *Journal of Adolescent Health* 1 at 56; Apter D

(2011). 'Recent developments and consequences of sexuality education in Finland.' BZgA Sexuality Education and Family Planning FORUM February 2011, 3–8; Van Keulen HM, et al. (2015). 'Effectiveness of the Long Live Love 4 program for 13- and 14-year-old secondary school students in the Netherlands: a quasi-experimental design.' Netherlands Organisation for Applied Scientific Research, Delf; BZgA (2017). 'Sexuality education: Lessons learned and future developments in the WHO European region.' Conference Report, Berlin, 15–16 May 2017 at 4; Breuner C and Mattson G (2015). 'Sexuality education for children and adolescents.' *PEDIATRICS* 138 (2) August 2015; Goldfarb E and Lieberman L (2021). 'Three decades of research: The case for comprehensive sex education.' *Journal of Adolescent Health* 68:13–27; Ezer P, Fisher C, Jones T, Power J. (2022). 'Changes in sexuality education teacher training since the release of the Australian Curriculum.' *Sexuality Research and Social Policy* 19:12-21.

In the Dark

1 Michael McGowan, 'Scott Morrison sends his children to private school to avoid "skin curling" sexuality discussions.' 3 September 2018, *The Guardian.*

2 Sophie Meixner, 'Does Australia's sex education curriculum need to include more on sex positivity, LGBTQI+ relationships and intimacy?' 27 January 2021, ABC News,

3 United Nations Population Fund, 'International technical guidance on sexuality education: an evidence-informed approach'. 10 January 2016 <https://www.unfpa.org/publications/international-technical-guidance-sexuality-education#:~:text=The%20International%20technical%20guidance%20on,the%20global%20Sustainable%20Development%20Goals.>

4 Katrina Marson, 'Milkshake video the final straw in consent discontent.' 20 April 2021, *The Sydney Morning Herald*; Samantha Pegg, 'Sexual consent really isn't like a cup of tea — but at least we're talking about it.' 2 November 2015, *The Conversation*; Belinda Karsen, 'Are tea and consent simple?' 26 August 2020, Sexual Violence Support & Prevention Office, Simon Fraser University, Canada.

5 Emily Ross, 'Why do Australian states need a national curriculum, and do teachers even use it?' 19 November 2021, *The Conversation.*

6 Sophie Meixner, 'Does Australia's sex education curriculum need to include more on sex positivity, LGBTQI+ relationships and intimacy?' 27 January 2021, ABC News.

7 Sex Education Forum, 'Young People's RSE Poll 2021', 1 February 2022.

Windows of Opportunity

1 Goldfarb E and Lieberman L (2021). 'Three decades of research: The case for comprehensive sex education.' *Journal of Adolescent Health* 68:13–27 at 22.

2 Ibid, 21; Pick S, Givaudan M, Sirkin J and Ortega I (2007). 'Communication as a protective factor: Evaluation of a life skills HIV/AIDS prevention program for Mexican elementary school students.' *AIDS Education Prevention* 19:408-21.

3 Taylor N, Prichard J, and Charlton K (2004). *National Project on Drink Spiking: Investigating the nature and extent of drink spiking in Australia.* The Australian Institute of Criminology November 2004.

4 Australian Institute of Health and Welfare 2020. Sexual assault in Australia. Cat. no. FDV 5. Canberra: AIHW.

What Do You Expect?

1 Australian Bureau of Statistics 2021. *Sexual violence — Victimisation: statistics about sexual assault and childhood sexual abuse, including characteristics of victim-survivors, victimisation rates, and police reporting*. 24 August 2021 <abs.gov.au/articles/sexual-violence-victimisation>

2 Ezer P, Power J, Jones T, and Fisher C (2020). 2nd National Survey of Australian Teachers of Sexuality Education 2018, La Trobe University at 39.

3 Schutte L, et al. (2014). 'The implementation of a school-based sex-education program in the Netherlands'. *Health Education Research* 29 (4): 583–597.

4 Zaneva M, Philpott A, Singh A, Larsson G, and Gonsalves L (2022). 'What is the added value of incorporating pleasure in sexual health interventions? A systematic review and meta-analysis.' *PLoS ONE* 17(2): e0261034.

5 Goldfarb E and Lieberman L (2021). 'Three decades of research: The case for comprehensive sex education.' *Journal of Adolescent Health* 68:13–27.

6 Carmody, M and Carrington K. (2000). 'Preventing Sexual Violence.' *The Australian and New Zealand Journal of Criminology* 33 (3): 341–361.

7 Michielsen K and Brockschmidt L. (2021). 'Barriers to sexuality education for children and young people with disabilities in the WHO European region: A scoping review.' *Sex Education* 21(6): 674–692 at 684.

8 UNESCO. (2018). International technical guidance on sexuality education: An evidence-informed approach (Revised Edition); Goldfarb E and Lieberman L (2021). 'Three decades of research: The case for comprehensive sex education.' *Journal of Adolescent Health* 68:13–27; Sarah Boseley et al., 'From 'consent football' to "pin the organ on the body": sex education around the world.' 27 April 2019, *The Guardian*.

9 Ezer P, Fisher C, Jones T, Power J (2022). 'Changes in sexuality education teacher training since the release of the Australian Curriculum.' *Sexuality Research and Social Policy* 19:12-21 at 19.

10 Ramírez-Villalobos D, et al. (2021). 'Delaying sexual onset: outcome of a comprehensive sexuality education initiative for adolescents in public schools.' *BMC Public Health* at 7.

11 Ezer P, Fisher C, Jones T, Power J (2022). 'Changes in sexuality education teacher training since the release of the Australian Curriculum.' *Sexuality Research and Social Policy* 19:12-21 at 12–13.

12 O'Brien H, Hendriks J, and Burns S (2020). 'Teacher training organisations and their preparation of the pre-service teacher to deliver comprehensive sexuality education in the school setting: A systematic literature review.' *Sex Education* 21:3 284–303.

13 Goldfarb E and Lieberman L (2021). 'Three decades of research: The case for comprehensive sex education.' *Journal of Adolescent Health* 68:13–27 at 19 and 22.

14 Ibid at 23.

On Our Watch

1 Ezer P, Fisher C, Jones T, Power J (2022). 'Changes in sexuality education teacher training since the release of the Australian Curriculum.' *Sexuality Research and Social Policy* 19:12-21 at 12.

2 Sophie Meixner, 'Does Australia's sex education curriculum need to include more on sex positivity, LGBTQI+ relationships and intimacy?' 27 January 2021, *ABC News.*

3 Social Research Centre (2021). National Student Safety Survey 2021; Jordan Baker and Wendy Tuohy, 'One in six university students sexually harassed, one in 20 sexually assaulted.' 23 March 2022, *The Sydney Morning Herald.*

4 Bullyingnoway.gov.au

5 <cowardpunchcampaign.com>; 'Stop the Coward's Punch Campaign' Media Release: The Hon Peter Dutton MP Former Minister for Home Affairs. Friday 25 May 2018.

6 https://www.respect.gov.au/the-campaign/

7 Anna Prytz, 'Teens take lead in anti-harassment fight.' 25 July 2021, *The Sydney Morning Herald.*

8 Fisher CM and Kauer S (2019). National Survey of Australian Secondary Students and Sexual Health 1992–2018: Trends Over Time (ARCSHS Monograph Series No. 118), Australian Research Centre in Sex, Health and Society, La Trobe University, Bundoora at 26.

9 Junkee.com (2022). 'Ending violence against women.'

Pounds of Flesh

1 Strnadová I, Loblinzk J, and Danker, J (2021). 'Importance of sex education for a successful transition to life after school: Experiences of high school girls with intellectual disability.' *British Journal of Learning Disabilities* 49: 303–315 at 310.

2 Hill AO, Bourne A, McNair R, Carman M. and Lyons A (2020). Private lives 3: The health and wellbeing of LGBTIQ people in Australia (ARCSHS Monograph series No. 122), Australian Research Centre in Sex, Health and Society, La Trobe University, Bundoora.

3 Hendriks J, Marson K, Walsh J, Laton T, Saltis H and Burns S (n.d.) 'Support for school-based relationships and sexual health education: A national survey of Australian parents.' (Manuscript in preparation.)

4 Mostafa Rachwani, 'Survey suggests four in five Australian parents support gender and sexuality diversity education'. 17 March 2022, *The Guardian.*

5 Hendriks J, Marson K, Walsh J, Laton T, Saltis H and Burns S (n.d.) 'Support for school-based relationships and sexual health education: A national survey of Australian parents.' (Manuscript in preparation.)

Fear and Self-Loathing

1 The World Health Organisation: 'Sexual Health.' <who.int/health-topics/sexual-health>

2 Goldfarb E and Lieberman L (2021). 'Three decades of research: The case for comprehensive sex education.' *Journal of Adolescent Health* 68:13–27; Mark K, Corona-Vargas E and Cruz M (2021, ahead of print). 'Integrating sexual pleasure for quality and inclusive comprehensive sexuality education.' *International Journal of Sexual Health*; Sladden T, et. al. (2021, ahead of print). 'Sexual health and wellbeing through the life course: Ensuring sexual health, rights and pleasure for all.' *International Journal of Sexual Health.*

3 Michielsen K and Brockschmidt L (2021). 'Barriers to sexuality education for children and young people with disabilities in the WHO European region: A scoping review.' *Sex Education* 21:6 674–692.

4 BBC News, 'Good sex can be safer sex, say WHO researchers.' 14 February 2022, BBC News.

5 Tony Sheldon, 'Could Dutch-style sex education reduce pregnancies among UK teenagers?' 5 January 2018, *The BMJ.*

6 Zaneva M, Philpott A, Singh A, Larsson G, Gonsalves L (2022) 'What is the added value of incorporating pleasure in sexual health interventions? A systematic review and meta-analysis.' *PLoS ONE* 17(2): e0261034.

7 Goldfarb E and Lieberman L (2021). 'Three decades of research: The case for comprehensive sex education.' *Journal of Adolescent Health* 68 (2021) 13–27 at 23.

Through the Looking-Glass

1 Patrick Wood, 'Australia's porn problem.' 8 July 2019, ABC News; Reuters, 'Billie Eilish says watching porn as a child "destroyed my brain".' 15 December 2021, *The Guardian.*

2 Byron P, McKee A, Watson A, Litsou K and Ingham R (2021). 'Reading for realness: Porn literacies, digital media, and young people.' *Sexuality & Culture* 25:786-805.

3 Ibid at 800 and 789.

4 Ibid at 793.

5 Herbernick D, Patterson C, et al. (2021). 'Diverse sexual behaviours in undergraduate students: Findings from a campus probability survey.' *Journal of Sexual Medicine* 18(6):1024–1041.

6 Hebernick D, et al. (2022). '"It was scary, but then it was kind of exciting": Young women's experiences with choking during sex.' *Archives of Sexual Behavior* 51: 1103–1123.

7 Jessica Wang, 'Former St Kevin's student claims school had homophobic, sexist, toxic culture.' 5 November 2021, *news.com.au*

8 Sally Wheale, 'Parents urged to talk to children as young as nine about online porn.' 16 December 2021, *The Guardian.*

9 Breuner C and Mattson G (2015). 'Sexuality education for children and adolescents.' *PEDIATRICS* 138 (2) August 2015 at e6.

10 https://www.respect.gov.au/resources/

11 Suzanne Dyson, 'Good sex ed doesn't lead to teen pregnancy, it prevents it.' 3 June 2016, *The Conversation*; Goldfarb E and Lieberman L (2021). 'Three decades of research: The case for comprehensive sex education.' *Journal of Adolescent Health* 68:13–27 at 20 and 23.

Lessons Earned

1 Strnadová I, Loblinzk, J and Danker, J (2021). 'Importance of sex education for a successful transition to life after school: Experiences of high school girls with intellectual disability.' *British Journal of Learning Disabilities* 49:303–315; Michielsen K and Brockschmidt L (2021). 'Barriers to sexuality education for children and young people with disabilities in the WHO European region: A scoping review.' *Sex Education* 21:6 674–692; Magenta, '"I realised how little sex ed prepared me for real world experiences": Living with a disability and learning about sex.' 7 December 2021, triple j.

2 Michielsen, K and Brockschmidt, L. (2021). 'Barriers to sexuality education for children and young people with disabilities in the WHO European region: A scoping review.' *Sex Education* 21:6 674–692.

3 Ibid.

4 Australian Institute of Health and Welfare 2020. People with disability in Australia 2018.

5 Australian Law Reform Commission (2010). Family Violence — A National Legal Response (ALRC Report 114). 'Sexual assault and family violence: The prevalence of sexual violence' at 1100.

6 Centre for Evidence and Implementation & Monash University (2021). 'Rapid evidence review: Violence, abuse, neglect and exploitation of people with disability.' Royal Commission into Violence, Abuse, Neglect and Exploitation of People with Disability at 37.

7 Strnadová I, Loblinzk, J and Danker, J (2021). 'Importance of sex education for a successful transition to life after school: Experiences of high school girls with intellectual disability.' *British Journal of Learning Disabilities* 49: 303–315 at 307.

8 Michielsen K, and Brockschmidt L (2021). 'Barriers to sexuality education for children and young people with disabilities in the WHO European region: A scoping review.' *Sex Education* 21:6 674–692 at 675.

9 Strnadová I, Loblinzk J, & Danker J (2021). 'Importance of sex education for a successful transition to life after school: Experiences of high school girls with intellectual disability.' *British Journal of Learning Disabilities* 49:303–315 at 307.

10 Travers, J et. al. (2014). 'Alignment of sexuality education with self determination for people with significant disabilities: A review of research and future directions.' *Education and Training in Autism and Developmental Disabilities* 49:2 232–247.

11 Caitlin Fitzsimmons, 'Disabled woman "furious" at lack of support over sex education.' 7 December 2021, *The Sydney Morning Herald.*

12 Franklin A, Raws P and Smeaton E. (2015). Unprotected, overprotected: meeting the needs of young people with learning disabilities who experience, or are at risk of, sexual exploitation. *Barnardo's.*

13 Strnadová, I, Loblinzk, J., & Danker, J. (2021). Importance of sex education for a successful transition to life after school: Experiences of high school girls with intellectual disability. *British Journal of Learning Disabilities*, 49:303–315 at 313.

14 Magenta, '"I realised how little sex ed prepared me for real world experiences": Living with a disability and learning about sex.' 7 December 2021, triple j.

15 Travers J et. al. (2014). 'Alignment of sexuality education with self determination for people with significant disabilities: A review of research and future directions.' *Education and Training in Autism and Developmental Disabilities*, 49 (2), 232–247 at 243.
16 Barger E, et al. (2009) 'Sexual assault prevention for women with intellectual disabilities: A critical review of the evidence.' *Intellectual and Developmental Disabilities* 47 (4) 249–262.
17 Campbell M, Löfgren-Mårtenson C, and Santinele Martino A (2020). 'Cripping sex education.' *Sex Education* 20 (4): 361-365 at 362–363.
18 Sexuality education: Lessons learned and future developments in the WHO European region. Conference Report, Berlin, 15–16 May 2017.
19 BZgA (2015), 'Sexuality education for persons with impairments.' Concept.
20 Commonwealth of Australia, Department of Social Services (2021). Australia's Disability Strategy 2021–2031.

In the Quietest of Places

1 World Health Organization. (n.d.). 'Sexual and reproductive health and research; "Sexual health".' https://www.who.int/health-topics/sexual-health#tab=tab_2
2 World Association for Sexual Health: Declaration of Sexual Rights.
3 Campbell M (2016). 'The challenge of girls' right to education: Let's talk about human rights-based sex education.' *International Journal of Human Rights* 20:8 1219–1243.
4 Natalia Kanem, 'Sexual and reproductive health and rights: The cornerstone of sustainable development' August 2018 *United Nations Chronicle* 2(LV): 2030 Agenda.
5 Report of the United Nations Special Rapporteur on the right to education: sexual education (2010).
6 Anna Prytz, 'Teens take lead in anti-harassment fight.' 25 July 2021, *The Sydney Morning Herald*.